The roundness of loss

Table of contents

The deafening silence. For my mother.	4
Letter to the birds	6
Johanna Wilhelmina Josephina van Haren	10
Shoes	12
Floating. The first meeting with my mother.	14
Sensitive teeth. The second meeting with my mother.	18
Bones. The third meeting with my mother.	27
My mother	29
The bag	30
The dead don't leave you alone	34
The non-grief	37

Nude	45
The rooms	55
An omen	61
Noortje	69
Memorabilia	76
The soul is more present than we think	79
Ke Lefa-Laka: Her Story	90
Oma Lola's things	93
Light	105
The parallel world	111
The angel wings	120
Farewell child (for Marike and Noah)	122
La Ultima Ascensión	125
Breathe in, breathe out, until there's no more left	134
I am serving a sentence	137
A pink cloud	148
Souvenirs of a loss	151
The depth below the surface	161
Love is All Alone. Together All Alone.	168
Reviving the word	173
Wessel Couzijn	182
Blue	183
I wouldn't have missed his death for the world	185
Father's wheelbarrow	196
Object for Opa	197
A house without a key	199
Her hand	212
The future is built with fragments from the past	215
Missing feels like a hollowing-out	227
Memory of a certain time – a marker on the timeline	237
Seven times around the earth	246
Carnival	249
Disappearing	258
Portrait of my father Hans Breedveldt Boer	264

Table of contents

Untitled (Portrait of the Artist's Father)	265
Was he not too lonely?	266
E.I.G Erik In Gedachten (Erik in our thoughts)	269
Broken eyes	277
The Wim-route	290
Fatum	293
Never is a very long time	299
A voice that glimmers in the light	307
with her voice, penetrate earth's floor	318
From one thing to another	321
Violence is a language. To craft is to care.	329
The passage through which we become (wo)men?	337
Death and water	343
Better not move	355
Living on air	363
Mending	373
Footnotes	378
Colophon	383

The deafening silence.
For my mother.

My fascination for lost memories is motivated by my mother's early death; I was 18 years old and for years I had already longed for the adventure of a brand new life. My life.

My father remarried within six months (where did she suddenly come from?). No photos of my mother were left in the house and her ashes were not scattered in a shared ritual beneath the beech trees in the crown estates, but they had been given to the undertaker by my father. We hardly ever spoke about her again, as if she had not only passed away but had also completely disappeared from our lives. Fortunately, I was able to start studying in another city, which enabled me to escape this absence, but no one knew her there so the conversation didn't really get going either.

The conversation about her fell silent on all sides. There was a still and empty aura around her. We have failed as a family by letting her slip out of our lives like that, as if we had forgotten her, which is unthinkable. But just the same, that emptiness has dominated for years and absorbed all the memories.

Memory lets go if there are no memory hooks such as celebrating her birthday together. Snivelling together on the anniversary of her death. Coming together, so that we can still laugh about her failed shortbread biscuits. My youngest sister got her purple fisherman's jumper and often wore it. I got her earrings, but they clamped my ear. I recently had them made into a pendant.

I'm quite a bit older now than she ever was. There's still time to make up for the deficiency of the silence. Here, a book for you.

```
You there!
On the mole-hole-grass
in the garden
behind the grey paved patio.
Breadcrumbs,
fast food for the birds.
The nestlings. The tame crow.
But now,
fifty years on,
the house has vanished.
The tame crow choked on a pebble.
The marigolds unsown.
The crumbs dissolved into the void.
Just like my mother's ashes.
```

Hello birds. Do you still remember my mother?

Do you still remember her apron, a cotton check with patch pockets, trimmed with plain piping, one of those aprons that looked like a dress, nice and loose, and sleeveless, with buttons at the front. She wore the apron every day because stains were attracted to her, far too much. My mother had the strange notion that she had fireproof hands and she was unusually proud of this. She didn't seem to feel all those blisters and kept on forgetting that fire is hot, and the heat of oven brutal. Her own stigmata. The tranquillity of the round table in the dining room, on certain days, at lunchtimes, we then sat there together. Us, a mother with her four children. It was just us together. While we children bit into our sandwiches (two with meat or cheese, then the cheaper sweet toppings, otherwise she couldn't get by with the housekeeping money), the birds outside pecked at the crusts and crumbs. Then the big window in the dining room was like a frame for the birds' meal, a film in which a sparrow hops up and down from the water butt to the grassed area with crumbs and back. We called this sparrow Spruitje.
A round brown little sprout. In the distance, the woodpecker is hammering away. One of us could already look forward to the evening because we were allowed to take turns to sleep in our parents' big bed, next to my mother. A body that purrs with contentment and relaxes and is having too much fun to sleep.

    After lunch, the day rolled on peacefully, on such days, the just-us-together days. The days when my father was lodging in a boarding house in Assen where he was stationed that year. As an army officer, you follow the postings and he didn't want to keep moving his family, that was noble, chivalrous. But the father-days were rougher, like going against the grain.

Each day around 5 o'clock, my mother put her apron on and once again embarked on the desperate task of cooking the evening meal. Cooking was her daily bugbear; she had no culinary skills. Bacon with soy sauce, yes, just something a little bit different. Or macaroni with sauce. Exotic. The four of us all pulled long faces and bent over groaning as if we had terrible stomach ache. Retch, retch. Everyone laughed, except my mother; she had tears in her eyes, but they were only seen by the birds who came every day to eat the crumbs. And tomorrow they'll get the leftovers of the bacon, although a squirrel will probably scramble down from the tree to get it, there's always a squirrel who likes bacon.

After the meal, *the* moment of the day arrived: would my father like the coffee today? My mother tried everything, a different brand of coffee, filters, a machine, spoonfuls of Buisman, but in fact it was never right. I don't know what kind of taste that man had in mind, perhaps coffee with rum or Cointreau. But I never heard: 'you know what, today do it yourself, I'm going to sit in the garden with my cup of tea. Hello birds, here I am again.' No, her brave face remained optimistic, but the birds knew better, they can read her soul. Her despairing coffee soul. Her desperate attempts to make everyone happy, or at least satisfied.

Every five years, I take the train to Apeldoorn, hire a bike and cycle through the area where I grew up. Past the endless flowering rhododendron bushes on the Burgemeester Roosmale Nepveulaan, along avenues with the names of fragrant flowers, the Jasmijnlaan, the Juniperlaan and finally the Excelsalaan. Number 3. I dismount and look at the number three on the house, I hear the birds, I recognise the surrounding trees, the houses next to it, behind, opposite, the street with its sharp pebbles, I recognise everything, except *our* house. I see a tasteless villa that no doubt has a home office. Our distinctive 1960s brick house with the garage next to it has vanished, dissolved, been wiped out. I app my brother. 'Yes, I'd already heard at an old school reunion, the house was demolished.'

'Was it really pulled down? Or maybe it was converted?' Although I can see for myself the impossibility of this. 'Completely demolished.'

That past of ours was cleared away radically. Firstly, a permit was issued to cut down two trees, then six spruce trees, and finally the town council issued an 'environmental permit' for 3 Excelsalaan, a permit for a new house. (Application for environmental permit Excelsalaan (3) 7313 BV Apeldoorn, erection of a dwelling.) And then that undersized villa appears there.

    The Excelsa has given up the ghost despite the Excelsa tree being a strong conifer variety, full of vitality. The tree has dark green shiny leaves that give off a mossy fragrance when they are crushed.

    There is nothing left to smell. The house has been pulverised, dissolved in the cosmic soup, irretrievably dissolved. Just like my mother's ashes.

p. 6, 10, 12, 18, 24, 25: Hanne Hagenaars, *My mother's wardrobe*, 2022, (photos: Paul Kooiker)

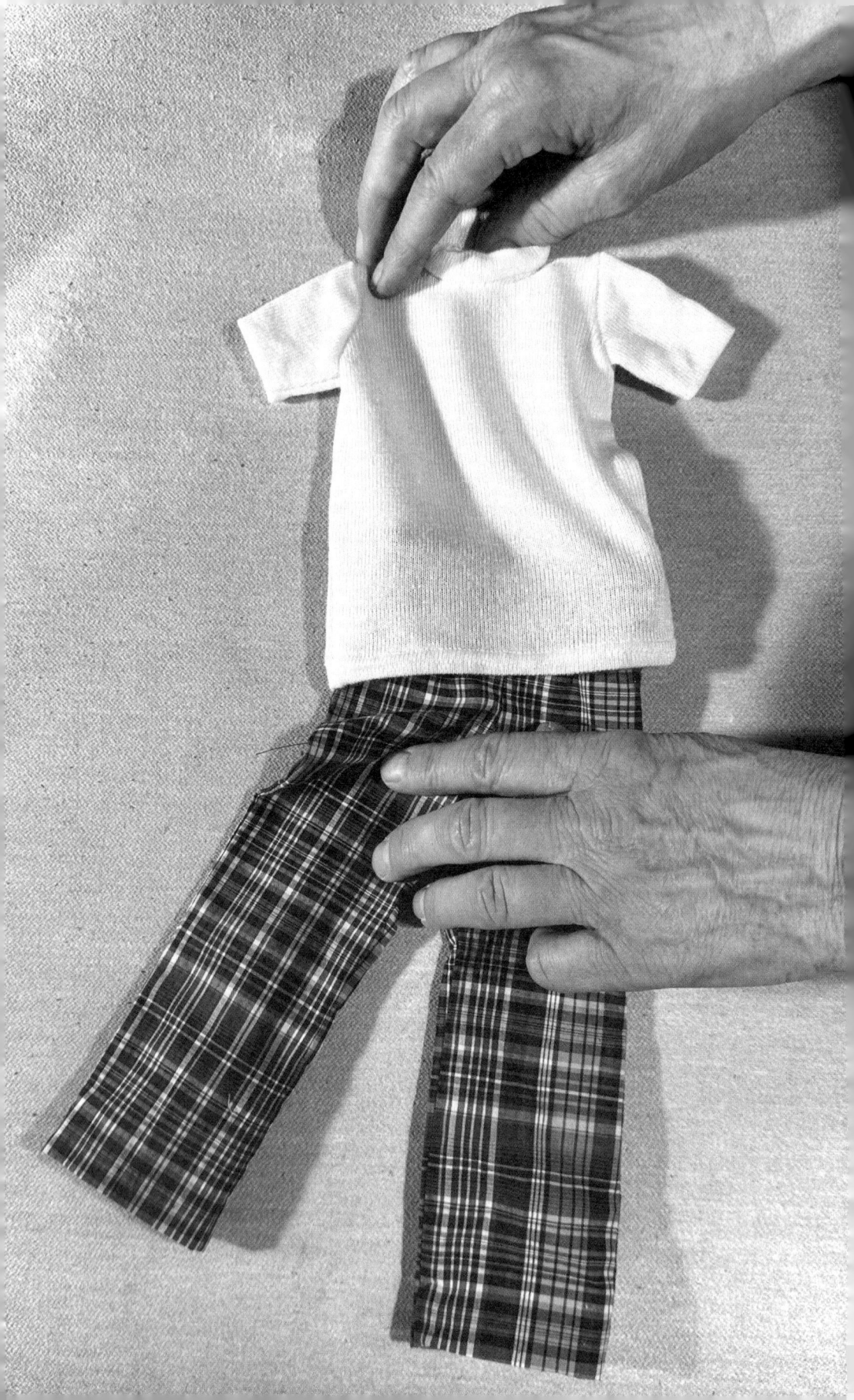

My family has a thing about names. On her birth announcement card, my older sister is still called Lettie. 'Oh, I'll let Ans—my mother—have her own way', my father must have thought at that time. But my mother's preference was swept away within a year; it had become Aldi. How? That remains unclear. My sister was happier being an Aldi than a Lettie.

I was named after my father's mother, and she was a kind grandma to me, even though she looked like a witch, with a sticking-out chin, and my father couldn't stand her. I changed my first name to Hanne (yes, Hanne Darboven, yes, a new life). Henrica Maria Aleida.

Baptismal names give children choices, that is a blessing. My brother even got four. My youngest sister, the favourite, the apple of everyone's eye, was named Marja, 'Sorrow of the sea'. Marja Dorothea. Why on earth Dorothea? Wasn't that the wife of my mother's brother? Rumour had it that she was found dead, naked, on the street in Mallorca, where she was on holiday. How? That remains unclear.

My mother's name was Ans, a name she warned us against; we must on no account name our children after her. She hated her name. No idea why. Her baptismal name Johanna means 'God is gracious', but I wouldn't know what his grace meant for her.

Her mother died when she was nine years old. This Alijda Johanna lived to be 47, and the stepmother on the yellowed photo doesn't look very compassionate. An imposing, strict woman who towered over her husband. My mother was sent to boarding school with the nuns and later on, we used to have a good laugh at her stories about the breakfast porridge. This concoction was cooked using the scraped off remains of the round communion wafers that were baked there in big ovens, and it consisted entirely of thick lumps. Morning after morning, she had to struggle to keep herself from vomiting. Sometimes she was able to sell the porridge for a few cents, then someone else ate it for her. Everyone in our family has a lump-phobia because of this.

Names.
For my love I will be named.[*1]

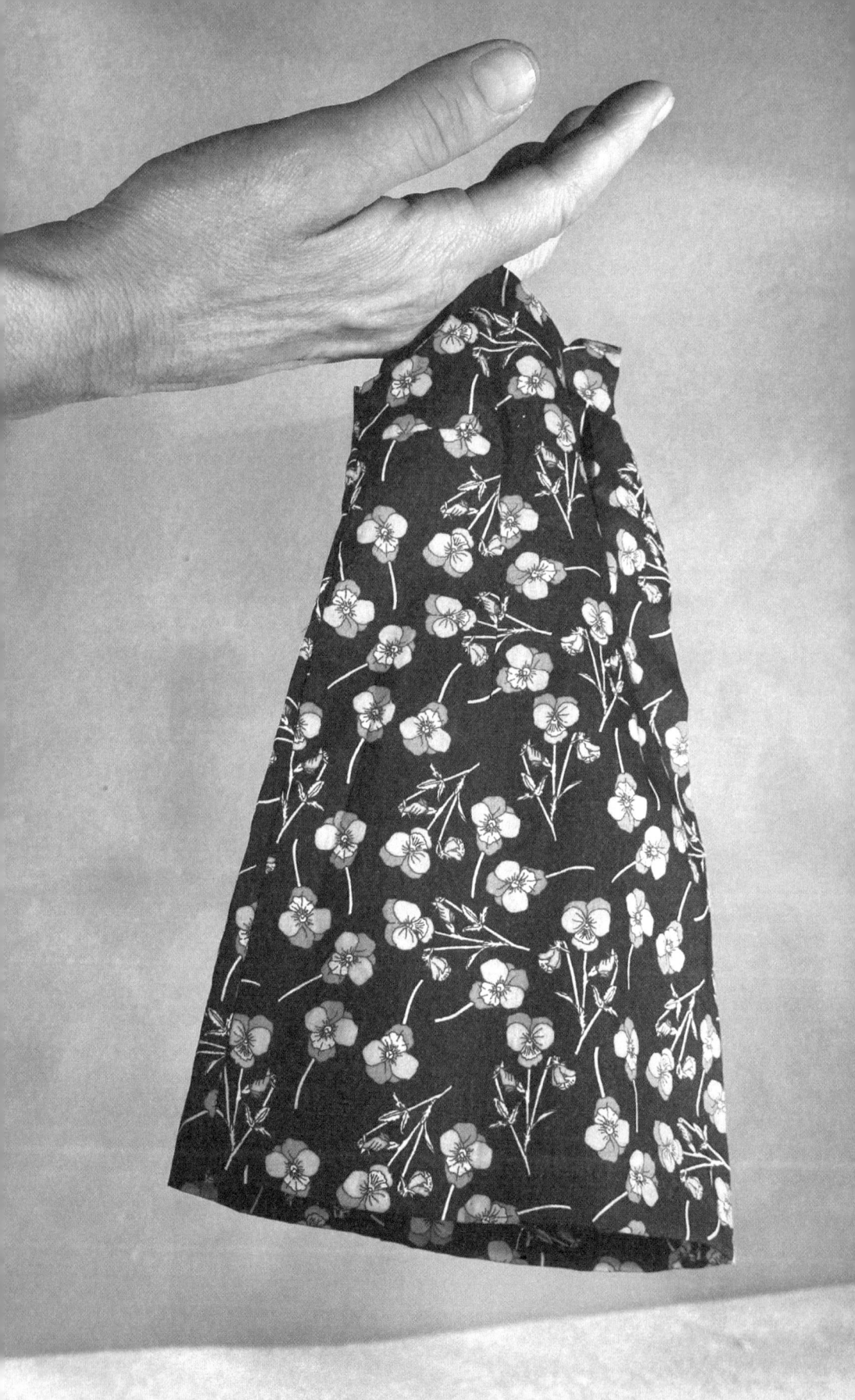

My mother was a daughter of the brother of the founder of the Van Haren shoe factory. Perhaps that's why her shoes were never comfortable. A lump on the side of her big toe always got in the way, she had a lot of blisters; her feet were sensitive, definitely not pedestals that carry you through the world. Van Haren shoes: she turned her nose up at them.

    Her favourite sister, my aunt Mimi, told me that she went to visit my mother in Grave, where my parents had moved into an upstairs apartment after their marriage. My mother was pregnant with the first, or the second, perhaps with me. She had forgotten the parsley and wanted to pop out quickly to get it. But, heavily pregnant or not, my father thought that his wife should go to the shops like a lady, wearing high-heeled shoes. Like a real woman. So my mother wore her heels to go down the long staircase from the upstairs apartment, but once she was in the street, just around the corner, she took slippers out of a bag, changed shoes and said to my aunt, laughing: 'Now everyone's happy!'

Floating.
The first meeting with my mother.

The owner of the hotel in India gives us the address of the town's best ayurvedic centre. My friend Marni and I take a cycle rickshaw and arrive, slightly dazed, outside a shabby house in a busy street. It looks nothing like the health resorts you see when you google ayurveda, but—who knows?—perhaps it's a well-kept secret.

Inside, the floor is covered with a soft, bright-red carpet and there are shimmery pink curtains in front of the windows. The floor is scattered with white boxes and small bottles of dark liquids, round jars with powder in every possible colour and opaque white bottles with colourful lids. A friendly, rather stout man is busy checking the medicines against a long list. A copper barrel with handles and decorated with rosettes remains a mystery, a piece of wood sticks out of it.

Behind the counter, the wall is covered with glass shelves on which yet more bottles and jars are lined up, awaiting a client. Right in the middle of the miracle cures, a young Jesus looks at me from a poster with a penetrating gaze, one hand stretching forward invitingly and the other pointing towards a pink heart that has been painted on his chest, below a cross. A pink cloth is draped around his shoulders.

First of all, the owner would like to show us the apartment that we could rent if we want to follow a longer course of treatment. It is on the third floor, where the sound of the street is very audible, as is the aircon, and there are pink curtains everywhere and the heavy wooden furniture is covered with, again, pink velour. I put my sunglasses on. It is overwhelming.

The doctor, appropriately dressed in a white coat, takes my pulse and writes a lot of things down on a piece of paper. His office chair is sealed in plastic and even the swivel feet are covered. Then he turns towards me and points out the stairs to the treatment room. A door has been made in an iron barrel and I'm told to sit on a wooden chair inside it. The jerrycan of petrol that is next to it provides the fuel to heat up the barrel. I have no idea how it works and as I sit down in that strange little stove, I can already imagine it exploding, and the newspaper headlines afterwards. The little pieces I'll break up into. But I tell myself not to be childish and I surrender to it.

Once I've been warmed up enough, I'm invited to lie down in my black knickers on a treatment table, where two sweet,

Floating.
The first meeting with my mother.

slightly built girls give me a synchronised massage with herbal oil that smells of liquorice, basil and sesame. My legs, back, arms, head. Then the other side, legs, stomach, breasts, shoulders and face. I slowly begin to float. Drops of herbal oil fall rhythmically onto my forehead.

Unhurriedly, they perform rituals and then leave the room quietly. And while I'm still lingering there, my mother's face appears: no, it's not a dream, and no, I'm not imagining it either. She is there, clear and tangible, floating in the air and she looks like the Hollywood star Ava Gardner from an old-fashioned chewing gum picture. We don't say hello because, after all, we already know each other. She speaks, and although the words aren't actually audible within the room, I can understand her clearly. She is looking her most beautiful, like she used to long ago, perhaps more like I know her from photos, with thick black, slightly wavy hair, that lovely wide mouth, eyebrows like fox tails with very light eyes below them.

Now that I think back on it, perhaps it was a wordless conversation, she was there, that's for sure, but I can't remember any sentences. She hangs in the air, being peaceful, and I lie as still as possible in order not to disturb the miracle. I stretch out my hand, perhaps I can touch her, perhaps that will make her more real. But suddenly, while my hand is reaching towards her, she vanishes in a puff of air; it makes me think of the explosion of common earthballs that used to spring up in the damp woods, and that we as children liked to jump on top of to see the spores come out in a black cloud. My mother vanished in a hazy black cloud like this. 'Stay! Stay!' I call wordlessly, but it still echoes around the room. I sit up to see whether the poisonous spores of the fungus may have fallen onto the white sheet, but no, nothing. I shouldn't have moved. But when I close my eyes, I can see her again, motionlessly present in the air. It is blissful. She stays close to me throughout my journey across India. It is as if the air there is better suited to carry souls than in our waterlogged country, because once I'm home again, she has completely disappeared.

Floating.
The first meeting with my mother.

Kochi, Kerala, India, 2016, (photos: Hanne Hagenaars)

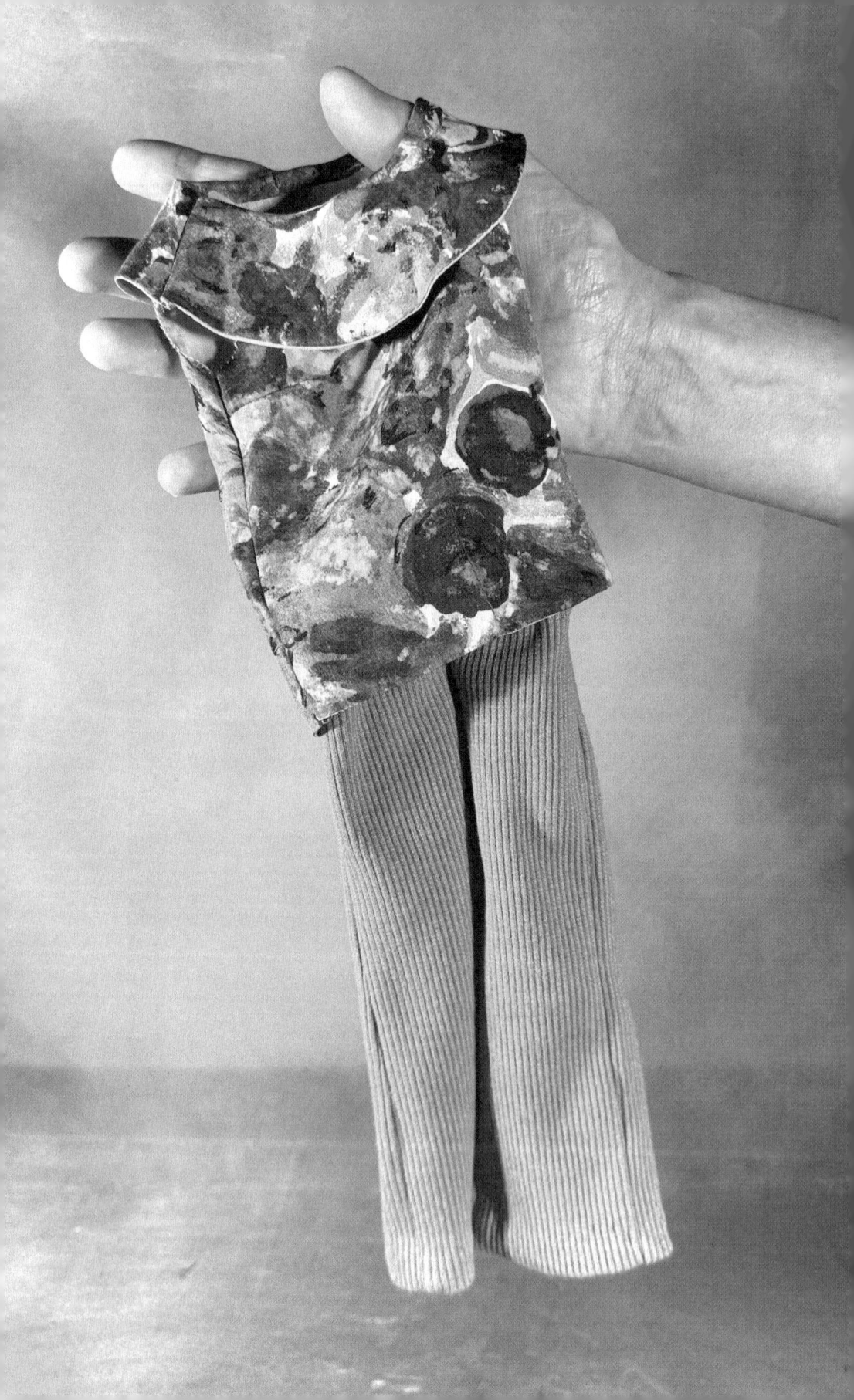

Sensitive teeth.
The second meeting with my mother.

My mother, I can see her face before me, but beyond that, what else, who are you, who were you? Memories have slithered away like slippery eels and trying to bring them back is like attempting to catch the fish in the water with my hands. I phone my brother, but his mind is rather blank too: we both keep coming back to the same moments, to the blue jersey trouser suit whose seat was so saggy, the suit that gave her a sort of independence, a trendy outfit, but with a touch of elegance too. In my quest to find who was hiding in or behind my mother, I book a session with an energy healer. Her website promises that, after meditating for a short time, she can receive a soul's energy.

The healer lives in an upstairs apartment behind Muiderpoort Station in Amsterdam and she greets me with a warm open smile. I trust her. A huge sofa, modular seating as they call it in the adverts, dominates the room, with a large television screen opposite it. There are soft toys, orchids, Buddha statues (of course) and there's a kind of stove giving off purple light. It turns out to be a HEPA filter to keep the air pure. Very down to earth. She unties her long hair because that's more relaxing and then we start.

    The healer meditates in silence with her hands together. Then I say my mother's name three times—Ans-Ans-Ans—and then the healer receives her energy. This all happens extremely quickly, and in short sentences she tells me what is coming through to her. I listen attentively for the first three-quarters of an hour because, although I trust her, I'm not yet convinced that she can make contact just like that with people in that parallel world. Does a soul really exist? And does the soul remain alive when the body is lying there so cold and forlorn?

    I make a mental note of all the things she mentions that aren't right: no, there was no dog, no standard terraced house with a front and back garden. Our garden wrapped round the house. No shop with a mullioned window. The bit about the sensitive teeth also seems strange to me. But then an image of my mother does appear that touches her core, in the way I remember it.

Sensitive teeth.
The second meeting with my mother.

The healer: 'Her energy is coming through unsteadily, as if she is living at the service of others and is self-effacing. Sensitive, very sensitive. She is not in her centre. A woman who senses and carries burdens; it wasn't always easy sexually either. A kind mother. Frustrated about life, it seems. She doesn't come over as carefree, her life was hard. She endured many fears.'

'Monday is washday, and I can see someone arriving by bike to do it together with her, it's nicer if you have company. The name Annie is coming through. Your mother isn't much of a talker, because even though she's very sensitive, she keeps it all to herself, nothing comes out. She's like a clam. Imprisoned in the small family circle, but what can she do? She has lost touch with herself. She would have like to have gone to university, to do something that inspired her. I can't see anything bad in her, but gentleness instead, a lot of gentleness. And unhappiness. She doesn't dare to come and go and do as she pleases.'

'A soft face of a man is appearing, light eyes. A long narrow face.'
    (Oh, that must be my father. Long and narrow, yes; soft, no. Dark brown eyes. A hard head.)
'She loved this person a lot. He was her safety.'
    (I don't believe a word of it.)
'Her husband and father seem to have become intertwined. The relationship with her husband is a good connection. As if they are standing together—and are one. But even now, your mother isn't showing anything, she's not communicating anything else, but I can see that they're standing next to each other. That is OK. That is what it is. Your mother needed attention and love, but it is dark in her aura. He was always at work. He did really love her, though. Perhaps she was used to living with scarcity.'

'And, yes, you shouldn't really say so, but your mother was happy to die. That sounds odd, but it's a weight off her shoulders. The suffering comes to an end.'
    Then I burst out laughing, which is inappropriate in the light of this sad remark about an unhappy life, but what the healer says fits too well with the image that has always stayed with me: after her death, my mother lay there so peacefully that I thought: she's much happier there than here.

'She had no pleasure in life', repeats the healer again.

Sensitive teeth.
The second meeting with my mother.

Then I ask questions: Did she love her children?
'Yes, but she is trapped inside herself and not accessible emotionally, not for herself and not for others. So not for you either, her children.'

'I sense a secret', says the healer, 'but nothing is coming, I'm not getting anything.'

Who was close to her?
'Her husband and children, of course, that was her world.'
'Men do what they like', says the healer, on behalf of my mother.

My father had a wartime past, I say to the healer, to shed some light on things.

'Yes, it is as if she understands him, she is carrying him. She isn't angry at him because she understands that if you've been through all that, it's just how you are, perhaps your mother accepts him. She loved him, she had no one but this man.'

'Shall I ask for your father's energy?'
That's fine, I say. *(He is there immediately. I can sense it, he's already in the way.)*

'A proud person. He walks with his nose in the air. A man who stands up straight, very different to your mother who prefers to hide. He looks powerful, but with a pounding sadness inside. That grief is choking his heart, it's beating against his arms and legs, making them kick and scream. A man of few words too, a tall heavy-set man.
(A short fat little man.)
He's the boss, it suits him to call the shots. Not someone who makes contact with your soul, but don't forget, that was also to protect himself.'
Then I say: just let him go, because I realise that it is all about my father again. He always dominated our conversations, even now, when I'm visiting a healer to learn more about my mother. My mother's energy enters the room again, mistily gentle.

'It's strange to say, but she is happy to die', the healer re-establishes her contact with my mother's energy.

Sensitive teeth.
The second meeting with my mother.

'No zest for life. It is as if very little makes her happy. Then it's a question of waiting until life is over and if you don't have much pleasure in life the days seem long. It's no fun being her, there's no joy coming through.'

What did my mother want to do in life?
 'I'm not getting anything.'
What did she enjoy doing?
 'Knitting, handicrafts. It seems she enjoyed making things.'
Yes, I say, she liked sewing clothes.
 'Yes, I can see it, she loved pretty fabrics. Timeless, elegant, wearable. That's how she appears now.'
Did she think she was beautiful?
 'She probably wouldn't go that far, but she did want to look nice, that's space for herself, receiving compliments, she can be real for a while. That's where there's least tension.'

But I don't feel anything at all, I say. My mother is in this room now, and I don't feel anything.
 'Yes, I also feel absence more than anything else', the healer replies, 'perhaps there never was real contact'. Then her energy disappears from the room, she is reluctant to come to this room. Although she is dead, she still doesn't want to open up. 'Please don't, leave me alone', is what I'm getting.

'You're the one who can break the cycle', the healer tells me. 'You are a happy version of your mother. You see things. I can also see anger in you. A red patch. Seek space, light, everything that brings happiness.'

'But listen. You did have a mother. She was there during the most important years. Perhaps you can shine a light for her, thank her, give love.'

My oldest friend reads the text and says calmly, 'This isn't new to me. Perhaps she senses you more than your mother?'

Hanne Hagenaars, *For Martha*, 2021

Bones.
The third meeting with my mother.

Mother is a distant word, so different from mama or mummy. Mummy in particular is like a cosy word from an old-fashioned book where everything is peaches and cream. Apple crumble-mummy, blackberry crumblemommy. 'Mother' is how I've referred to you for 48 years, my mother. Once upon a time, I used to call you 'mama', in that white house surrounded by tall slender pine trees, a lawn around it with flower beds full of orange and red marigolds (one of the few plants that you can't possibly call beautiful but that I love anyway because that's what memory does to you). Our shared blueberry-passion, blackberry-love, and walking-fervour, the empty buckets we took in search of chanterelles in the woods and brought back full to the brim. Luckily, I was the only one in the family who enjoyed this, maybe so I could be together with you for a while, the ultimate pleasure. The warmth and delight swirled around me on those days, accompanying me into the damp woods. 'Together', the magic word 'together'. But mama, mum, mommy, or my favourite word 'mutti', because it clings on to 'gemütlich' like a desperate little animal, we have lost each other and I am going to a shaman to find you.
    Mama.
    Dear mama (who art in heaven).

The shaman is embarking on the journey to the ancestral field and, if I breathe in and out slowly, I can accompany her and will perhaps encounter your spirit, my mother's spirit. The shaman tells me that you are energy now. Yes, energy. The underworld lies concealed deep in the earth, but we can make a very good connection from this small room on the first floor of a terraced house, if my mother's spirit allows us to, because the worlds somehow exist synchronously alongside each other. The shaman drummed and sang and took me along to the ancestral field or drew your energy towards me, that's also possible. I heard 'Johanna' rolling over the field like a long soft echo, Johanna -a-a-a. And while I lay there on the mattress, surrounded by singing and drumming, fragrances and colours, by movements and by cosmic crystals, I sometimes felt a cool hand on my face for a moment, and my skin seemed to explode with pleasure at this gentle touch. While I allowed the smell of cloves and cocoa, cedar and sweetgrass to drift inside me, your energy approached me. A big lotus opened from the pubic bone, a pink-white flower that diffused a sweet fragrance and blended with the spicy smells that the shaman had wafted over me.

Bones.
The third meeting with my mother.

A coldness took hold of me, chilling me to the bone, the sheet was suddenly far too thin, and without me asking, the shaman laid a blanket over me. Does that coldness come with you from the ancestral field that is so elusively distant? At the same time, I felt surrounded by fluffy protective air, a thousand arms were carrying me, no, I didn't rise up off the bed, I would have happily allowed myself to be carried away, but it didn't work, I was still lying down. Here.

And although perhaps I don't totally believe in the shamanistic view of death—because why of all theories should this one contain the truth?—I really did see that flower, with my eyes closed. Yet I felt contact with you, perhaps for the first time in my earthly life. It was there, unmistakeable.

This is what the shaman was able to convey to me about her journey to the ancestral field: 'There was a black thread running from you to the ancestral field, going back seven generations, a thread that turned gold later on. At a certain moment, I saw a grave and flowers were starting to grow there. Those flowers formed a bed of pink energy that closed around you, where you could surrender yourself to feel the connection and the love that's always there.'

'Your mother is present in your bones', the shaman explained to me. That seems to me to be the deepest depths of my body, it's what holds me up and it's what remains intact in the ground for longest. 'The fact that your mother's spirit has crept into your bones says something about the unbreakable, intense connection; it's no longer about remembering or loving, but about what cannot be broken. Of course there is love for your mother, even though she wasn't always able to envelop you in warmth, of course there is. If you want to receive her wisdom from the ancestral field, make contact with your bones.'

The invisible contact with my mother's soul, the lotus, the roses: the loneliness I felt somewhere, always deep down in my soul, had eased a little, but I have no idea how to make contact with my bones so I can feel them, without breaking or bruising them. I could go and meditate. I can also leave things as they are.

My mother

I am four
You are my mother

But I can't see you,
my short-sighted eyes.
The wild boar from the nearby forest are rootling
a hole through the hedge.
The wind is rising, the tall thin trees,
there, in the forest, are still standing.
In our garden they've had enough, and
one by one, they're falling, bang! on the gutter.
The house shudders.
The squirrels leap away to the neighbours' garden,
But I can't see you.

The front door is ajar,
one by one, I put the dolls outside.
When will the gods be satisfied?
Not yet, the back door is banging
The man
His house
No one's house.
We wander through the passages,
Meet no one.
The air is damp and above all heated.

This woman.
Who's been to Lourdes after all
Her weakness for bonbons
With so much warmth in her heart.

My mother

The bag

The bag

I still carry a small lump of guilt around with me, I can locate it in that thickening of my left middle finger that has a strange bend in it, towards the right and back to the left, with a cartilage bump at the top. That is where my guilt lies for remodelling my mother's wonderful snakeskin handbag into a watch strap when I was an adolescent. The bag was no longer used and lay gathering dust at the back of a big wooden cupboard. I kept on nagging until I was allowed to have the bag.

I was so eager to make something beautiful, something real. Never again having to open that drawer during craft class, to choose a picture to copy. And so I cut the snakeskin bag into strips and, in utmost concentration, I made a wide strap with a buckle, with a narrow strap inside to hold my discreet lady's watch. The result was a big bold thing that suited me much better. I got an eight for it.

I'm highly effective at hiding away feelings of guilt but the doctor calls the bump arthritis, so there's nothing to worry about. Until my brother sent me a mega web-transfer on the 2nd of September with 340 family photos after visiting my father's widow, when he took home a big box of photos that had been there in the attic for years and years.

Then I see the photo. At the town hall. My mother is watching while my father is signing his name. He can be seen clearly on the photo but my mother is dissolving into the light that is streaming into the picture on the left side, speckled black full of dust particles. After signing the marriage certificate, the couple steps outside, truly radiant, and they pose briefly on the pavement for the photographer. My father and my mother. Their hands are close together and form a swirling spot together with the leather gloves that each is holding or wearing. They are smiling broadly. Quite logical, most people will think, on such a festive occasion. Together forever. My father is wearing his beige military jacket with brass buttons and his officer's cap. My mother is wearing a dark, somewhat flared coat with a fur collar, an elegant scarf, and a hat. The bag is dangling from her arm, yes, a real lady's handbag, made of snakeskin with a click closure and a narrow strap. That mysterious handbag made of genuine snakeskin, with small satin pockets inside as a finishing touch, for the powder compact, for a comb, peppermints. For a small purse, a handkerchief, perhaps a pen, everything a woman needed in those days. The handbag that was the witness at their wedding.

However many doubts my mother may have had about this man, as I later heard from her sister, my aunt Mimi, if you receive a bag like that as a present, you can't resist. What a wonderful, precious bag made of snake leather. Python. And I can't detect any doubt in all those photos. The mystery of a relationship is as opaque as an opal. Perhaps she really did love him, felt sorry for him because of his traumas and nightmares, or perhaps she was charmed by his handsome face. Perhaps she felt his pain and wanted to take care of him. Not only on the wedding photos, but on all the photos, my parents are looking at each other with a sort of twinkle in their eyes or are smiling broadly.

I always assumed that my father's thick red ring finger was caused by a snake bite, when he had seized that bag from a snake, in my feverish child's imagination. It was probably a gunshot wound where the doctors had done a pretty good job of saving the finger. Only just back from the colonial war, he brought a big snakeskin with him, together with trauma and a lock on his emotions. Such a beautiful and important gift—how could I have cut it up? As if it symbolised my dark thoughts about… about everything. The guilt-bump.

Until I met the Mexican artist Dodi Espinosa, whose work contains a lot of snakes. 'Wonderful', he cried, 'it's the passing of time. Transformation.' The snake is temptation. A Mexican god. A snake is slithering over the earth, in eternally undulating cosmic energy. Take your pick! The snake is a mythical creature that is both a cosmic creator and a destroyer, and a sacred being. It slithers over the ground and picks up centuries-old knowledge via the vibrations it feels when its body makes contact with the earth. A snake smells with its forked tongue and hears via its skin. It never blinks its eyes, is always wakeful. The jaw of a python can come loose from its hinges; I saw a photo online of a cut-open python that had swallowed a man whole—you could see his legs lying in that long body. I also read that a snake can mate for days or weeks, which is why the snake represents active phallic energy, endless potency. And so that was also dangling from my mother's arm.

My mother, who never protested; gentle soul that she was, she complied with my father's moods, like an ideal pancake that adapts itself to the shape of the pan, but never burns, never falls apart, in the worst case turns out a bit too colourless and limp for fear of being burned. But what do I know about their love, their hate, their relationship? Only that I was afraid. The handbag became a watch strap, and that strap has got lost somewhere. Perhaps it fell into the dust on the ground, then a car drove over it, and it was destroyed by the rain and the sun. The transformation of the snake goes on and on. Through the dust, through the ash, sand, and mud. Right through the phallic energy. Perhaps the snake has been transformed via the watch strap into gentle kundalini-energy, the energy that slowly winds its way upwards through all your chakras. Divine energy. Perhaps their smile to each other was genuine after all.

Sometimes I sit on the sofa and sometimes my mother is suddenly sitting next to me, just like a flash in my mind. My hand moves, but of course it touches an empty space. Then I caress the emptiness for a moment. The dead never leave you. Sometimes I cycle through the city and see the magnolia in bloom and a few weeks later the fallen petals lie on the roof of a car and cover the street. My dear sick mother, who so bravely pretended nothing was wrong. A well-meant but uncomfortable game. 'Take care of your father', she said to my older sister, just before she died. She was worried, needless to say. But dear mother, at that time you didn't know that within a few months a blonde schoolteacher would be parking her car outside your front door. Our front door. That she would be cooking a lousy pasta on your stove. Your sheets—no, the sheets you shared—took on her smell.

Then I think about your garden, Aldi, dear sister, where tufts of blue flowers grew in the white flowerbeds; those were my favourite speckles of colour in that beautiful garden. The blue of our mother's eyes.

My mother was laid out in her very best summer dress of loosely woven, mustard yellow linen with copper-coloured buttons and a belt. The sleeveless dress drew attention to the inactivity of her bare arms. They would never again put clothes through the wringer on Mondays, never again take a deliciously moist brioche loaf from the baker. Her hands lay folded, never again to sew green hockey skirts for her three daughters, or those troublesome white flannel shirts that we didn't like at all, because we wanted the official clothing from the sports shop. She would never again pull staples out of a brown cardboard package. I looked at her face for a long time, at the expression of quiet happiness on her face, and sighed deeply. The eighth of September 1974. My mother… I don't believe I was with her when she died, but I'm no longer absolutely sure, my autobiographical memory (my hippocampus? the ventral frontal cortex?) has dark, almost black areas of mould when it comes to this period. I loved my mother intensely, but did she love me? I used to stand by her side like a brave knight and tried to protect her from that almighty man beside her, my father, but I think that this was more of a hindrance than a help to her. She liked to make herself invisible, to prevent arguments. I thought that she ought to stand up for herself, but that was not in her character. And who stood up for me?

After her death, my grief retreated immediately, I thought I had lost it and looked everywhere: in Delft, in the neighbourhood full of stark new-build houses and the tall block of flats where we lived for a while, in the house my parents moved to, just before my mother passed away—a semi-detached house in a quiet square in Pijnacker, just outside Delft. I spent one last summer there. In my attic room, I looked at the family photos over and over again, gathering dust in a cardboard box, and longed for a new and different life, although I had absolutely no idea what that life might look like.

Perhaps my grief was broken? Could it have been crushed by my father when he stood yelling by my mother's sickbed in the hospital? If that were so, was it lying broken under a chair, watching, during that evening when my father stood waiting in a corner like a bullfighter and attacked my younger sister who, in his opinion, had come home too late? It turned into a real fight, but without blood. My sister soon forgave him again, but I didn't, I remained angry for days or perhaps even weeks. Being angry is also a feeling and, at any rate, a clear feeling. So I did have feelings but all the other ones took the form of a dark fog in my head and I could only think: go away. Or I maintained a bitter silence. My warm body felt desires, many desires, for something different and better, and shame too, immense shame for all the rows I witnessed when my father was angry again, at the neighbour, at a car driver, at all the members of my mother's family, and his own brother. At my younger sister, at my older sister, at his only son. Going into a shop with him was risky because a sense of suspicion could flare up at any moment and if he felt slighted, you'd better watch out. A lot of fear was dissolved into that grey fog in my head, nebulised fear, intangible and unrecognisable.

But the grief was not in that mist. Perhaps it had hidden behind that teacher at school, that popular art teacher, whom I only knew from stories. But at the graduation party he suddenly offered to drive some students home in his orange-painted Volkswagen. Okay! After he'd dropped my boyfriend off, there were just the two of us in the car and he'd asked me to come and sit in the front. His right hand touched my hair fleetingly. But he didn't drive to the block of flats where our family was living temporarily, on the 20th floor, no, he drove to a mill just outside Delft. 'What are you doing?' I remember asking. He parked the car, and then that fog again. Wisps. Like the Spanish painter Zurbaran's bound lamb but without ropes around my ankles and wrists, simply paralysed. No, I didn't need to worry, he'd 'leave before the gospel', that's what he always did with his wife too. He drove me back home nicely.

   I was eighteen at the time and the hormones were raging through my body. My mother lay critically ill in bed at home and at the same time there was that lust, and the urge to investigate, so it really seemed as if I'd asked for it because of those inappropriate thoughts. Perhaps God had read my desires, like on that painting where a man goes to take communion, but God sees that his thoughts are not pure: the devil is already dancing around his hands and quickly snatches the host away. No purification for bad people. That's what I thought. I did not trust in this 'leaving before the gospel', and so I wandered through a quiet, cheerless neighbourhood on Sunday morning until it was time for my appointment with the weekend doctor.

The pills he gave me made me tired, so tired that at home I couldn't lift another box. We were in the throes of moving house. My memory is blackish even today, but I do remember that the doctor came to our house after I collapsed. I lay in bed among the boxes and slept for days. No one asked me anything. I hid that secret away, perhaps together with the fear and the shame.

I didn't like going back to that new house on the square in Pijnacker, a town close to Delft. My father had remarried soon after my mother's death. Where had she come from so suddenly? And now she was lying in the bed in my mother's place, in the same bed where my mother had gone through so much pain. Unbearable. But my father drew me onto his lap, 'I understood that, didn't I? I was no longer a child'. Then he recalled memories of his amazing sex life with my mother. When they were still young. He was still wearing his pyjamas and I sat there again like a meek lamb. Paralysed. I was sick in the attic, very quietly, and that green feeling came up again immediately whenever I saw him. He stank, I shivered. And when I did go to that house in Pijnacker I secretly poured spirits into empty bottles I took with me, as a surrogate for the bags of vegetables and homemade apple pie that my friends' mothers gave them. I warmed my heart with sips of Cointreau and a few drops of cognac.

After this art teacher, I also had a short, wonderful affair with an Alan Delon-like boy in Tours, just under Paris. We were allowed to use his brother's flat. Never did scrambled eggs taste as delicious as then, never was an affair so profoundly beautiful. The taste of heaven. But my mother's death, shortly afterwards, had a far-reaching effect: no mountains of grief but a heavy blow to my lust. It was as if my mother was watching me rebukingly from heaven, no, there was something she didn't like at all. It was with a pitiful remnant that I moved to Utrecht, finally free. Or so I thought. My body thought about it differently, it refused, became paralysed, would no longer join in with me. It took a long time before I was able to to lure back the lust.

Years later, I plucked up all my courage in a moment of clarity and rang the doorbell of that popular art teacher. My plan was to hurl curses at him, preferably with his wife there too.

Yes, that's how I envisaged it. That he had to stay away from me if he didn't want to stay for the gospel. To shout at him that he had strangled all my hormones to death, stabbed the life out of them, drained them dry. But the door was not opened. No one at home.

Perhaps that is why the grief was waiting for me in a corner of my student room. I was studying psychology, to make the world a better place—how arrogant or how foolish. I was nobody. An unhappy girl who went along with the group to the bar, who felt no grief. Yes, my fellow students were interested to hear that I had just lost my mother; that made an impression, especially during the psychology seminars. 'I haven't been through so much', said the girl who came after me apologetically. But I didn't show anything. There was nothing. Just that emptiness, and that intense longing, for love, for warmth, perhaps even for a hug from my mother. Maybe it was not surprising that when the figures were published from ground-breaking research by Nel Draijer [*2]—one in seven women is sexually abused—my girlfriends looked around, counted to seven and then said aloud: we thought of you. I did not even ask why. I fled, into that black fog. Remaining silent. All those men's secrets were extremely well hidden. I don't feel as cold as I used to, but I don't have access to the black areas of my memory. The grief emerged shyly. Not that it will ever stand up straight beside me, so we can look at the world proudly, hand in hand, no, I think of it more like a parcel that I always carry with me under my arm; sometimes it lies on the table, sometimes under my bed. It now has tissue paper wrapped around it with a loose string. Yet I can only unwrap it every now and then because it soon becomes too much for me; it will simply go with me into my grave and that's fine.

GOLD

I was ten years old when Nan Goldin's older sister took her own life by lying down on the railway tracks. 'It was an act of immense will', writes Goldin in her foreword to the photobook *The Ballad of Sexual Dependency*. Goldin sensed that her sister was unable to go on because of all the limitations and stifling norms that were imposed on her, a woman's life in the sixties. In the week that followed, Nan Goldin was seduced by an older man, and it is the first time that I read how lust and loss can come together, how the primal forces of sex and death can get in each other's way. For Goldin, it may well have been her salvation because she ran away from home to live a life according to her own views. She was fourteen at the time.

> 'The diary is my form of control over my life.
> It allows me to obsessively record every detail.
> It enables me to remember.'

She starts taking photos, to record details, in order not to forget. And she writes:

> 'But recently I've realized my motivation has deeper roots: I don't really remember my sister. In the process of leaving my family, in recreating myself, I lost the real memory of my sister. I remember my version of her, of the things she said, of the things she meant to me, But I don't remember the tangible sense of who she was, her presence, what her eyes looked like, what her voice sounded like.'

And she dedicates her photobook with the photos of the life she has chosen for herself 'to the real memory of my sister, Barbara Holly Goldin.'

The wild nightlife that Goldin celebrated with her friends, her new family, produced a constant stream of photos. The camera seemed to be attached to her hands so no one noticed it any more. No one poses. They are themselves with all their zest for life and partying. Beneath a classical erotic painting with curvaceous female bodies in a rather frumpy hotel room, a woman sits contentedly in bed. On the bedspread with yellow flowers lies a present and a bunch of roses. She is rolling a cigarette, or a joint, full of concentration.

The photo next to it: A woman in a gold top and trousers is asleep, nestled in a thick, luxuriant, gold-flowered throw that is draped over a black sofa, next to a television, but the world goes on without her and her friends taking part in it. They live in their own world. A world of drunkenness, a life of sex and drugs that takes place at night. After the death of her sister, Goldin has an extra sense for what is the authentic and she finds it in these people, swirling around with all the beautiful and ugly sides.

The non-grief

A diary is what she calls the photos, but it also seems as if she, in defiance of her family's silence and concealment, wants to show everything here, holding nothing back. As if she is shouting loudly, just look, this is my life, just look how I'm enjoying it, and judge away! She explains that she never wore her glasses so her life became even more of a blur of undulating and dancing patches and colours. "The diary is my form of control over my life. It allows me to obsessively record every detail. It enables me to remember."

The real memory, that of complete honesty. *The Ballad of Sexual Dependency* is named after a song in *The Threepenny Opera* by Kurt Weil and Bertolt Brecht. The book is like an opera that takes place in the nocturnal life of a big city, where ecstasy and drugs and sex, and yet more drugs, love and loss, tears, intimacy and independence and mutual dependence are consumed with voracious gulps.

I have the impression that great photographers should also press the shutter with their eyes closed at the perfect moment, that photography is first and foremost intuition. Nan Goldin preferred not to wear the glasses for her short-sighted eyes. Without those glasses she could not choose and focus precisely, but she had a real gift for the snapshot. And it prevented her as a photographer from selecting, from letting her norms define the photo. What is the real memory? Without selection. Without norms. To show it exactly as it was.

Nan Goldin's words brought me comfort because they showed me that it can simply happen, that death and sex can end up wound up together. And I saw that Goldin dived into that crazy pool of friends, lust and love, instead of remaining seated, frozen, on a chair, as I did. Where could I have thawed out? That desire, that greediness in Nan Goldin's photos, there's the party, the life I dreamed of in my attic room, and later in my lonely first-floor-at-the-back student room. That intense life which I am going to seek out in my next life.

Nan Goldin lost her family once again; most of the people on the photos are no longer alive. Aids. Drugs. It is a memory, gone forever, the moment that lasted until Nan Goldin stepped outside again after rehab, into the sunlight. But that takes nothing away from the shiny, turbulent life that she shows us.*[3]

Nude

Nude

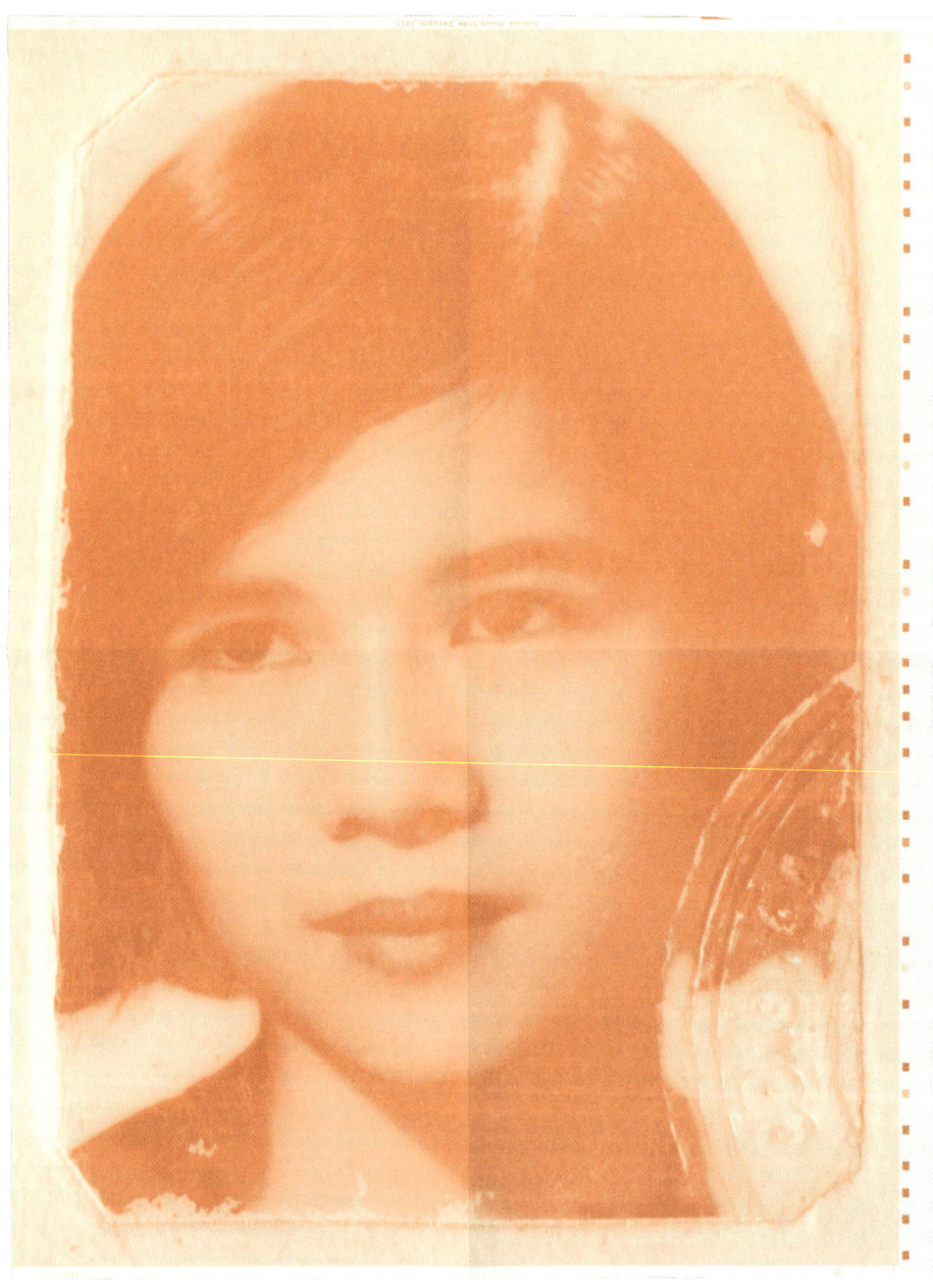

Simone Hoàng, *Hoàng Thị Như Hảo*, 2019, 74.5 × 60 cm, aluminum offset plate, (photo: Gert Jan van Rooij)

Nude

Simone,

Going back through my notes, I see that the photo of your mother is to be read universally. 'It must go beyond what is personal', you said. 'The work may well be about my Vietnamese mother, yes, it is her portrait. Or rather, no, it's the passport photo from her ID card, that is important.' I can barely recall the conversation from my scribbled notes. About how you set to work with laboratory assistants to develop an acid enabling you to separate the colours of a negative. About brushed stainless steel. Confrontation mirrors, reinforced glass. It was a nice intense conversation, full of technology and full of black holes. 'Black holes confront us with the greatest challenge in physics: how to reconcile the largest structures of the universe with the smallest structures.' *[4] The universal and the personal. So much scientific research in order to give the love for your mother a right to exist—flashed through my mind. And at that time I did not yet realise how special your love is.

I saw the work *Nude* in the living room of its brand new owner, Joep van Lieshout. There she was again: your mother. Three differently tinted prints of the same passport photo. A parting in her hair. Her gaze, modest and shy. Infinitely gentle. Elusive. I look at her, but she is looking just past me with her eyes directed slightly upwards. In the yellow print, the face has almost disappeared into the paper. In the red version, the hair frames the young face, which lights up like a narrow heart-shape. The brown version is readable as a black and white photo. The blocks of colour lie under the three upright portraits, brown, red and yellow, as a response to that sweet gentle face. As if the colours have leaked downwards and have been caught there by three equally sized pieces of paper. They marble the sheet. Title: *Nude*. Sometimes her name: Hoàng Thị Như Hảo.

Little by little, the story emerges, the story about you and her. About how your mother came to the Netherlands as a boat refugee and met your father on that boat. The programme *Andere tijden (Different times)* reports on the rescue of an overcrowded boat like that one with Vietnamese refugees.*[5] The splashing water around the boat turned out to be caused not by people swimming but by the sharks that were swarming around it. The refugees floated around for days without food or drink. Parents gave their children a burial at sea.

A Dutch ship took them on board. 'I can still remember that moment very clearly. There was a strange smell coming from that boat; I've never smelt that odour again but I have the feeling that I smelt death then', the captain relates.

The smell of perfume becomes visual in your hands because you develop rolls of film in perfume baths. Anachronism. You immerse a roll of black and white film in boiling water and this produces a blue print. Conversely, it appears that the most horrifying moments are often stored as a sensory experience. All that a conductor remembers of the car accident in which he lost his wife is their daughter's scream. That intensity became the yardstick for his music. Perhaps those images are too heavy for the eyes so they let them go. Falling images. Smell is a powerful force, perfume can intoxicate, tempt, repel, obscure. The streets of Vietnam smell of jasmine, of the faintly sweetish smell of the river *6 but no exotic fragrance can drown out the smell of the war.

The ten-part documentary *The Vietnam War* contains an unparalleled amount of found footage. After two episodes of the series I have to take a break. Not only because of all those mutilated bodies, the atrocities that must have taken place beforehand, but above all the realisation that there was no escape possible, not from the incessant bombardments, not from the fluctuation of the concepts of good and evil and the deadly consequences. Eight more episodes to go. 3,387,148 deaths.*7 In April '75 the fall (or the liberation?) of Saigon marked the end of the war. The conflict continued, about who was right, who was wrong, re-education camps, brutalities, a civil war full of booby-traps. Your mother grew up in this torn-apart country. We can only surmise what her eyes saw. Or the smell from which she can never escape. And then *you* are there. Simone. Your name means listening or hearing. What a wonderful name for an artist. You are true to your name because there is a beautiful sense of compassion floating among all those chemicals. You grew up without many photos being taken, first in your mother's arms, later in foster families. But without pictures to look back into the past. The writer Dubravka Ugrešić divides refugees into two categories: those who have photos and those who do not. The photos are the facts of life of a vanished existence. And even though the photos only show the cherished moments of life, the wider universe filters through those images. If you read carefully, an image of a period in time comes to the fore, of peace, of war, poverty, a part of the world. Photos tell so much more than just the life of the main character. Ugrešić describes the existence as a refugee as a dreamlike state in which fragments of the past come and go. Without the photos that bring the memories to the surface or to which your memories willingly conform, the past is a blank sheet of paper. Without something to cling onto, the memories withdraw into their own uncertainties. The photos serve as punctuation for the memory; they make it possible to read it like a story that we weave around it afterwards. While I am writing this text, my list of questions grows: when did you visit Vietnam as a child together with your mother? An artist in residency in Ho Chi Minh City. But then I read the following sentence by Ugrešić:

> 'One more thing: the question as to whether this novel is autobiographical might at some hypothetical moment be of concern to the police but not to the reader.'

There is absolutely no need to sift through your past; fragments are enough and the work is a touchstone. Those are the facts.

In our second conversation, you tell the story of you and your mother. About how she was not able to look after you. And how you received four photos after her death, including the one from her ID card. There she was, your mother. You looked at the photos again and again. A country and an era hover behind her image; she is your mother but at the same time so much more. You notice that her skin tone takes on strange colours, sometimes even a dark spot, and you set out to investigate. It turns out, a very sobering thought, that the first colour films were designed to portray white skin. Of the three very thin emulsion layers on the negative, the red-sensitive layer is at the bottom. This means the colours that are needed to portray a different skin colour are less likely to appear. Yellow, brown and red. An explanation that is consistent with a chemical formula. But at the same time, I think about the French who colonised Vietnam for a century, who regarded the Vietnamese as an inferior race, and who, with their refusal to give up the colony, form the origin of the Vietnam War. They were white, just like the Americans who took over the war. As a hard-core scientist, you dive into the chemical formulae. Unexposed rolls of film go into an acid bath so that the colours of the emulsion layer come to the top and are then separated again using another procedure. The image of your mother rises up out of the colour baths, from the colours yellow, brown and red. Unmistakable. Using these processes, you make large prints of the difficult colours brown, red and yellow as an act of reparation for everyone whose skin is not white.

You suddenly send me a number of documents. About 'securing your place' with the foster family, about your name change, and a death certificate for your mother. In the latter document I read the incomprehensible line: 'Approved the deletion of 21 words and 3 punctuation marks.' I check—it is correct. The institutions that noted this so precisely could do nothing for her, they were unable to make contact with her. Authorities. 'Why was there no one who simply rang her doorbell?', you wonder. When you are 31, you decide that you want your own name back. Yes, I understand that, why can't you belong, with all your individuality? Why that adjustment? Being Vietnamese and having a name like Klomp (wooden shoe) is an uneasy combination.
   'There is a certain expectation, an assumption, that anger dominates my life, that I am angry with my mother. But I *am* my mother's daughter.' Yes, fortunately you are her daughter, standing up for her. 'Immense sadness lies behind her choice. That she must have been so lonely, despite my being there. I was actually never with her, even though I was there. Because it takes a lot of courage, knowing that your daughter is going on with her life without you. I felt that there was love, a form of devotion, she gave love. I felt it.' I find it intensely moving. In the Netherlands, therapists teach children to distance themselves, to be angry, to stand up for themselves. But do we teach love? Or does love lie in those big abstract sheets of paper, and can we absorb some of it by looking?

'Night sensitivity' is your latest project. Somewhere beyond the Atlas Mountains in Morocco, towards the Algerian border, is one of the places where the world is darkest; the darkness is at its most intense just before the sun rises. The night, the negative of seeing, that shrouds who we are; you make images emerge from that dark night. Just as our memory can creep out from the darkness of what has been forgotten, like a softly whimpering little animal. By developing the negatives lovingly and with miraculous chemicals, an image is created, not a realistic image but a beautifully scented image of a flower. That is love. Those are the arms that embrace your mother.

'I still remember that, when we first met, you asked me whether this work is an ode to my mother. We are now somewhat further in the process and I think more and more that it is an ode to *the* mother, not per se *my* mother. An ode to the origin, the beginning, the source.'

The more we talk, the better I understand that it is without doubt also an ode to *this* mother. Wherever she is, your love will reach her. And we can feel it—with you.

Nude

Simone Hoàng, Nude, *Hoàng Thị Như Hảo*, 2019, 210 cm (3 times 70 × 50 cm), brushed stainless steel, tempered glass, confrontation mirror, perspex, HCL LED, Ilford Gold Fibre, Chromolux, dibond, museum glass, maple wood, (photo: Gert Jan van Rooij)

The rooms

The rooms

Marenne Welten, *Kitchen Cabinets,* 2022,
(photo: Art in Print, Middelburg)

For twenty years now, Marenne Welten has been wandering through the rooms of her childhood home in her mind's eye, like in a film, and she paints those rooms: the hall, the kitchen, the bathroom and, in particular, various versions of the living room. Sometimes the brushwork is thin and transparent and sometimes, by contrast, extremely thick. Green, blue, white and brown dominate but there are few places with just one single colour because everything has become entangled, nothing is solid. Only when you look at it for a bit longer does a chair, a desk or a lamp emerge from the paint. The dank colours show a room in desperate need of a window being opened for some fresh air. The seats are heavy armchairs. A cloth on a small round table touches the floor all around it.

A small girl with blonde hair and a green face is standing beside a plant that is almost as tall as she is, and she has been painted the same colour as the window and the kitchen cabinet behind her. Yet all the attention is drawn to her because of the dashes of white paint highlighting her clothes and face. Her sweater looks much like a brown-green vista surrounded by her arms that form a thick frame in the same colour. Her two yellowy-green legs slant to the right like bamboo canes. Unsteady. There is a plant, a window, and a kitchen cabinet, but that shy girl dominates the image.

A little girl is sitting cramped up in a huge chair, watching TV, with her thin purple legs on a footstool. Expressionless. An island. It is as if time has been squeezed out, as if then and now are clasping hands. A living room with a piano, a cactus, a chair with a cat, but all this still doesn't make it homely. Everything looks awkward, dissolving into the paint, and you can barely grasp it with your eyes. As if the memories also prefer to run away from it, in pursuit of time.

As she paints, Marenne travels back into the past, especially to the living room: the place where she was told that her father had died, although at the time she did not really understand what death meant. 'An uncomfortable memory but when I looked at it through the eyes of a painter, as if I were looking at an unknown room with its own colour and composition, the tension vanished. That was the key to painting my past, and the letter Ted Hughes wrote to his daughter Frieda about the power of disguise helped me too.'

> 'The emotions of a real situation are shy, but if they can find a mask they are shameless exhibitionists. So — look for the right masks, cast about and experiment. A feeling is always looking for a metaphor of itself in which it can reveal itself unrecognized.' *8

Marenne paints the room and not the scene in which her mother told her about the death of her father. The paint packages the painful moment that Marenne remembers in strokes, in colours and directions until the pain slowly disappears from it. The story becomes liveable. By always painting the room from a different perspective, she is able to distance herself from that one story. The intensely deep grief that comes up in waves is also allocated a colour and composition. The room can put up stiff resistance against that memory or flow away before your eyes like melting ice.

In this way, Marenne's painted rooms each trigger an emotion that you can pick up simply by looking closely. You can walk into the rooms and feel what she feels. 'The oil paint combines with the brain and while I paint an area opens up within me that I don't yet know. That's where logic flies out of the window. I used to use photos, but I definitely don't do that anymore; I destroy the picture that I encounter in my mind and build it up again using the paint. The front door is polished; the rubbish, the trash, is by the back door and I that's where I go. From there, I can go on.'

The rooms

Marenne Welten, *Room*, 2013, (photo: Art in Print, Middelburg)

An omen

Lorena Torres, *Tu y un presagio (You and an Omen)*, 2022, 100 × 150 cm, oil on canvas

An omen

I'm longing for the sun. It's raining outside and despite the fact that I live in the middle of the city, aeroplanes are roaring low over my upstairs apartment. It seems to have something to do with the wind and the rain. The din is deafening. It's already been raining for weeks and, if the rainfall radar is anything to go by, it has set in for a while. There's always sun after rain, but I'm afraid that it could just as well take four years, eleven months and two days, the time that the primal-mother Ursula had to wait in the book *One Hundred Years of Solitude* by Márquez until the rain finally stopped and she could die peacefully. Joyless and rain-weary, I wander over the internet, via via via I come to a painting by Lorena Torres: a person with a red ear and a moth on their forehead. *Tu y un presagio / You and an Omen,* 2022. You and the omen: a greyish moth as an omen to remind you that life is short (as if I don't know that). A memento mori moth, which spreads its wings or flies into the lamplight to remind us of the cycle of life and death. In the Old Testament, the moth (asj) is mentioned as a small butterfly that prefers to ensconce itself in clothing. The moth stands for transience and destruction. I know that from my own experience: little holes in my favourite cardigan, my endless battle against the larvae. Compared with a butterfly, the moth is a step-animal, an ugly sister. But even the moth gives you unexpectedly beautiful moments, such as a moth that drinks birds' tears or feeds itself by drinking the moisture from the eyes of crocodiles and turtles. A scene from the book *One Hundred Years of Solitude* has crept into real life. 'There is not a single sentence in my novels that is not based on reality. But the sense of reality of European readers prevents them from seeing that reality isn't limited to the price of tomatoes or eggs', Márquez once responded in an interview.*9 His thick book lies under my bed, in case I wake up at night and want to go on adventures. I keep Lorena Torres' paintings for the daytime. I print a few of them out and hang them on the wall beside my work table. And online I read Lorena Torres' motto.

> 'My painting and, in general, my artistic explora-
> tion are one; they are life after death, like my
> grandfather Manuel del Cristo, who was born once and
> died twice, although no one believes me. These are
> not stories to tell, and they are stories to watch.'

An omen

I decide to write to Lorena and through having read *One Hundred Years of Solitude* I can say to her from the bottom of my heart:

```
Dear Lorena,
I do believe you.
Who was your grandfather?
Can you tell me something about him?
Hanne
```

In a long letter, she tells me the fascinating story about her grandfather. My grandfather was born and raised in the small town of Puerto Giraldo, on the north coast of Colombia. I believe I only saw him about ten times in my entire life. I remember him as a man who was usually dressed in white shirts and trousers but it's just a memory that I'm not a hundred per cent sure of. Since I never had the opportunity to share intimate moments with him while he was still alive, I grew up creating an idea of who he was, based on the stories my dad used to tell me about him. Our family called him Manuel del Cristo or 'El Viejo Mañe'.

The day when I truly met him was the day he died. I was living in Bogota and sometime around midday I received a call from my dad letting me know that that my grandfather had died. As I didn't have any kind of attachment to him, I just answered with a cold: 'I'm so sorry for your loss'. One hour after this call, my dad called again, telling me that my grandfather had somehow woken up from death. Later in my life, someone told me that this is not particularly uncommon but for me this was the beginning of my relationship with El Viejo Mañe.

A huge magical door opened before my eyes. Two days later, I was travelling back to Barranquilla, the city where I was born, and taking a car down to Puerto Giraldo. I remember my dad telling me to dress in white and grab some 'carnival' jewellery for me and my mother. I followed his instructions. On our way there, my dad was telling us that, the night before, the coffin with the body had stood in the town centre. Open. People had danced around it and a band played some traditional local music. For me this was so surreal that I could hardly believe it until I had the opportunity to see some videos taken by my aunts and cousins. When we got to Puerto Giraldo, the coffin was in my cousin's house. There were people dressed in traditional carnival dresses and his daughter was wearing a long dress with yellow butterflies (just like in *One Hundred Years of Solitude*) embroidered on it. People were talking about his life and it was my only opportunity to learn who my grandfather was. At around four o'clock in the afternoon, when the temperature was 30°C, more than 300 people were walking in a procession to the rhythm of a band playing, while several men were carrying his coffin. We arrived at the cemetery, which was full of dust and very old monuments. The sky was pink and suddenly there was a gentle breeze.

After that, I discovered that he had been planning his funeral for about four years. He wrote some of the music for his funeral, he paid for all the alcohol so everyone could drink for free, he asked old women to dance around his coffin in long skirts and without panties. It was his own way of making how he had lived his life something to remember, both for those who had met him and for those who had never known him. This event was surprisingly overwhelming for me because it coincided with the moment when I decided to become a painter 24/7. So, it was the beginning of a personal healing journey for me and the culture where I belong. I made a series of paintings called *La Muerte vino y yo me fui* (Death came and I left) which is a description of my experience through this new bond with my grandfather.

An omen

Lorena Torres, *Naranja en sol negro,* 2020, 100 × 100 cm, oil on canvas

An omen

Lorena Torres, *En cada tumba dejé una lagrima y un beso*, 2020, 100 × 100 cm, oil on canvas

Noortje

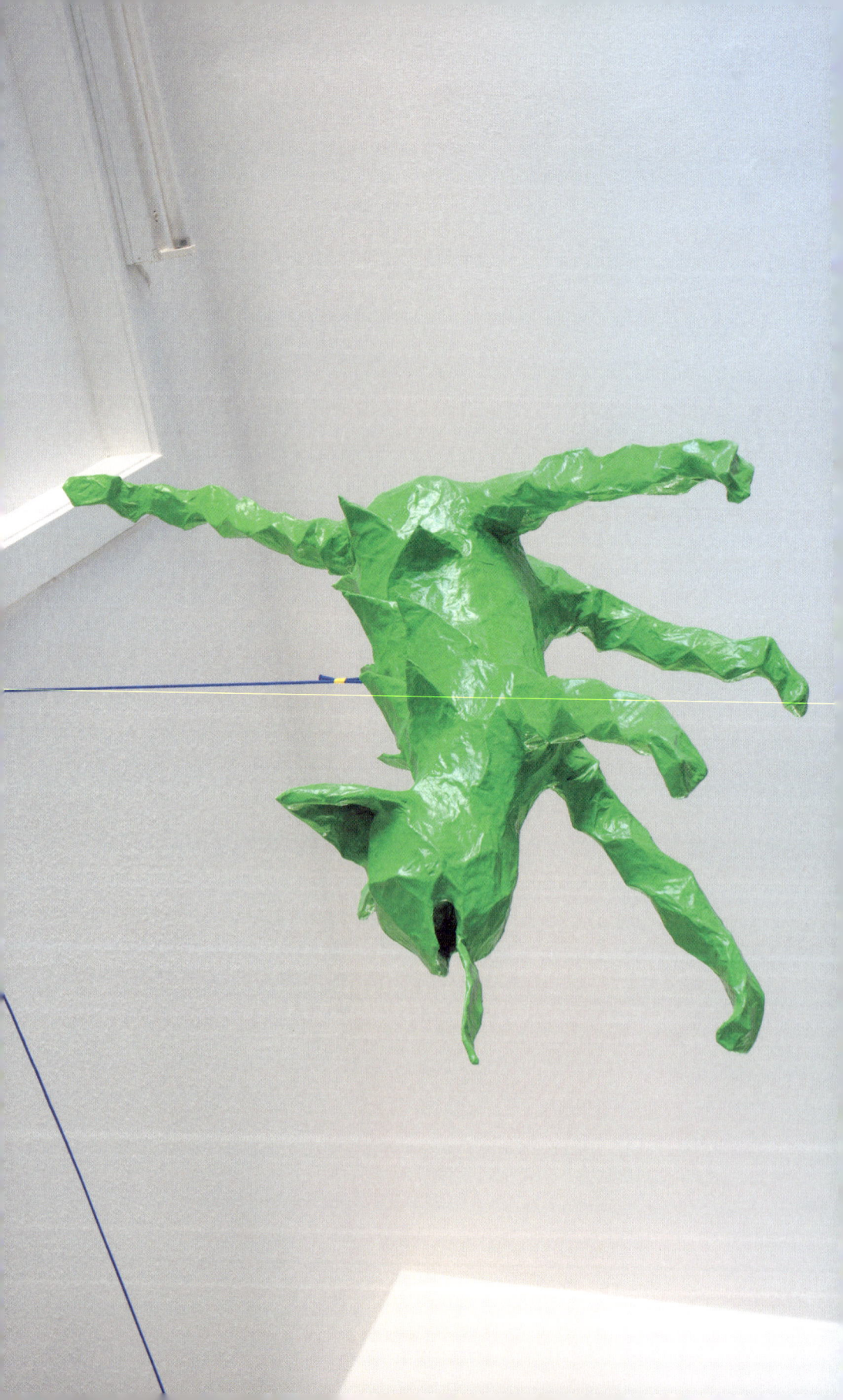

The vast majority of dog-petparents-owners-possessors are crazy about their pet because they receive so much love from them. An inseparable companion who is never critical but always wags its tail at you, licks your hand, and gazes at you loyally. In her book, *Dan neem je toch gewoon een nieuwe*, Antoinnette Scheulderman describes her bond with her dog Bubbels. 'When I sat on the sofa, and it was deafeningly quiet without the companionable click of her nails on the wooden floor. When I grated cheese, and no one came rushing towards me. When I came home and was no longer greeted as if I'd just returned from a trip around the world—even if I'd only just popped across the road to Spar for a carton of milk. When I sat crying on the sofa and didn't feel something tickling my neck; her warm head resting against my cheeks comfortingly.'

How different this was for the artist Mariëlle Videler: she chose a cat from the rescue centre that was traumatised and had an autistic disorder. She wanted to give this animal love.

When Noortje had just moved in with her, she regularly sent me photos of a cat that would barely show itself, just the tip of the tail, paws under the radiator. A hazy blob under the sofa. At first, Mariëlle couldn't make any contact with the shy creature. Noortje vanished as soon as Mariëlle entered the room on her stockinged feet. The cat was terrified and felt most at ease in the spare room in the attic that was full of green plants. Mariëlle used to put the radio on softly so that its hum would neutralise other unexpected noises somewhat because Noortje remained jumpy.

During the first weeks and months, Noortje's invisible presence filled the entire house like the pervasive sweet fragrance of cultivated lilies. When Noortje crept away behind the sofa, Mariëlle lay down in front of it and talked to her softly. 'I can still remember so clearly that she was sitting behind the sofa, looked at me for a moment and started to purr very loudly. She drooled a bit too because her teeth weren't quite right. It was heart-wrenching. Her entire being was longing for contact but she could not yet bear to be stroked. We spent the evening like that, and she eventually came to lie down in front of the sofa. The ice had been broken a little bit. And when I was finally allowed to stroke her, a shiver went right down her back.'

As an artist, too, Mariëlle wants to contribute to a better world, although she is only too aware of the depressing fact that her input can be no more than a thimbleful. And yet, every small contribution helps. During the bird year, she got up at six o'clock every morning, rain or shine, with iron discipline, and drew a bird on a sheet of paper, a creature that stemmed from her mood at that particular moment, inspired by all the birds she had ever seen and elaborated in her imagination. During *Bird Bath,* the walls of Lumen Travo Gallery were filled with 365 drawings of birds, each placed on a small piece of wood. It was unparalleled. During *Bird Club,* a cat was also present. In the centre of the room, there was a rug with the silhouette of a cat draped over a low bed so that her guests could lie on this cat to relate a special experience with a bird. In this way, the person was placed at the mercy of the cat for a while. In Mariëlle's view, a 'pet-animal', such as a dog or a cat, is a bad human fabrication; the word 'outside-animal' does not exist because that is where a cat belongs, instead of on an upper floor with walls on all sides. She took Noortje out of the rescue centre to salvage what she could of this cat-life, rather like caring for a discarded circus animal, but participating in the system of pet animals is something she doesn't ever want to do. 'I don't want to encourage that process.' The sinister number of pet cats in the Netherlands (2.9 million) disturbs the balance of nature to a significant extent. After high buildings, our sweet pet cat takes second place as a serial killer of birds. 'We fatten the cat up and then it goes outside to eat snacks, out of sheer boredom.' In Canberra in Australia, a law was introduced stating that cats would have to stay indoors in future because their impact on the biodiversity of vulnerable indigenous animals was too great. There were protests, and cats are now permitted to go for walks outdoors if they are on a lead.

Mister K., the previous cat who strolled through her life, always made a terrible din: he yowled at the most ridiculous moments and because he was deaf it sounded incredibly loud. It drove Mariëlle and her friends mad. 'Then you do start to think you might take him back to the rescue centre. You really do.' A heart-rending dilemma. Mariëlle embroidered a small banner, saying 'Stop the eviction' and placed it behind Mister K.'s food bowl, giving him a voice too. 'You take an older cat home with you, and you know it comes with a past. But you don't know in advance that the baggage it brings is an infernal din. But as soon as we were able to accept that this was just the way the animal was, a switch flipped and we were able to live with each other.' Just as in a human relationship, hidden forces play a role, such as unspoken thoughts that hang in the air, a tension that the animal feels too. Mister K. gradually made less noise.

In addition to being traumatised, Noortje also had a fragile body and after four years the deterioration couldn't be reversed: despite all the good care she received, she died. It happened shortly after Mariëlle had composed a paper plant every day for a year.

'I haven't really made a memorial for Noortje because I can't think of anything for something as big as the relationship with a cat. It is too extensive to capture those feelings in an image; it's not possible.' But after Noortje's death, she did make a wild, green, papier-mâché cat. At the end of the bird year, Mariëlle hung a homemade bird in the rafters of her bedroom, but after a year of drawing plants she couldn't produce another plant. After the silent plants that she cut out with the patience of a saint and then painted with ink, and a Noortje who always had to be approached with caution, something had to break out and it took the form of this fire-breathing energy-tiger. An idol, a power-Noortje. 'Have you noticed that it has a pulley on it, so that the cat can come down? If I need extra power, I release it.' She first painted the cat egg-yolk yellow, but it had to be this bright green after all. A green blowing cat. Green with envy and rage. Exploding outwards, look, his hairs are almost tiny wings.

Mariëlle and Noortje lived together in a space while they gradually got to know each other. Their bond was not via a conversation or by touching, but you could say that they experienced a spatial relationship in which they skirted round each other, warily looking, listening, sniffing. And although Mariëlle did not see the cat most of the time, she was always very much aware of her presence, just as a powerful gemstone also emits its influence into a room, unseen.

The autistic cat Noortje required an intuitive approach, sensing the air with one's fingertips, whispering nonsense words, or pricking up one's ears. Embodied seeing. Mariëlle learned this concept during a residency in Colombia where she met Abel Rodríguez (Mogaje Guihu), a man who grew up in the Amazon region and learned everything about the plants in the region from his uncle (a 'sabedor', someone who understands the secrets of plants and animals). Dom Abel shares his knowledge of plants by means of drawings that are often called 'a gift from the jungle'. Knowledge originates from so much more than objective facts and observing the world with your eyes and Don Abel introduced the concept of 'embodied seeing', inhabiting the world through your senses. 'Knowledge resides in your *canasto*,' Rodrígues told her, 'in your chest, together with your heart.'

Perhaps that green blowing cat was indeed Noortje's twin-energy and what the house was now urgently calling for. The wild, green version of Noortje is also inspired by the symbol of the jaguar that helps the shamans in South America as an assistance animal when they undertake their dangerous trance journeys. They paint themselves with the pattern of small open circles and spots of the jaguar, so that they are transformed into this animal and can undertake the dangerous journey using its power. In this sense, you could also call a cat an assistance animal because it challenges you to activate your intuition.

Making art happens via the body and that means that Mariëlle never outsources anything and produces all her work herself: drawing, cutting out, watercolouring, embroidering endlessly, she gets branches from the forest, drills holes in the wall, and puts in countless hours of work. Hand, head, heart.
 'I experience the world based on this body and the energy of the moment. I always try to establish contact with myself as the source as well as possible, and to explore the world starting from that position. In fact, I turn myself inside out to discover where my boundaries lie, what my language is. Where can I find freedom? Beyond my shame, beyond my fears, because otherwise I can't give everything.'
 She wants to give everything in her art. She explores the world outside herself carefully and takes it inside: everything can be found in that universe and usually in duplicate: light and dark, good and evil, eating and being eaten. That is what makes life special, and it is a matter of accepting those two opposing forces.

The sparrows are happy that Noortje is dead; they have more peace and quiet now that Noortje has stopped chasing them with her watchful eye, from behind the window.

Noortje, 2018

Memorabilia

Gábor Arion Kudász, *Memorabilia*, 2010–2014
The artist made an inventory of all the belongings of his mother, the painter Emese Kudász, who died on 22 November 2010.

The soul is more present than we think

Let's start with the biggest thing, the universe, the cosmos, the unfathomable. A photo taken by the Hubble space telescope shows us a pitch-black area, with an infinite number of luminous dots and ellipses, that scientists tell us is expanding on all sides. Boundless. Each ellipse-shaped speck is a separate galaxy, each with about 100 billion stars. We can see this thanks to the telescope; we can believe it, but it is impossible to really understand it.

I can believe in much more with my eyes closed than with my eyes open, for when my eyes perceive, they register only the things that reflect light; things with mass that take up space. Matter. With my eyes closed, I can imagine that, after 35 years, the soul of Ana Mendieta has found a place in the body of the artist Natalia Ossef. Completely covered with brown mud, her bent arms raised, Mendieta stands stock-still against a tree. Individual blades of grass are creeping up from the ground via her body. *Tree of Life:* like an earthly goddess, she is the central point of the planet; the distinction between human and tree has been removed. Her being is earth, grass, and tree. *[10]

Natalia Ossef (1983) and Ana Mendieta (1948). Two searching souls. Both grew up far away from their homeland and that very earth, mother earth, turned out to be the core of who and what they are. Both were in search of something profound, something that determines us as humans, the soul (or what may be called the soul).

As a twelve-year-old in Cuba, Mendieta was sent to America where she grew up without her parents. Her work was not understood for a long time, as if the world was not yet ready for it.

Natalia Ossef came to the Netherlands from Syria with her parents when she was four, from El Kamechli to be precise. Her parents are Orthodox Christians and speak Aramaic, an ancient language that is at risk of dying out because the minorities that speak it have been forced to live in diaspora. Syria, a beautiful country with a rich past: archaeologists have demonstrated that Syria was home to the oldest civilisation in the world. The country was part of what was often called the Fertile Crescent and the Neolithic culture goes back to 10,000 years before Christ. 'Where do you come from?' is usually the first question that Natalia is asked.

'Ten years ago, you could easily say that you came from Syria, people were open and curious, but now everything is coloured by the war.' People approach her with a series of assumptions, and that goes much further than the civil war. Perhaps the preconceived view that Edward Said described in 1978 in his book, *Orientalism,* still plays a role. In his opinion, the Western sense of superiority lies in the view taken by Europe, a view that was also fuelled by art with images of the Middle East as a sensual, exotic world full of voluptuous nudes, preferably in a harem. 'Orientalists presented the Islamic culture as static, as 'eternal, uniform and not able to define itself', which automatically made the West dynamic, innovative and enterprising.' *11 And the current situation with the war comes on top of all this. Images that are correct and incorrect tumble over each other: Syrian, Aramaic, Islamic, Christian, unbeliever, black hair and brown eyes, woman, artist? Or are these superficial labels, and do you need to go down a completely different path to find the essence? 'In order to know who I am and what identity is, I had to go and dig into the past.' What is the meaning of this existence, so far away from her native soil and in total oblivion of the ancient cultures that preceded us?

In order to unravel this, she set out for Antwerp to do a Masters. It gave her an introduction to a wide variety of works by women artists and both the recognition and the radical approach were like a breath of fresh air. Take *Semiotics of the Kitchen* (1975) by Martha Rosler. In a small kitchen, Rosler presents the cooking utensils in alphabetical order with dramatic gestures. Apron! Bowl Chopper! Dish! With restrained anger, she throws away the imaginary sauce that she scoops up with a ladle, she stabs the kitchen knife threateningly in the direction of the viewer. She expresses all her fury and frustration at restrictions placed on women in the sharpness of her gestures. Rosler depicts the last three letters with her body, throwing her arms in the air to form a desperate *Why* to indicate the letter Y.

> 'I was concerned with something like the notion of 'language speaking the subject', and with the transformation of the woman herself into a sign in a system of signs that represent a system of food production, a system of harnessed subjectivity.' *12

The paintings based on photos that Natalia made in the past suddenly didn't seem 'real' enough anymore, not sufficiently part of the world. Would the act of creating also be able to speak directly and hence reveal the meaning? To start with, the hands, like independent characters, separate themselves from the performance. Hands that reach, embrace, greet, desire. Can the actions that had entered her paintings from photos perhaps be translated into real gestures? Doing is after all a dimension that precedes language and that surpasses saying something in immediacy. It is difficult for a gesture to feign something.

In the East, mudras—a certain position of the hands or posture of the body—have been used for thousands of years in dance and rituals. A mudra attunes the flow of energy from the body to the universal, cosmic energy. Each gesture has its own meaning, the simple act of pressing hands together as a gesture of greeting (namaste) focuses the attention inwards and opens the heart. You could also interpret putting hands together in a Christian prayer as a mudra. Sometimes people hold their hands in front of their eyes in order to increase concentration, to turn inwards.

In the photographic series *Be my Contemporary,* hands play the leading role: they embrace a face, cradle a head, open, hide, weigh, and indicate. Natalia covers her face with her hands that emerge from black sleeves under a white jacket. Her fingers can be read like a detail of the moon with small pools of skin on the phalanges and under the nails. This mysterious black and white photo, which speaks to you without words and without sight, is called *Bird Face.* Cone cells that are sensitive to ultraviolet light enable birds to see the urine trails of mice, for example, or they see colour differences where we only see black. They experience the world differently than we do. Yet we should be able to expand the field of observation by being more alert to invisible energies. The love that can well up in your heart is an energy like this, or the ominous vibrations that you can feel in a room where an argument has just taken place. Her photo with the hands in front of the eyes reaches you without using voice or eyes.

It was scary, but Natalia Ossef had to make a new start, 'perhaps just as radically as John Baldessari', she says, smiling.

What she learned from that imposing American was to let go of her fear. In 1970, Baldessari was so dissatisfied with his semi-abstract painting that he decided to take all his paintings to the crematorium to have them burned. 'It was a very public and symbolic act,' he said, 'like announcing you're going on a diet in order to stick to it.' *[13]

Natalia Ossef embarks on a quest for her origins, and her family line guides her back to Syria, deep into the history of the world's oldest civilisations, and that brought her close to herself again. 'Although I was only four years old when we left our country, my being is connected with the earth there and my body feels the destruction. The war seems to have been set up to destroy the holy cities in Syria, to break contact with the sacred ground, the primordial soil where the feminine energy—the goddess energy—roams.'

History is an open shape, like an amphora; one person may throw tar into it, the other rose oil. The problem is that it is imposed on you every day, that single point of view taken by parents, books, and stories. You don't know any better. Written history is like a vessel that is always filled from a certain perspective. In search of the essence, Ossef not only dived into the past by symbolically travelling to her native country, but she also sought a zero point from which to make a new beginning, and that starting point could only be her own body. The body that is so concretely present as a casing that holds thoughts, bones, organs and impressions together, but how do all those impulses intermesh with one another?

In March 2020, she set off for a residency in the south of Spain, an isolated place with barely any internet coverage and where only women were gathered. The ground there was dry and desert-like and the area was dotted with Aleppo pines, those evergreen conifers with their soft, yellow-green needles that were planted there centuries ago. Surrounded by nothing but the rustle of the needles and the vibration in the air, the silence there was loaded. Never before had she listened to the silence like this. The energy simmered and lifted her up as if she were being carried. Actions come to life there: two powerful, proud women stand facing each other while they each hold a half sphere of clay, connected by a rope, against their navel. They look each other in the eye but the energy also circles round via the connected half spheres—the stomach area is after all the region where the emotions come together and are digested.*14 In the background, the mountains are silhouetted like breasts. 'We humans are replicas of mother earth', Natalia says to me. 'We are one with the earth; that is my true identity, and my desire is to bring that back. Everything else is a label, any category constrains reality.'

After the residency, her life is turned upside down. Her soulmate Wouter decides that his existence on earth has lasted long enough. After a spiritual experience that was like a near-death experience, it seemed as if his spirit was too big to return to the limited shape of the body. This time the silence is full of noise and it is crushing. Rationalising is of no help whatsoever. How can you possibly carry with you something that is too painful and too heavy to bear? 'Everything I knew—nothing was the same anymore.' The loss links up with that question about the essence of her being and she notices that she remains in connection with him beyond what is known, a deep connectedness, the realisation that the soul is endless, 'because I felt him, I had a lot of dreams in which he returned as if he wanted to say: there is something unmeasurably big, hang in there, go on, go on.' 'The soul is more present than we think. We believe in science nowadays, in seeing and measuring, but that excludes so much.'

```
And I don't believe in the existence of angels
But looking at you I wonder if that's true
But if I did I would summon them together
And ask them to watch over you
To each burn a candle for you
To make bright and clear your path
And to walk, like Christ, in grace and love
And guide you into my arms
— Nick Cave
```

'I no longer knew where I was and ended up between heaven and earth. The transparent dresses in my exhibition also hover like this, as if I am making a place for myself there': *Carry me along, The Domain of Intimacy.* The dresses carry precise quotes about the body, the scope of the senses, the connectedness of everything. They embody a fluidity where dialogue and thoughts flow together. There can also be heaviness in lightness, such as some observations on those ethereal dresses: *As though I were hearing some magic formula uttered in a foreign tongue.* As we read, we hover along with them; as we think, we hover further.

'We are replicas of mother earth', says Ossef, and it sounds like a gentle echo of Ana Mendieta's thoughts:

> 'I am overwhelmed by the feeling of having been cast from the womb (nature). My art is the way I re-esthablish the bonds that unite me to the universe, an omnipresent female force. The after-image of being encompassed within the womb, is a manifestation of my thirst for being. It is a return to the maternal source.'

In a photo, Natalia is nursing a round shape made of red-painted plaster that could be a womb. It makes no difference whether it is inside or outside the body. In the drawing *Primal Images 6*, a person is embracing another round, red shape like this, perhaps his belly, perhaps a child. A womb? Humans originate from mother earth, so the earth can be seen as a wonderful, immense round womb. We originated from the earth, or as Mendieta expresses it: we are 'cast from the womb, from nature'. Both artists regard themselves as part of the cycle of creation: earth, life, earth, and that will go on and on.

'I don't feel lonely anymore because I am more in contact with my own soul, with souls around me; now I've opened myself up to what manifests itself outside the physical. Like a dress that flows smoothly when you wear it or hang it up, the system in which I live has begun to move. Senses are awakening, sometimes voices rise up within me, and my intuition is becoming heightened. An invisible, endless stream has been set in motion.

What began in Spain has deepened, following the death of Wouter. Death has gained a significance that I was not aware of before. The soul or spirit does not disappear, and it takes the experiences of our human existence with it. That makes your life on earth really matter.

The death of Wouter was a great revelation about what reality actually involves. It was as if I had entered a hologram and saw the connecting filigree where universal love forms the core. At this moment in time, many people avoid the spiritual;

they don't believe in it. The ancient knowledge from long before religions with their male dominance seems to have vanished, but it remains stored in the body and that knowledge was awakening in me. A universal message from within. I don't belong here and yet I am here.

Returning to the origin means finding the healing, connecting energy again. Mother earth is our access to the spirits, as if you are diving back into that womb, being born again.'

> 'My art is grounded in the belief of one universal energy which runs through everything: from insect to man, from man to spectre, from spectre to plant from plant to galaxy. My works are the irrigation veins of the universal fluid. Through them ascend the ancestral sap, the original beliefs. The primordial accumulations, the unconscious thoughts that animate the world.
>
> There is no original past to redeem: there is the void, the orphanhood, the unbaptized earth of beginning, the time that from within the earth looks upon us. There is above all the search for origin.'
> – Ana Mendieta in 1983

Natalia Ossef scrapes the soil away. She makes space for her body. She presses herself onto that place against the great rocky wall. She lies on the ground, covered or uncovered with soil, always in perfect unity. Reaching from the earth towards the cosmos.

p. 80: Natalia Ossef, *ANKH III*, 2022

The soul is more present than we think

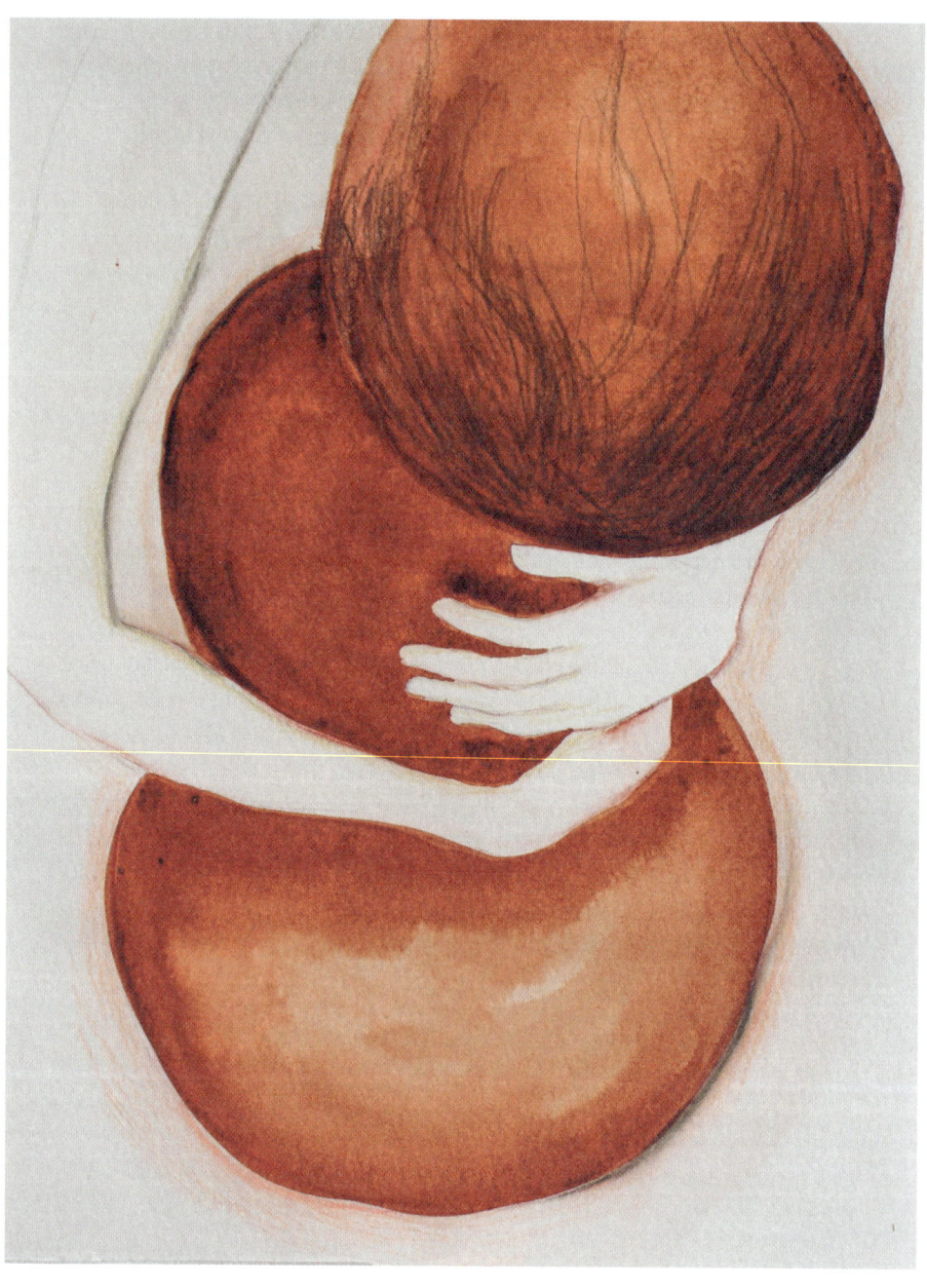

Natalia Ossef, *Primal Images 6*, 32 × 24 cm, shellac ink and coloured pencil on paper, 2020

The soul is more present than we think

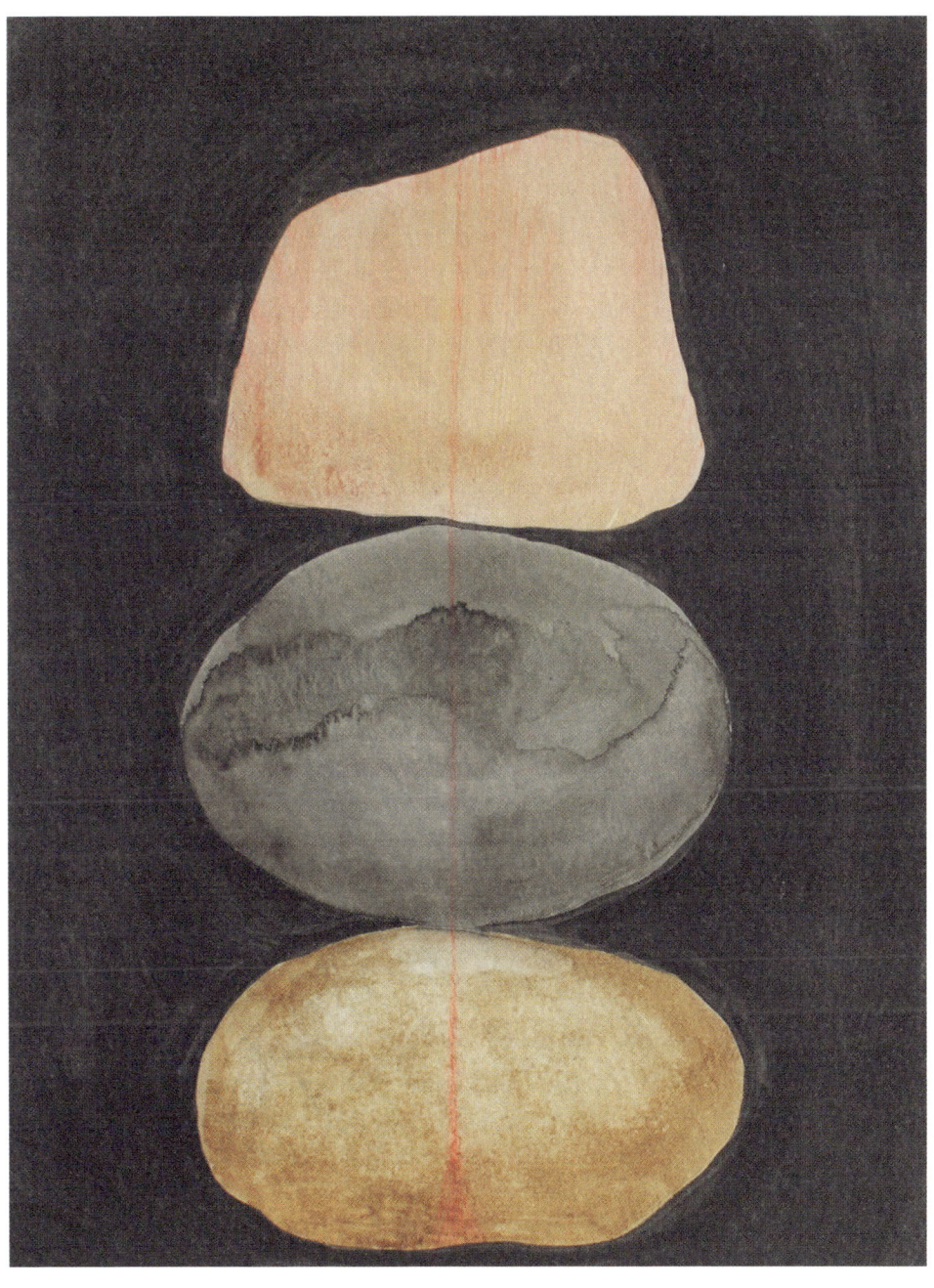

Natalia Ossef, *Primal Images 7*, 32 × 24 cm, watercolour and pencil on paper, 2020

Lebohang Kganye, *Ka mose wa malomo kwana 44 II*, 2013

The first photo of a spirit was made in 1861. The young photographer William H. Mumler was pottering around in his studio and decided to make a self-portrait. To his consternation, a shadowy portrayal of a young girl appeared on the negative beside his own image. At first, he thought it may have been due to his lack of experience with photography, perhaps he hadn't cleaned the glass plate properly. But spiritualists claimed that the first photo of a spirit had now been made and their assertion was supported by the fact that the spirits kept on appearing in Mumler's photos. In this way, photography seemed to provide proof for the presence of a 'soul' or a 'spirit'.*[15]

When her mother died in 2010, Lebohang was only 20 years old. 'My mother was my main link to our extended family and past, since we all now live in separate homes. Her death sparked the need to trace my ancestral roots and to locate myself in the wider family on some level and perhaps also to explore the possibility of keeping a connection with her. The idea of 'the ghost' started to emerge in my work.'*[16]

In her mother's wardrobe, there were dresses and suits from 20 or 30 years ago. They had been waiting there quietly on a hanger all that time and the clothes were still in perfect condition. Lebohang leafed through the family photo albums and there were lots of photos in which her mother was wearing one of the outfits that had been kept, and she looked fantastic. A beautiful woman with an elegant sense of style, posing amongst large luxuriant plants or in front of a stone wall. Her grandma often still remembered when a certain photo had been taken and helped Lebohang to find the locations. Lebohang poses in her mother's clothes in precisely the same settings, adopting the same pose, or she hunted for clothing that strongly resembled it. She superimposed herself into the old photos. In the spirit photos, the ghost appears in the form of a shadow behind the person, visible but hazy and intangible.

On Lebohang's photos, the reverse is happening: the mother is clear, and the image of her daughter is indistinct. In these photos, time is slipping away. Like a guardian angel, Lebohang appears around her mother, as if she still wants to look after her. The closeness is what counts. Or is it the distance that matters?

Oma Lola's things

If I were a thing offered for sale on the Alibaba site, I would rebel against my own superfluousness. Suppose I'm a lettuce-sandal, one of those green sandals with an upper like an elongated lettuce leaf: I've been made too cheaply by too-small hands, of plastic that harms the environment forever. Then I travel in the confined space of a shipping container to a distant land to walk around on sweating or manicured feet, on a fluffy carpet. I'm never cleaned, and I probably soon end up in a stinking rubbish bin with leftover tomato sauce. My life ends just as miserably as it began. And, what's more, I'm a copy of a lovely green lettuce-sandal of which only a limited number were produced, using environmentally friendly raw materials, completely vegan; you could make soup out of them. Yes, then I'd be a miracle, to be found on the feet of the model Bella Hadid, and I'd be wiped clean carefully every day using a soft cottonwool ball because I am pretty unique, and everyone feels I deserve a long life.*[17] When the vegan sandal is tired and worn out, it can go into the compost bin, which is suitably smelly, like an object that is diving back into the cycle of life, without harming the earth. This is something every object would wish for, and why do we humans sometimes want something different, like a freaky sandal made of polluting raw materials?

The artist Doina Kraal feels boundless love for 'the things' she cherishes with her hands and eyes, by touching them, caring for them, and especially by also using them. A colander hangs on a hook in her kitchen. A sorry-looking thing. The individual parts—the base, the body, and the handles—are held together with screws and, during the course of its existence, the round shape has been stretched into an oval with bumps and dents. 'My colander—I laugh about it every day, such an odd thing, but I do use it. Keeping something just for the sake of it, is so pointless, I take care of the things by living with them. The way we treat things is so careless and polluting nowadays. I'm an advocate of loving care for objects. Life is time and anyone who doesn't have time to cook a nice meal or to play, or to care for their surroundings, is in fact forgetting life itself, which is nothing more than a certain amount of time on earth.'

    As an artist, she arranges personal home-made or found objects in a big wooden cupboard with drawers and pigeonholes, a cabinet of curiosities, in order to share her life with the viewers. Like a commercial agent for these things, she travels around the world, constantly adapting the objects to new places and situations.

When her dearly loved grandmother, Oma Lola, died, she created an installation as a tribute to her, with her grandmother's belongings floating freely in the air, an ethereal construction of insignificant little things. *The Survival of the Faintest.*

During my visit to her studio, she carefully takes an object out of a moving box, an empty brown perfume bottle that Kortmann Art Packers & Shippers has wrapped meticulously, with the fine cord on which Doina has hung it rolled into a little bundle and a number on the label. Her hands touch it delicately and carefully unfold the bubble plastic. Slowly, a procession appears, of silly, touching, sometimes incomprehensible small things, a sort of parade that doesn't file past in a straight line but ends up on the table as a dishevelled heap, as if old age means that the things can't do anything but lie there, breathless. And so the life of her grandma curls upward in between us via the odds and ends, the stories, the memories. There are small individual embroidered flowers that you used to get for free with a packet of cigarettes in the early thirties, a loose Rennie, a rolled-up tape-measure that age has stuck together as a solid object that can never measure anything again. This useless thing has also been kept. Small handwritten cards hang on the objects with instructions about what to do with the item or they tell you something about their history. A little card on a broken vase explains who dropped the vase and what you could still use the broken remains for.

The articles have their own rules here, Grandma's rules: Gloves: only suitable for going out, concerts or opera. Perfume bottles: only for looking at. Snakeskin shoes: don't wear them when cycling. 'I was sometimes allowed to borrow the shoes and then had to hand them back immediately after the party', says Doina. A mysterious bit of wood, from which nails have been pulled out, leaving it full of small holes that have then been circled in pen, has a big round hole in the top. 'This can go in a cupboard with a rail through it for the clothes', has been written on the wood—an utterly incomprehensible article for which Grandma nevertheless sought a purpose. Lots of small round boxes—Rouge Fin de Theatre, made in Germany; 'Feinste Lippenschmincke' in a refined, powdery green cardboard box;

Reichert's 'schönheitspflästerchen', in a small box, the edge of which has been repaired with adhesive tape but is coming away again—there is a small box on which the word Mousseline is written in rounded letters, like a circling doodle line. Ichthyol ointment also appears in the original glass jar, but with an Albert Heijn peanut butter lid. 'I still remember where this jar stood on her dressing table and my Grandma used to smell of this ointment', says Doina, as she sniffs the aroma. 'My memory is triggered by sensory aspects such as scents, faces, tastes, objects or sometimes just words. This gives me access to time, the past, because each object carries a history that immediately comes to the surface. These things bring me into contact with my Grandma, with the past, with our shared history.'

It is in these things that Oma Lola lives on. A muslin cap with lacework lies on the table, a cap worn by the family's maid, when Grandma was young and lived in Germany. A white cap has a little card, on which I read: 'Our cook used to wear this cap. KÄTE. In 1935/36 she was no longer allowed to work for JEWS, and sadly had to leave us.' The family used to lead a good life in the Germany of long ago, with a cook, a chambermaid, a car to drive to a small lake on Sundays to go swimming.

Her father Franz was an orthodox Jew and theatre doctor; he married Omi Koch (Grandma Koch), a Protestant operetta singer who only later converted to the Jewish faith. A year before Kristallnacht (the 'Night of Broken Glass') in 1938, they fled with their daughter Lola to the Netherlands, where they ended up in Amstelveen. During the war, their union as a mixed marriage was noted and at first mixed-marriage Jews were not rounded up and deported by the Nazis, but that soon changed and that was the reason why her father had to go into hiding. Fortunately, the house had a space where that was possible. Doina has made a short film about it, where you see a man sitting at a small table in a cupboard. Little Lola was alone at home when the Gestapo burst in to search the house. 'Open up!', snarled the soldiers at the little girl. There she stood, with the key to the cupboard deep in one of her apron pockets. 'That's the linen cupboard with sheets, the key's downstairs', she came up with. The soldiers let it rest. Father was saved by a brave little girl who was able to control her indescribable fear.

Life continued.

This father fell in love with Lola's Dutch teacher during the war and the family was torn apart. As an only child, Lola was adored by her father, but the divorce drove them apart and they fell out. 'The breach with her father was incomprehensible because although Oma Lola was somewhat straitlaced, she was also forgiving. Many Jewish people, understandably, had an aversion to everything that was German, but she did not. My Grandma loved Germany, she was eager to continue with life, with her neurotic, restless, full life. But she was unable to forgive her father.' When the Jewish Oma Lola was eighteen, she married Adriaan, twenty-five years her senior; they had two daughters including Gabrielle, Doina's mother.

In that once well-to-do family, Lola learned to eat nicely by spooning her soup with newspapers propped under her arms. In her, you could see a glimmer of that past at various times, through the faded glory. She was an amazing person, headstrong and fearless and she interfered with everything. She pulled the cigarette out of the mouth of an unknown passing girl to diligently explain the dangers of smoking to her and that she'd really better stop. In every situation, she was so much herself that you couldn't help but love her. She used to walk into Doina's mother's house all the time to first check in the rubbish bin whether something useable had been thrown away, meaning useable in her special eyes. Her love for unsightly odds and ends was boundless. With fiery zeal, she looked after all the things she took under her wing. Her house contained at least fifteen built-in cupboards that were organised with great care. Oma Lola. 'The cupboards at our house were a mess', explains Doina, 'and Oma Lola taught me how I could tidy the cupboards: make a layout, fold the clothes, make small piles and then she wrapped a ribbon with a snap fastening around the clothing to keep it together. But she also used to tidy my cupboards when I wasn't at home and I took the door handle off to stop her. We have a deep connection with each other. Oma Lola is often in my thoughts and I wonder: how would she do this? She'd be thrilled that I've given her little belongings a third or even a fourth life in my artwork.'

Yes, things, that fantastic amount of stuff around us. Too much.

Too little care and love. We should love these things more, and we can best do this with objects that are worthy of our love. A monobloc chair is printed in a single piece from plastic in a shape that is calculated on the basis of the lowest production costs. It is an ugly, wobbly thing that you don't automatically fall in love with. A using-thing, not a love-thing. But nevertheless, we need to cherish everything; a plastic shopping bag can't help having come into the world. But a handmade wooden table contains life, culture and thoughts within it; hands have planed and filed it. A wooden ruler absorbs time into itself by fading, staining, and becoming greasy. Take a plastic ruler, though, and time slides off it; at most, it gets a bit scratched. Care keeps an object alive for as long as possible. You can re-upholster a sofa, you clean a mark away; we could consider thanking the maker and the materials.

A house reflects its inhabitants, we live there together with our belongings and afterwards it's the things that bring the inhabitants to mind again. Yet, in sociology, as a science that aims to describe society, 'things' seldom play a role. If, however, we want to know something about the past, it is by means of objects that we do so. Every little bowl or fragment that is dug up, however damaged it may be, is cleaned carefully and picked up using gloves to place it in a display case. In the Jewish Historical Museum in Berlin, by means of about a thousand objects, a picture is given of the Jewish life that was swept away, the life before the Holocaust. The things appear to be riveted to the past, they tell stories of human lives and the community. These things also have a biography of their own, perhaps they have already moved house ten times, been saved from uncaring hands, fallen off the table, been repaired again, taken on a journey.

Oma Lola's preference for the insignificant, for what is overlooked, the leftovers, for paltry little bits and pieces that she cherishes with labels and instructions, cannot be seen in isolation from her past. She built her own museum with all those little things as a monument to innocence, that is a reminder of the time when her family still had the right to live, when thoughts were not yet tainted by the Nazi ideology. In the light of the unfathomably great evil of the Holocaust, a father who has to regularly live in a cupboard and survives the war perhaps seems like a footnote in history.

When I walk in the Anne Frank house and see photos of signs with the measures that were announced one by one against the Jewish citizens, it sends shivers down my spine. Anne enumerates them in her diary: 'Wear a Jewish star. Jews may no longer be on the street from 8 o'clock in the evening until 6 o'clock in the morning, may not go to the theatre or cinema, may not go to a swimming pool, Jews must go to Jewish schools.' A banner with 'Jews not welcome'. It's not that I'm hearing or reading these rules for the first time, but in this emotionally charged place I connect them with a small girl. How do you explain these rules to your child? Lola's family may have been able to take their own bed and other furniture from Frankfurt with them, but they still lost everything: their safety, the right to live.

Oma Lola always kept the little boxes, caps and pots from Germany with her and pledged her heart to other useless, defenceless, broken little bits and bobs, as if she wanted to set an example that there is no such thing as 'superfluous'. She heard the stories about the camps, the atrocities, and the lack of everything. In the camp, every scrap of paper had great value, everything was precious. Old newspapers. Bits of ribbon. Little boxes. A pen.

After the war, nothing was ever the same again for Jewish people; people who had survived the Shoa were totally devastated when it became clear that even their possessions had disappeared, held back by heartless Dutch people. Words can hurt and slowly result in us starting to see a person differently, as happened in the lead-up to the Holocaust. Things can also cause pain, for example when they are deliberately stolen by another person and are not given back, as Jewish people experienced after the war. Powerlessness once again. Injustice.

'The things of the past were the things of evil', it says in a review of the book *Nagelaten Dagen* by Marga Minco. The story takes place after the Second World War, about the harrowing situation where people kept their Jewish neighbours' things safe but didn't want to give them back after the war. 'Yes. Now I remember it again. I had stopped by the door, I noticed that the Persian carpets were partly overlapping. Probably because of lack of space. I recognized them immediately. You'll think it's crazy but for I moment I felt a sense of joy. Yes, really.

You get that when you suddenly see someone again who is dear to you.' Eva rings the doorbell of the neighbours from the past. She sees the Persian carpets there and her mother's blue bowl is just standing there on the table in the living room. She lives in America now and comes into contact with the first-person narrator in the book and asks whether they will look for her mother's things in the house. The narrator finally takes the blue bowl to Eva but then it shatters into fragments. It seemed the only way to bear the pain, to erase the injustice.

From the perspective of the Jewish faith, everything in the world has a vitality: objects help in ritual acts. Words have meaning, a vibration, a rhythm so that each word you speak becomes connected with life. It breathes its meaning into the world. If a word has value, a thing certainly does!

The Survival of the Faintest symbolises the life of Oma Lola, but there's an entire nation standing behind her. As I read Marga Minco's story, the names tumble over one another; I sketch a family tree on a scrap of paper to distinguish between the people who are mentioned. I do the same during my conversation with Doina Kraal because the events and family members are presented to me in a chaos of time and space. A warm chaos, full of memories, too many events to relate, stories from a past that don't fit into a distinct production. Stories that have arisen from too rigid a vision. But the heart has its own rules and sees that everything in the world is of equal value, a little broken box, a dented colander, a mouse, and a person. There is not a sliding scale, so it makes sense to regard the insignificant things as precious friends, family members. Diamonds. These things, they lead us to the past and the future. It's up to us.

p. 94, 102-103: Doina Kraal, *The Survival of the Faintest*, 2009, (photo's: Peter Cox)

Light

Hanne Hagenaars, *Money for Lucy*, 2020

Dear Lucy,

Yes, I know, you're no longer there, but I think each soul takes its own time to move away slowly. A student told me that in Afghanistan they believe that the spirit of the deceased returns home in the days following the death, until the sun goes down on the third day. So, who knows, perhaps you're still close by when I bring you this letter. I think you are. Lucy, the name that means light, and how perfectly this name suits you, with your luminous hair and your eternal optimism, a bright star who meant so much to me. We recognised each other in our tough start to life, but as time went on, you and I both took on a more cheerful perspective, looking ahead more than behind us—sometimes wandering and sometimes fully grounded in the here and now. We went to a spiritualist evening together in a school opposite a beautiful church that had been transformed into a bizarre bubble gum paradise, a candy-Disneyland for little girls who loved everything sweet and pink. The school hall was full of disconsolate people and the great spiritual man looked unkempt and told corny jokes. No, we couldn't expect any good to come of this. A sad disappointment, because we were so eager to believe in higher forces to lift us above the events of the past and also to beat back your illness. Yes, the illness that was suddenly there, that didn't even turn everything upside down because you didn't allow it to. You fought the evil force with optimism. And Lucy, my admiration for you rose far above sea level, above my own height, rocketing into the sky.

Your courage gave life colour, your courage was like a sewing pattern that I use again and again to make a new apron that I then put on, and once I've done that I can go on again, frying an egg or putting a celeriac and bean dish into the oven. Your courage always gave me a push in the right direction, to embrace life.

So much hope, so much faith too, you were the light, in your ability to live in the moment, following each test result, whether good or bad; you absorbed it and then you were able to immerse yourself in a film again, an observation, everything that life had to offer you. You sent me this photo from Istanbul, and I love it. What a delightful family: two beautiful daughters with blue eyes that shine intensely, Jelle looking like a rather grumpy old man,

Contents of the wallet: *Money for Lucy*, 2020

having probably dashed into the photo from behind the camera, and you, you are surveying it all and laughing, with an understatement like 'just look at us!' A headscarf-family who has just arrived in the city from the countryside, but who, I think, believe in one another above all else.

Lucy, who tirelessly continued to give lessons, to make her jewellery, who even published a stunning booklet about her cross jewellery in September, a pale salmon-pink family production. 'As if time is hanging still for a moment', wrote Jelle. Fingers crossed. Time is hanging still now, because your eyes are closed, because we are already missing you although you are unmissable. Because the significance of each cross has come to an end, especially the Egyptian cross as a symbol of life. There is a cross after your name now.

Dear Lucy, my dear brave friend, you were a great example to me with all your courage. When I think of you, there is not just the loss but above all warmth, love, light and laughter, life.

The parallel world

The parallel world

Aline Thomassen, *Untitled*, 2018, 215 × 114 cm, (photo: Jan Zweerts)

The parallel world

As I open an old book, a photo falls out and so I unexpectedly find myself looking at the child I once was; it is one of those compulsory school photos in which I am playing with Meccano while one of my beloved dolls sits unheeded in the background and says nothing. I look into the bright eyes of this little girl with her thick fringe and feel that this child's soul is also my soul, her eyes, that I've never before realised shone with such power, radiating the desire to live and to survive.

I had to think of this moment when I looked into the eyes of the women Aline Thomassen draws on paper. Their clear, fiery gaze permeates me, and I can't help but surrender, to measure myself with their glance, making a connection, because their gaze reminds me of my own powerful childhood gaze. Dear women in Morocco, how I would love to speak with you about this uncompromising gaze. About life, the children, about your mother too, perhaps your father. Amidst the waves of life, you walk on, in a wounded body, with a too-big child in your arms, with your belly ripped to shreds. I taste the energy of these women and my tongue grows round and soft, my body absorbs it and stands upright resiliently.

Aline walks up to me while I'm looking at her drawings; what is her relationship with these women? 'It's all in the drawings— as soon as I start to put words to it, I'm afraid of not doing justice to the complexity. That relationship is loving, layered and full of contradictions.'

Hesitantly, Aline later tells me about the loss of her child, before the birth. In softly spoken, stumbling sentences. I'm familiar with that pain, I know it, and especially how the coldness of the silence that surrounds it almost strangles you. How no one puts their arms around you to cradle you, but everyone withdraws in embarrassment, in not knowing what to say, and then slams the door to run away from this calamity, your calamity, my calamity. Aline tells me that the women in the Moroccan city where she lived for two years and where she still spends a long period each year, were able to embrace her and shared their experiences with her very openly. Their deceased children brought intense grief but simply remain part of the family, they just belong: for example, a woman can say that she has four children, two here and two in the parallel world, that unknown, mysterious place where their souls hover. They remain part of the family in the words that are spoken, in the mention of their name. Their parallel life has a warm place in the mother's heart and the effortless mention of their existence softens the grief into a breathing experience. *Fridge light*,*[18] that's what suddenly strikes me in relation to my own experiences after the death of my newly born daughter. Cold light, functional light, blue and unbearable.

Women live in close contact with their body: having their monthly period, a child that grows inside you, that is part of you, like an organ of your own, that lives thanks to your blood. Giving birth to a child is no small thing, a very intense, painful, and sometimes even traumatic event, and the vocabulary we have available is too limited to describe it. That body is a powerful, proud, unique feature about women, who can give life.

That physicality is wonderfully and all-encompassingly present in Aline's drawings, organs that appear outside the body like purple flowers, blood vessels that transport their nourishing substances within and outside their body. Their leftover waste. The inside coming out, the body that carries the emotions and stores every feeling within itself. 'The accepting interaction with the body by the women amongst themselves was also a breath of fresh air', says Aline, 'in the hammam, naked and without inhibitions, they scrub each other's skin, wash each other's long hair. They are far less bothered than we are by shame and discomfort about a body that is too fat, too thin, too saggy, or too old, and all those other norms.'

'My perspective varies depending on whether I'm here or there', says Aline. 'Over there, I speak about the freedom that I experience from the Netherlands, for example about the fact that I can travel alone for my art while my husband looks after the children, but once I'm back in the Netherlands I defend the women *there* because of the positive things I observe and experience, in the contact with the women. At the same time, I notice that despite the possibilities in the Netherlands, most people don't take up the freedom that could bring them closer to their dreams. Many people are stuck in a straitjacket of certainties, like in a prison they have chosen for themselves. In Morocco a lot is determined from above and there are social and economic constraints, and how you manage then is what interests me.'

The women in the drawings carry the pain that comes with life, and they keep going with an incredible lust for life. The pain is absorbed by their body and soul, that tragic dimension is more present in countries where life is harder. 'Yes, sometimes there is an unequal position between men and women, I can't deny that, but isn't that conversation about this possible inequality often used to position our own Western value system above it? There is a hornet's nest of problems over there and how, regardless of those problems, people still manage to stand strong in life without denying the pain. Yes, I admire that.'

The first time Aline visited Morocco, she immediately had that amazing connection, a *coup de foudre* that is based on hidden mechanisms. Now, after she has spent so many years in the country, she understands it better, and she shows that rapport in her drawings. How can I characterize her, Aline? Perhaps with the sentence: 'There she is, a human being, diving into the unknown, and she is wide awake'. She travelled through the country on her own, observing, absorbing everything, and learned Moroccan (Darija) along the way. She bought a house in the medina and moved with her husband and children to spend a number of years there and was embraced by the community. Now, she returns there regularly.

The women she draws life-size are powerful, and in particular their gaze is imperturbable, steadfast, unwavering. A self-confident woman with heavy eyebrows looks at me, so intensely that I almost forget what else is happening in the drawing. Her hand is grasping something that is lying on her body, a viewing-hole to another world, the inside flows into the outside. An inner self makes us think of something inside us, but perhaps it is in fact outside, something big that takes care of us and cradles us, in the same way as a deceased child stays with you, outside and inside at the same time, with whom you remain in contact. In cohesion with everything.

And then, at the end of the row of large drawings, and slightly apart from them, there is the drawing of her mother, in earth-red watercolour as a homage to this exceptional woman.
    The mother is portrayed so intensely physically, naked with a focus on her face and her vagina. The legs and one arm are cut off brutally so that the attention lands on the middle of the body,

the breasts, belly, the vagina of course, the modest face, and then the hand gesture that looks like the *Jnana mudra,* the hand gesture of teaching. The tips of the index finger and the thumb come together, but this time the gesture is not pointing towards the chest as it usually does but towards the vagina. The drawing is astonishing, and I only really understand why it is so seared into my brain when I follow a lecture by care ethicist Inge Van Nistelrooij a month later. She speaks about the ambivalences of motherhood, about how both care and comfort are expected from the mother and a continuous striving towards letting go, otherwise the child would just suffocate. And she speaks about *The Mother Other,* philosophy's silence about the role of the mother in the formation of the self and how the body of the mother was subsequently cast aside by technological developments. By making the unborn child visible, her body slowly vanished from sight. An ultrasound of the foetus is cherished as a precious image and what we see is an independent little being with the mother's body playing no role. Yet every budding little human is completely surrounded by the mother. The first dialogue of every human begins with the interchange of substances and noises, the rhythm of her heartbeat and her breathing.

Our Western society sees humans in the first instance as individuals who can make their own choice and thereby create their own world, but it is open to question whether that is true. Because this means we forget that everyone's beginning is totally intertwined with another body, that of the mother. And what influence does that have on our self? Are we only complete when we no longer need anyone else? We develop in constant interchange with our family and surroundings. That begins with the mother, but as *mater* in the sense of 'matter' she is becoming ever more absent.

Aline Thomassen makes an all-encompassing drawing. The vagina as *L'origine du monde* does not have a sexual connotation but is the source of life. After all, you come out of that body. 'Not that I ever saw my mother so naked', says Aline, 'because she was rather prudish, but she did have this posture. Perhaps I have given her more of the attitude of a Moroccan woman.' Just as in her other drawings, there is again that intransigent physicality and with it the plumpness of this body in which you can take refuge. The mother has an inward-looking expression with eyes that have been painted away.

'Yes, she was enigmatic. If I asked her: 'What are you thinking about?', she would reply: 'Oh, just leave me alone'. But she was not floaty, a wise mother who lived in the here and now with earthly solutions. She uncovered connections that you as a child did not yet understand.' In the drawing, these links are visible in lines that Aline traces over the drawing with a tracing wheel, intended for transferring sewing patterns onto paper.

'My father was an artist, a fierce man, with whom it was almost impossible to live, but she could do it. Despite all the uproar, I didn't have the impression that she was a victim, she kept a tight hold on the reins. She stood her ground, held her head high proudly. And she did not judge. Although we didn't have much money, my father cherished his two Bugattis, and she let him. Everyone with a good heart could do everything and be everything, as far as she was concerned. Her compassion even extended to a murderer, 'how awful that someone has become like that', she would say. The drawing combines the gentle absorbent body with an imperturbable gaze.

Everywhere in the paper there are holes that look like they've been made by a small explosion, making a passageway. They make a connection with the unknown but in the form of a wound, a blemish. It is after all also a farewell.

Aline Thomassen, *Untitled,* 2017, 253 × 151 cm, (photo: Jan Zweerts)

The parallel world

Aline Thomassen, *Untitled*, 2014, 236 × 152 cm, (photo: Jan Zweerts)

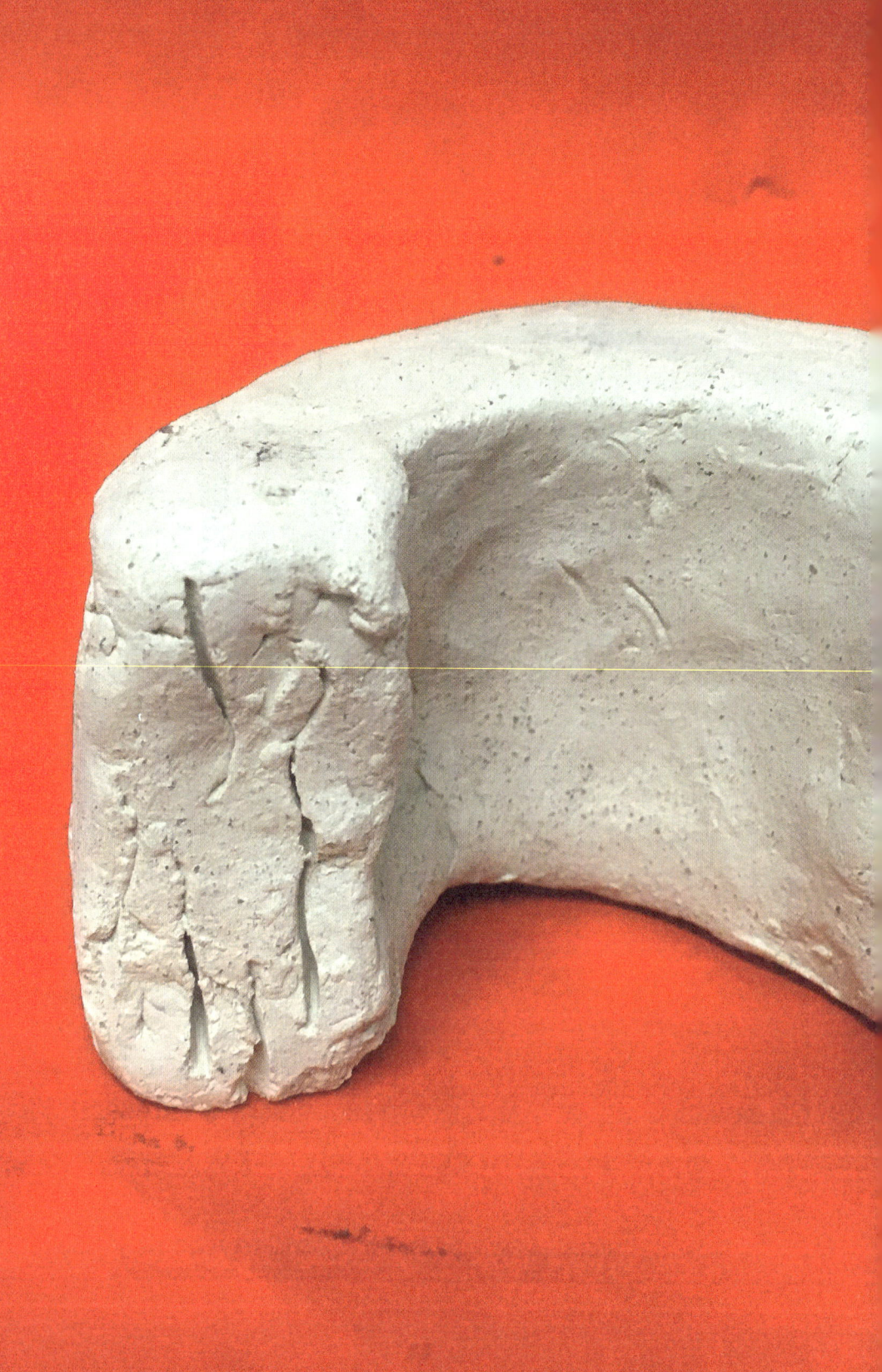

The angel wings

At secondary school, Djoeke Scheepmaker was given an assignment to make three objects out of clay and, as you would expect with girls of that age, she came up with a heart, a flower and angel wings. The teacher gave her an 'F' because she didn't think the clay angel wings looked enough like real wings. What do we actually know about angels? In the Bible, they are almost always described as beings without wings. Yes, really.

Tears welled up in Djoeke's eyes because, to her, these were real angel wings. The grave of her little brother Noah has a semi-circular wall that embraces the flat gravestone like the wings of an angel. What else can you do but let a deceased child depart with his guardian angel?

As a two-year-old, Djoeke was too young to consciously register the death of her four-year-old brother, yet the grief had still stored itself away inside her. That 'F' really hurt.

The death of her brother left a deep gaping hole, and everyone in the family did their best to close this wound. As a child, how do you deal with your mother's grief? 'My mother worked so hard to keep on going, for our sake; she is a wonder woman', says Djoeke. 'And when my mother was very sad, I would empty the dishwasher, or sometimes I would tiptoe through the house, very quietly. I was also really afraid to speak about Noah, I was afraid that by mentioning his name I would disturb that great intense grief and wake it up. Now, I know that we as a family are all carrying it together.' This meant that her own pain was also able to gradually float to the surface. 'After experiencing this immeasurable grief, we can cope with anything', declares Djoeke. 'Now I'm also increasingly curious about who he was, my little brother Noah.'

Lifeblood that never dries into a spot to be cleaned away but continues to be a soft, warm spot that moves together with the family.

Marike Hoekstra, fragment from *Child*, 2013

for Marike and Noah

Farewell child

A human body is too small
for such great grief as this
that swells up
from inside,
against your eyelids, ears and mouth.
The words that glide over your lips
mean nothing at all.
It is over.
The air seems too heavy.
Your head mashes life
It lies there at your feet
On the ground.
It won't wash away
It stays
It remains
While you are perishing, yet must go on.

La Ultima Ascensión

Kevin Osepa, *La Ultima Ascensión,* 2022, film stills

```
We understand
this endless moment
of being one
through unmeasurable ages
of being and becoming
– Aletta C. Beaujon in 'The Beauty of Blue'
```

For years, there was a large wax crayon drawing on the wall of my hall: WOEDE (RAGE). A ferocious whirling ball was spinning round against a background of heavy green streaks that were flying in all directions. During my teaching period at the Nola Hatterman Institute in Paramaribo, one of our students became a father. Glowing with pride, he came to show his little treasure and our hearts just melted for this pearl of a new being. The baby girl was passed around the circle and we kept extolling her virtues. Everything about her was perfect. The father continued to attend classes faithfully until one day his chair remained empty. We heard the news through the grapevine: his little daughter had died, but no one knew how. His furious drawing made an overwhelming emotion visible. Because how can you deal with your grief, and above all, your anger? By yelling at everyone who offers you sympathy? He asked whether I would buy the drawing and I took the rage with me, across the ocean. The force of the rage shook in my hallway. That wonderful anger was hanging there as a tribute to a sweet baby daughter who had also taken hold of my heart and would never let it go. Anger. I understand it.

'I wanted to make a film in which the impossible could happen. One of our greatest desires is for a deceased person to return in some way or another, but that is one of the few things that isn't possible', states Kevin Osepa (Curaçao, 1994) with regard to his film *La Ultima Ascensión (2022)*.

    The stunning film, full of mysteries, shows how the main character, Rowin, deals with a major trauma, the loss of his brother who drowned in the sea. But this story isn't served up to you as clearly as I am now describing it; you discover it while you are watching. The film unfolds at a slow pace, scene by scene, without explaining much. A lamp with water streaming out of it while the floor stays dry. Stones in a circle on the red earth. The terrifying water. A comet in the sky.

The synopsis of a film goes back to the grief and powerlessness that seized everyone when Kevin's little brother died before he was even a year old. Kevin doesn't want to say much about it, because it is of course primarily the story of his father and his wife. But that intensely felt desire to be able to erase events, to make them undone, that is the origin of the film. The death of a child; you can easily lose one another in that too-big and too-bitter grief, like in a vast labyrinth where each person goes in a different direction in search of the way out. Everyone gets lost.

Rowin looks at a photo of two men with straw hats: he is still standing next to his brother. He looks at the past, full of melancholy. The mother strokes the folded orange polo shirt that is lying on a brown wooden side table, beside a hand mirror, a statue of the Virgin Mary, and a candle with matches to light it. A Bible. A rosary is dangling from the small wooden cupboard on the wall that contains a photo of her deceased son. This altar is the straw she clutches onto.

While the wind whistles, brown leaves blow between the rocks. The image turns black for a moment. In the following scene, Rowin washes his face with water from the garden hose, puts his knife into the holder hanging at his waist, and takes his things to go fishing. 'Wouldn't it be better to stay at home today? Please', his mother begs. 'The sea already took a son from me.'

Rowin is fishing. Two legs are drifting under water. A second. A ringing sound is heard from the distance; Rowin turns and sees a tall man with long hair on the hill. Just for a moment, in a flash. Something black shoots by but when I look back at the film, image by image, I can't find it at first. Did I perhaps imagine it? Or has the mystery crept into the film? The knife is lying in the water.

The scenes in the film correspond to the inability of Kevin's family to move forward together after the death of the child. The loss had an enormous impact on the family and of course each person deals with such a great loss in a different way. One person wonders why fate treated them like this. Someone else will shut themselves up in a winter quilt of grief, zipping it closed around them. The great 'why' hovers around an event like this but there is no answer. They are not used to speaking openly about feelings on the island, which means that a wall of loud silence arises between the family members.

The island itself is also in pain. That pain is hiding in the salt of the water, the red of the earth and in the dusty heat; suffering that is washed up from the colonial past. 'I see a community of pain and a longing for this pain to be recognised. I am looking for rituals for healing and wanted to portray what it might mean to have contact with the power and rituals of the indigenous population, the Caquetios.' Rowin meets the man from the distance, the indigenous spirit Shi who protects himself with amulets, chains, bracelets, feathers, and shells. He gives Rowin a new knife. He makes fluid gestures, like in a dance or incantation, and Rowin imitates his movements. Shi teaches the fisherman about the bushes that grow in the dry red soil. A meeting between then and now, between lost knowledge and the emptiness of the modern age. An approach, a struggle, and intimacy.

'The spirits feel pain too, they want to be seen', says Kevin. 'Not everyone believes in those spirits, but things really are smouldering underground. The anthropologist Richenel Asano told me the story of a man who kept running into problems while building his house. After maize and rum had been put out to appease the gods, everything went ahead smoothly. The people believe that you can't build everywhere just like that because the indigenous land does not belong to us. You must leave it alone.' There are many places and many separate stories like this. 'You need to live together with the spirits', says Kevin, 'also with the evil forces that you can keep happy by means of recognition and offerings.

'The spirit Shi is a descendant of the Caquetios, the original inhabitants of Curaçao. They were carried away en masse by the Spanish. Their language has been lost. An entire culture has been wiped out and little is still known of their beliefs and rituals. The facts tell a sad story: in 1499 the Spanish explorer Alonso de Ojeda set foot on Curaçaon soil and that changed everything. At first, he called the islands 'islas de los gigantes', which means island of the giants, because the inhabitants were taller than the Spaniards. When there was no gold found and the agricultural ground turned out to be poor, the name was changed to 'islas inutiles', useless islands. After that, big money was earned in Willemstad with the slave trade from Africa.

The intimacy between Rowin and Shi is a moment of healing that Kevin cautiously allows to happen in his film. His homosexual orientation is something they prefer not to speak about in his family and on Curaçao, and the emancipation of the black queer identity on the islands is therefore an important element in his films.

I recently read an interview with the South African preacher Mpho Tutu van Furth *[19] in which she makes a link between the resistance to LGBTI relationships and colonialism: 'The English came to Africa and India with their very limited ideas about sexuality and gender. In most ancient cultures there is certainly space for gender fluidity, for sexual preferences, experiences and expressions outside the heterosexual box. In the original languages, there were also all kinds of words for this.' It offers a comforting thought and will also apply to other oppressed countries where the original values have been swept away, such as Curaçao.

Perhaps, probably, the spirits are our forefathers. They are present in us, and we secretly hope that they will stay close to us and that they are still watching over us. Forefathers are 'flown souls and a floating presence', I read in an apt description. But however it may be, we are always connected to our forefathers—those who went before us—whose DNA we carry within us, whose traumas still reside in our bodies, whose joy is handed down to us. 'But,' Kevin always stresses, 'there is good and evil. Forefathers can also take possession of us by haunting our psyche like evil spirits.' 'Pain can corrupt,' warns Kevin.

The human psyche is vulnerable. I recognise that: an unstable spirit is receptive to everything. During a period when I wasn't so strong, I kept losing things. A magazine, a book, my indoor socks, a pencil case. One thing after another silently disappeared from my house. I thought it was burglars, changed the lock and even thought I might be under a curse. But it was probably my own unbalanced spirit. I cleansed my house with incense and felt a sense of peace.

'The spirits also form part of a psychological game. Imagine there's a package with a dead rat on your doorstep—that is so unsettling that you can imagine all kinds of things behind it. Perhaps it's even a curse. Perhaps coincidence. Such a simple package can drive you crazy.'

Many old customs have stayed alive. Kevin comes from a big family and when a family member dies, the names of all the relatives are mentioned in the newspaper. Writing down those names together is also an enjoyable get-together, although it is most certainly not the intention to forget anyone. A favourite aunt of Kevin's died recently and lots of things came up during the name-meeting. That she was always late. Her jokes. And, oh yes, that particular joke, they tell that one again. A lot of laughter and fun. It is healing to talk about someone and it is confirmation that the person still belongs. And then there is the tempting superstition about numbers. The coffin in which the aunt was buried had a number and lots of people rushed out to buy lottery tickets with that number. Aunt was born in 1966 and that was an important number for the lottery. And if someone wins with those magic numbers, they think: look what she has given us. Because of the value that is placed on numbers, people also buy lottery tickets based on the registration plate of a car that has been involved in an accident. Perhaps something good will come out of something bad. There are many ways to ward off evil spirits, such as the laundry bluing that almost everyone in Curaçao uses. People apply the powder to the soles of their feet or to a baby's head as protection against the evil eye. 'At the same time, the question arises of what you are seeking protection from. What is the threat? Sometimes it is good to show your vulnerable naked soul and to have a conversation with the spirits. In this way, there can be relief on both sides. Interacting with spirits has beautiful sides and shadow sides and I don't want to over-romanticise it. I want to investigate it.'

While they dig in the earth, a skeleton appears. Shi puts the bones and the skull into a big earthenware pot, one by one. Rowin gives his knife as an offering, and they bury the pot and cover it with leaves. One of the few traditions that are known about the distant indigenous past is that of the second funeral. We know from gravestones that most dead bodies were buried in large, covered pots. But sometimes the body was put directly into the ground and the bones were dug up again after a number of months or years, and were put into a pot in the ground after that. A second funeral. We see it in the film. There are indications that the Caquetios had a cyclic concept of life and death and that they believed in a two-tier afterlife. In the first afterlife, the dead person still remains present among the living as a ghost.

They can issue warnings, make contact, and offer comfort, and sensitive people can feel their presence. The deceased person slowly transforms into a more mythical being at a distance. These are the spirits with which shamans can communicate. The cycle has come full circle when the spirit returns to the earth again as a human or is reburied, ready to travel on to the second heaven.

During an interview with Kevin, the presenter is afraid of giving away the ending of the film, but the story is not important in that sense; it is about the way it is told, the way it makes you empathise and experience it with the characters. 'In the film, I want to communicate spiritually. In a sensory way. In order to say more than what is there. To look at something for longer. Through touching. Hints. Coincidence. The scratching scene was not in the script, it came about while we were filming.'

The magic can take place in the scorching heat of the landscape because the forces from the past are still present there. There is space for inexplicable events. Furthermore, it's all about an interplay of the magical landscape of Curaçao and the ghosts and spirits that wander through history.
    The sun is so red that it is as if you can see the sun sweating because of its own heat. The landscape is panting and sizzling. The rustle of animals, branches that moan. It's a different type of landscape to the Netherlands. More nature, more spacious, more colourful. Ground in which the umbilical cord is buried. The landscape reflects the nature and the thoughts, the soul, of the people in the country, is how it seems. The Netherlands has a rational landscape, even the trees in the forest grow in cultivated rows. The last patch of primeval forest near Ugchelen disappeared when a motorway was built through it. The landscape is as sober and rational as the long white line on the road.

The little brother was called Gyan. His name is mentioned. The stories slowly get going, from grandma, an aunt, a brother. A process of healing is slowly beginning, although everyone knows that the death of a child never leaves you.
    In *La Ultima Ascensión* Kevin makes a miracle happen: the drowned son does not come back, but a tiny baby, scooped up out of the water, does return to earth.

the washed colors of the afterlife
that lived there long before you were born
— W.S. Merwin, 'Rain Light'

Kevin Osepa, *La Ultima Ascensión,* 2022, film stills

Breathe in, breathe out, until there's no more left

Judith Jockel, *You breathe from a garden in your neck*, 2016

The photographer Judith Jockel gave me a book of photos of roses entitled: *You breathe from a garden in your neck.* Following the death of her best friend, Mieke Van de Voort, she inherited her large-format camera. The camera was old and broken, and Judith first tried to repair it as a sort of occupational therapy. That didn't work. Well then, she'd simply set to work with the broken camera. Each summer for five years, she photographed the roses in the garden behind the studio they shared.

The name Mieke Van de Voort has always stayed in my mind thanks to a poignant article that appeared in the newspaper *[20] after her self-chosen death: 'Mieke's death was not tragic, her life was not pointless.' I have never forgotten this sentence either because it summarised the viewpoint of her parents so succinctly. They fully accepted their daughter's decision. 'We had children in the firm conviction that the world would become more beautiful because of them. And that was so', said her mother, Dorijke, at the beginning of the cremation ceremony. 'She was completely autonomous', the father added. And hence also in a decision about whether or not to continue living. Her parents respect the decision she made.

The article sketches Mieke as a strong, creative woman, perfectionistic, brave, and social. She embarked on major initiatives, such as moving house with a South-African freedom fighter, ten years her senior, in order to live and work in Johannesburg.

But she also suffered from depression and when that blocked her creativity, there was no longer an outlet. She was unable to work in that gloomy atmosphere, and the pills to combat the depression made her feel numb. She took the decision to step out of life.

'A garden without roses is a sorry thing', it says in *The Magic World of Roses.* Thanks to this book of Judith's and this garden full of blurred roses, there's no 'sorry' in the world without Mieke. There is a painful feeling of missing her, but also the roses to commemorate her, full of memories.

I am serving a sentence

I am serving a sentence

Alice Neel, *Dead Father*, 1946, 50,2 × 71,4 cm, oil on canvas,
© The Estate of Alice Neel, courtesy The Estate of Alice Neel
and David Zwirner

Perhaps Alice Neel didn't like nice people as much as distinctly awkward characters; this is what you might conclude from the fact that she painted her mother from life at least four times and never her father. The father was a friendly man who never hurt a fly but Neel has little appreciation for this, as is apparent from her comment: 'My father's life was a complete sacrifice'. In an interview with Ted Castle she explains her preference:

> TC: 'Did you have a lot of conversations with him?'
> AN: 'I was more interested in my mother because she was brighter, she knew more and she was quicker on the draw.' *21

Dead Father

Neel painted her mother in 1930 as a strict woman with grey hair in a bun, who is looking around, alert, from behind her round glasses but comes across as rather distant. The white background makes you think of ice rather than a living room wall. In *Last Sickness* (1953), you see her in a checked dressing gown, sitting uncomfortably on a ramrod straight wooden chair. A woman who is undergoing the last part of life with resignation. In her body and her tense gaze there is a retreating movement, shrinking back, and you wonder from whom or what. Perhaps her situation, in which death is already combing her wispy hair with his long fingers? She is looking him in the eye fearfully. Her expression also reads like an admission of guilt, like an anxious question to her daughter. 'What now?' Her facial expression also reflects Neel's own dissatisfaction about how she suddenly got a sick mother in the house in addition to caring for her own two children. 'What are you doing to me?', Neel seems to be painting into her mother's face, because more than anything else Neel simply wanted to work behind her easel. She partly solved that by using her mother as a model. On the dresser in the background, lemons gleam in a transparent dish on a tall stem.

Alice Neel only painted her father once and that was on his deathbed, with the simple title *Dead Father*. 'My father died in May, 1946, when he was eighty-two. He was buried near Philadelphia, and I went to his funeral in the little town of Colwyn, where I had grown up. I realized that I would never see him again.

He was a good, kind man, and his head looked still noble. I did not set out to memorize him because I was too affected. But the image printed itself. So I did him in his coffin next day, after I returned to New York.' *22

It is a tranquil, even rather dull, portrait compared with all those other intense portraits through which an entire life resounds. Here, the life has departed, his face is already sagging slightly. Silence. His arms lie straight beside the body and not, as is usually the case, bent with the hands together on the belly. The black of the sleeves forms a single area with the rest of the suit. A powerful, deep black expanse that dominates the painting. Between his curved hands lie two individual roses on the black of his suit, almost like two light red testicles: like a variation on the wound in Christ's side on the cross in the shape of a vagina. The death of Christ is, after all, also the re-birth. So these roses could refer to his role as progenitor, as father. And, of course, roses are the symbol of love. The father is lying on pleated satin fabric and a frieze of white lilies mixed with a touch of pink forms the top edge. Their sweet, rather sickly smell hangs heavily in the air. Because of the blunt cut-off on the lower edge of the painting, as a viewer you can't distance yourself, you are immediately poking your nose into the coffin.

Santillana del Mar Enríquez

Alice Neel and children was a tricky combination, as it was for all women with talent and ambition in those days (and the centuries before). She tells Patricia Hills frankly: 'I should have had some birth-control because then I was simply an ambitious artist. When people would mewl over little kids, I just wanted to paint them. But anyway, when I got pregnant in Cuba, that was it.' The father was the Cuban painter Carlos Enríquez whom she'd met during a summer course in Philadelphia and with whom she, despite all her ambition, travelled to Cuba instead of studying.

Santillana is born in Cuba in 1926, and half a year later Neel takes her baby daughter to her parents in America. She takes care of her, and paints, and takes cares of her. Santillana, an adorable little girl with blazing dark eyes, dies of diphtheria just before her first birthday.

In *After the Death of the Child* (1927–1928) Neel paints a world from which all pleasure has been removed: a tree without leaves stretches its bare black sticks upwards, in a small playground children swing and slide unsupervised, while in the distance adults wander through the streets like black zombies.

Isabetta

'In the beginning I did not want children, I just got them. But then when she died, it was frightful. After Santillana's death I was just frantic. Then I was already in a trap. All I could do was get pregnant again and I did.' And then there is Alice, Carlos and Isabetta. In 1930, Enríquez goes to his parents with their little daughter and the plan is for Isabetta to stay with them while Enríquez and Neel travel to Paris together. But it turns out differently: while Neel is still staying with her parents in Colwyn, Enríquez goes to Paris on his own and leaves Isabetta behind with his family in Cuba. Neel is bewildered and her heart is dismayed. 'Because he was weak, I was abandoned', she says. Neel begins to paint like one possessed, day and night. Painting is her mission in life and the only way not to succumb to that crushing desolate feeling. Just before the nervous breakdown that followed, Neel painted the horror-like *Degenerate Madonna* (1930) for which a girlfriend posed. The unhappy, exhausted mother has the profoundly sad baby on her lap with her swollen head and spindly legs but who, despite this, sits there like a little princess, as a radiant white centrepiece. In the background, her after-image looms, her soul perhaps, her future? When Neel speaks about that period, she makes the famous remark, 'You see, I always had this awful dichotomy. I loved Isabetta, of course I did. But I wanted to paint.'

Her nervous breakdown began with a persistent fever. The reason, Neel indicates years later, is that she was unable to express her grief. Her mother does not understand her artist's drive because when Neel asks her whether she may live together with Isabetta in the parental home so that she can continue to paint, she refuses. Despair creeps into all her neural pathways.

Neel provides a comprehensive account of her mental illness. 'I died every day, sweats break out. You are positively sure you are dying but I never made a sound.'

I am serving a sentence

Alice Neel, *Futility of Effort,* 1930, 67,9 × 62,2 cm, oil on canvas,
© The Estate of Alice Neel, courtesy The Estate of Alice Neel
and David Zwirner

Carlos comes to see her again and still wants to take Neel to the City of Light, but she was already too hopelessly lost in that pitch-black darkness. An attempt to take her own life fails. She is hospitalized again and Carlos goes to Paris anyway. And so Isabetta remains with his family.

Neel wrote the poem *The Great Renunciation:*

```
I was full of theories
Of grand experiments
To live a normal woman's life
To have children — to be the painting and
the painter
But now I have no strenght
My mind is weak and tired, my body sluggish,
My belly's fat — my gums receding
I 've lost my child my love and all the god damn
business
That makes my life worth living
```

In memoriam voor Santillana

After spending a year in various psychiatric hospitals, Neel paints an 'in memoriam' for Santillana in 1930: *Futility of Effort.* The work was prompted by a newspaper report about the death of a baby that crawled through its cot and got stuck between the bars, while the mother stood ironing around the corner. It is a minimal and bleak work in sober white, grey and black. The child is hanging lifeless in the arch of the foot end of the bed; on the right, the sketchy unfinished contour of the mother is visible, and on the left, a window where the curtains leave a dark diamond shape open. A thin line cuts across the fragile child's body. Neel calls this black line the fate line, which is the palm line that is associated with achieving one's own destiny in life. The life line, the curved line on the bottom right side of the hand, is meant to say something about the length of life, which you would perhaps rather expect in connection with Santillana's premature death.

The inclusion of an inborn palm line in the painting refers to fate, the belief that your destiny is in fact determined in advance. It expresses a resignation and equanimity that is striking for Neel because most people she portrays are, by contrast, bursting with energy and do not simply bow to fate, or at least bear their fate with fortitude. Neel herself is also a strong woman who distanced herself with verve from all the stereotypes about what was expected of her as a woman. But there's no escaping from the immense amount of care for the welfare of a totally dependent baby. The realisation that such a tiny life can slip through your fingers just like that, while you are, for example, doing the ironing, is devastating. Reading between the lines, you sense the despair about the death of her little daughter, but the prevailing feeling is of guilt. An unbearable, unnecessary feeling of guilt.

Alice Neel already stood up for herself in her statement about the work *The Intellectual* (1929). 'That child is my child. I'm that blond with the three arms and the three legs. I was so conscious about taking care of that child. You see how I am, I'm looking at the child.'

Pictures of People

Alice Neel paints her husbands, her family, her children, her grandchildren, but Neel prefers to call her images of all these people 'pictures of people' rather than portraits because she reflects the spirit of the age in the people she paints. Even if her family members pose, it is about a bigger story. About the disadvantaged position of women, about social dilemmas, the choices you have to make as a mother. She struggled enormously with motherhood. Nowadays there is more space in a woman's life, more choices. 'I'm not dogmatic about not having kids', writes Rebecca Solnit. 'I might have had them under other circumstances and been fine—as I am now. But I really wanted to write books, which as I've done it is a fairly consuming vocation.' *23

Death does not often appear in Neel's work where, on the contrary, strength, alienation and seduction resonate through the works. Pregnant women look at you in a daze, children stare with frightened eyes. How will this far too big adventure of life end? Her third child, her little son Hartley, sits on his rocking-horse with huge, terrified eyes: 'Where in God's name have I ended up?'. The bewilderment at having been placed in this world emanates from every child she paints. Nowhere is the drama of being more present than in the eyes of those children.

Isabetta

Isabetta grows up in Cuba. In 1934 she visits her mother in New York and Neel paints a portrait that still ruffles a lot of feathers. The nakedness of the young Isabetta is criticised from all sides, as well as, later, by Isabetta's daughter who calls it 'disgusting'. A sexually suggestive portrait? I see, rather, a bold child, and above all a self-aware, autonomous being, a child that can fend for herself, with rather large feet and her hands on her hips, one foot slightly more to the front. An unabashed gaze, a powerful—I am here—gaze. A strong child, of whom Neel hopes that she can find her own way, even without her mother. Neel possibly underestimates the impact of her own absence that began with her breakdown. The portrait is not *per se* more sexually coloured than all the other children, men and women she paints. Neel is proud of this portrait of her daughter, and she poses together with this work and her boyfriend Kenneth Doolittle for a photo. Neel lays her arm on the top edge of the standing painting as if she has her arm around Isabetta. In an unprecedentedly furious, jealous rage, Doolittle destroys hundreds of drawings and more than fifty of her oil paintings, including this depiction of Isabetta. Neel paints the portrait again, and in 1981 she makes another new, rather bleak version of this portrait of Isabetta, with the title *Memories*. It is her *in memoriam* for this daughter with whom she already lost contact during her life.

Alice Neel was a free-spirited woman who painted herself throughout life. You have to be courageous. Success comes late in her life and she enjoys it. She does not tremble while awaiting her own death—no, she is already stretching out her hand to him before he comes strolling along.

> AN: 'Oh yes! Death and I live here together. I wonder how I'll die.' 'But human beings can bear anything. Dostoevsky said that man is the animal that can get used to anything. I love that! [...] 'I often say that I'm serving a sentence here.'
> TC: 'What do you mean?'
> AN: 'Well, life.' [24] [25]

I am serving a sentence

Alice Neel, *Last Sickness,* 1953, 76,2 × 55,9 cm, oil on canvas,
© The Estate of Alice Neel, courtesy The Estate of Alice Neel
and David Zwirner

I am serving a sentence

Alice Neel, *Isabetta,* 1934/1935, 109,2 × 63,8 cm, oil on canvas,
© The Estate of Alice Neel, courtesy The Estate of Alice Neel
and David Zwirner

A pink cloud

Marit Dik, *Pink cloud*, 2019

Marit Dik:

A little sister is a project about my sister Alice, the oldest of four girls. She was born in 1953 with Down's syndrome, but little was known about it at that time. My parents were worried about her slanted eyes, but the doctors reassured them, 'that would sort itself out'. This painting depicts my mother with my sister and it shows how unsteadily she is standing in her new future with her first child. She was still young and had to stop working after getting married (you had to, in those days!). From spending her time with girlfriends, she now found herself at home with the baby, with whom she fell in love at once, although she was rather puzzled about her. While I was painting, I was overcome by the feeling of loss for both my sister and my mother.

There was a lot of ignorance about Down's syndrome and people could make pretty blunt remarks. I heard some women whispering to each other about a boy with Down's: 'look at that unhappy child'. I then felt ashamed, as if we as a family had done something wrong, but it can still make me angry now. Besides, it wasn't true; on the contrary, my sister was often very happy! My sister was ambitious, stubborn, sweet, my big sister but also my little sister. Fortunately, there were also friends who supported my parents by just behaving normally. It is fascinating that acting normally is a real breath of fresh air in such circumstances.

My mother told me what was wrong with my sister when I came home one day and told her she was being teased by children in the neighbourhood. I was 7 at the time and found it very confusing. Everything about her was different: her life, her future, her appearance. When she was 17, she moved to a group home and worked at the sheltered workshop and later in a day care centre. There was little variety in her life. She died aged 64, but years of dementia preceded that. I saw her change from a headstrong, energetic woman into a little sister in need of help, with whom I again had the wordless intimacy of the past.

Souvenirs of a loss

Mirthe Berentsen, *The right to be forgotten – fabric and patterns*, 2021

A thing without an owner is ripe for a rummage sale although that is an unworthy place for a thing to end up: this expresses undisguised contempt for the person who once collected it. For years I used to buy things at the flea market, thinking I could sense like a clairvoyant that this particular owner's honour must be restored. That shiny purple apple cider jug with the spout indicated a good and beautiful person's love of things. I carried the debt of honour for many people. Until an artist commented, while looking around in my house: 'It looks just like a rummage sale here', and that was the signal to have a clear-out.

Things have sentimental value in relation to the owner: the famous helmet of Jan Hanlo lay on a cushion in the Literary Museum,[*26] purely and simply because the author had worn the helmet while he chugged away on his moped.

You make direct contact with the owner through things. My shy mother loved Maja soap with that exotic picture of a fiery Spanish dancer wearing a billowing red dress. Every day when I walk up the stairs I see the stale bottle of Maja perfume on a small ledge, bought at, yes, the Noordermarkt. It reminds me of her delighted face when she took a packet of Maja soap out of the gift-wrapping paper and also the rather sad realisation that my mother was more apron than red dance dress.

Stuff.

Things.

Our houses are full of them. Sometimes I think, with a big heart full of compassion, about my son who will have to empty this house after my death. Poor child.

It happened to writer Mirthe Berentsen early in life after both her parents died at the age of 54, soon after each other. First her father, then her mother. She was 25 years old. The death of her mother was not unexpected because apart from MS she also had a hereditary kidney disease; of the large family with fourteen children, the ones with this condition died young. Mirthe also has to live with this disease. The burden of everything she has seen weighs heavily and when her mother died all those memories hung above her head like thick, dark clouds. The grief, the loss, but also the leaden realisation that above all you must make something of your life. 'It is constrictive', says Mirthe, 'as if I must not only live for myself but also have to do justice to the dead. And yes, you can certainly think of the fact that the only thing to do is to live in the moment but how do you do that, without God or parents to help you?'

When I think back to the conversation with Mirthe, I see pink, dark red and even bright yellow shells forming the outline of a squid on the snow-white sandy beach of an island that is surrounded by every shade of blue that water and sky can have. An exceptional blue. A nirvana. That otherworldly beautiful place full of shells that gave her a gentle nudge to live on with the grief.

We discuss the awkwardness of talking about such a great loss: it almost always falls like a cannonball between you and the other person, who then flinches with shock. It is as if you are burdening the other person with it. 'I am a master at putting people at ease', says Mirthe, 'like when my father had just passed away and I decided to go to the Venice Biennale anyway, after much hesitation. "Have you already got over it a bit?" was the first question that came my way. And a girlfriend commented: "You've not really been yourself lately, so dejected."'

I would like to swear wholeheartedly on Mirthe's behalf. Yes, what do you expect? But my silent swearing fizzles out immediately. If you have to deal with such complex things at such a young age, then it's difficult for your contemporaries to understand. The loneliness dances around you continually like the devil, and grins at you. Where is God?

During the last little bit of her mother's life, Mirthe rented an apartment on a farm in the area, half an hour by bike from her mother's house. It helped her. Nature is always a loyal ally during tough times, for comfort and peace, perhaps even acceptance.

The day her mother died, the mother horse on the farm also died. At the end of the day, the animal was lying at the side of the road with a tarpaulin over it, waiting to be collected. 'I went to the dead horse and stroked its warm body for a long time. It may sound vile, but it was very comforting. The body of my mother turned cold so soon, and hence so far away. A horse has such a large body that it takes a long time before it cools down. The other horses were blowing and snorting with grief, but the fact that the days eventually went on and foals were born again also brought relief.'

Death is cold, I remember that too.

What is left is a house full of things. Things embody the remains of an existence, what has been left behind on earth, the dregs of a life. Due to her mother's lingering illness, dust had gathered everywhere. The rooms, the passages, the bathroom, the shed, the studio. 'How in heaven's name must I do this?', Mirthe wondered. 'All those things, all that sadness. I couldn't keep all the things just because I simply couldn't bear the thought of life in this house coming to an end.' Plates and spoons lay immersed in some cold soapy water in the washing up bowl. Remains of toothpaste still on the toothbrush, the cap next to the tube. On the last evening, Mirthe had cooked her mother's favourite meal; some leftovers were still waiting in the fridge to be warmed up. The leaves of the plants turning brownish at the edges.

Together with her sister, Mirthe set to work. To begin with, they were getting on each other's nerves because they didn't know where to start, until her boyfriend advised doing it room by room. So obvious. The first layer is easy, all the rubbish can go, the obvious things that no one wants to keep. Then they used a sticker system and when there were double stickers it was settled with arguments.

    What is left over after that is a tricky group of things that no one wants to take, but that are so personal that you can't really get rid of them either. A favourite worn-out pair of pyjamas. The tube of hand cream that always stood next to the dishwashing brush, a cherished book with the bookmark halfway through it. The tin of aniseed sprinkles. Notes in the margin of an existence. It was these very everyday objects that emphasized their mother's absence: she wasn't able to wear out these socks, the toothpaste hasn't been used up. Death has shut the house down. All that clutter that may have lain in a drawer for twenty years—what is most ordinary may actually be what is closest, but it's of no use to you.

Mirthe photographed all these things that she was unable to throw away and didn't want to take. The 'souvenirs of a life', is what she calls them. Each room produced its own imprint, its own postcard. The study, the bedroom, the bathroom, the living room, the shed.

Mirthe Berentsen, *The right to be forgotten – bedroom*, 2021

The small pieces of fabric with chunks missing felt very close and tactile, reminiscent of their shared life that also had so many chunks missing from it. Nothing of value, simply some miserable leftover bits of fabric and patterns, red, blue, shimmering, fluffy, velvet. Cut-off corners, cut-out half circles, strange block-cut edges. On the photo, they are neatly arranged on a sheet of white paper. Things are tangible, memories cling to them, and those fabric scraps trace a line towards the dolls' clothes that her mother used to sew for her and by extension towards everything that she did for Mirthe. The photos of these things are brought together in a rectangular photo and framed, with the outline of the things sandblasted in lines on the glass, like an echo calling out after them.

Nicolaas Matsier wrote the book *Gesloten huis* about clearing his mother's house. The standstill of the title ultimately leads to a cheerful departure from the house: 'I can be missed here' is the last sentence. Matsier photographed the emptiness, the dismantled house, the absence of his mother, of everyone. But no photos of the garden, her garden, 'the long-term artwork by my mother's hand'. The pale-pink clematis that Matsier said continued to grow so vigorously after an accident his parents had in Romania. 'I don't want to think about the garden. Because that garden will change too quickly into someone else's garden. [...] Perhaps the best thing I could have done would have been to bury the camera with film and all here in the garden. Right now. For example, at the foot of the jasmine.'

Each gesture of keeping, photographing, the fullness, the emptiness, shrinks back at the depth of a loss. Later, he describes the clearing of the house, and each object brings back the past. *Gesloten huis* becomes a book full of memories. The disappearance of the house and its contents is accompanied by the fear that the memories will dry up, and may even disappear for good. His book makes it possible for him to leave the place behind him with the slamming of the front door, because all the memories are stored in the book. His mother now lives on among many people.

'People consist of memories', Bernlef once wrote. And as a person you have only really disappeared if no one thinks about you anymore, because memories crumble away over time as part of the great mill of life: everything is crushed. Always. Why is there no clearing-the-parental-home-leave?

We talk about mourning, and Mirthe stresses that there is no quick fix, no app, and that in this neoliberal society there is in fact no time for mourning. Something that is normal is pushed into a classification system. 'Yes', says Mirthe, 'as if feelings of loss and mourning can be calculated in an Excel sheet. As if your deepest being can be summarised in a form.'

There is for example a mourning meter: so you can work out for yourself whether help is needed. Do you perhaps have a persistent complex bereavement disorder? (PCBD according to the DSM-5.) Mirthe has difficulty with those boxes into which bereavement is placed. 'After my father's death, following an intense sickbed, I started to live very hard and loud, lots of partying, sex, work, a lot of escapism basically. And I thought that I was really happy because everything felt so intense. It was more like dancing on the edge of the volcano.' I think I score as abnormal, because how can you, in what is pretty much the tail end of your life, suddenly be preoccupied with your mother again? Haven't you got over it yet? Hopeless.

Suddenly you're an orphan. Mirthe. A bit further back in time, that sad house was a familiar and warm house, where she saw her mother. Normal. Death means that something ordinary falls away, the care and concern of your parents for you, their child. No safety net anymore. Alone in the world. Mirthe has a family now, and a daughter. 'After the death of my parents I was so eager to experience new life and not only death and loss. That was a pretty difficult decision because it seemed there are so few good things in the world, but a child means something big, so big that everything changes.' Her daughter also symbolises the fact that it is possible to break through certain circles. Her arrival felt like a new page in a long deterministic line and her daughter was given the name Lillit, named after the first woman on earth. A new beginning.

Loss continually changes its appearance. Missing evolves. But in that first year after her mother's death, it seemed simply too big, too much. With her birthday coming up, Mirthe took the decision to no longer celebrate that day until she was 55 years old. 'Gloom and doom crept into every fibre of my being.' Because yes, everyone celebrates the fact that another year has been added, but for Mirthe it felt more like counting down, one year less.

Her partner, Constant, surprised her with a holiday, so she didn't need to celebrate her birthday. 'I had no idea where we were going and I didn't particularly like it. First off to Düsseldorf, then to Dubai, changing planes, then a small plane, a sign with a name I'd never heard of before, then the next change onto a seaplane. After the long journey by air, we arrived at a resort in the Maldives. All inclusive.'

'It was so ridiculously beautiful there, I was finally able to relax. The fishing, the underwater life, the clear ocean, it all had nothing to do with my life in the Netherlands.' Kindled by the transparent water, all the beauty and the intensely pleasant feeling that all this beauty brought, the realisation came that grief can be so raw that you simply forget that there were good times, without illness, without arguments, without annoyances or lack of understanding. Every morning, she went for a walk across the island and noticed how the grief took hold of her. She was walking there, two legs, two arms, a being filled with grief in that immeasurably beautiful landscape. She picked up the shells that sparkled in the sun in all the colours of the rainbow and laid them in a pattern on that pure white sand, took a photo, and threw everything back into the ocean. *(It is forbidden by Maldivian law to collect coral, shells or sand from the Maldivian waters,* 2021) 'It gave me so much solace, especially because I wasn't allowed to keep it. Normally, you want to take something that is so beautiful and special with you, but I suddenly understood that something as beautiful as these shells or love can simply be there without you having to hold it in your hand.'

In this way, she was able to take a different kind of souvenir home from this holiday, a head full of clouds and shells, and a gust of wind.

The depth below the surface

The depth below the surface

Katinka Lampe, *40068,* 2006, 40 × 40 cm, oil on linen

> 'Art is a perpetual sacrifice of sentiment to truth'
> – Proust *27

'I try to understand the world better by painting it', says Katinka Lampe during our conversation. Those boys and girls on her canvases with pink or orange hair, with veils, headscarves, or even crowns of thorns, look unfazed in their attire and array of colours. But beneath the skin, something is smouldering that is beating against the surface and sometimes permeates into their expressions. Emotions. Maybe and maybe not. These young people live in the here and now, but we can already read something about their future, as if in a crystal ball. Or, reasoning backwards, I detect something of my former self in a curious painting of a little girl with long black eyelashes and half-open, pale cornflower-blue eyes, even though I had dark hair and green eyes. This little girl radiates a mixture of expectations and suspicion, perhaps some hesitation. Is everything really going to come up roses for me in this world? Katinka takes a young face as her starting point, not so much to promote 'youth' but because she can utilise these smooth faces as a blank canvas. Her own children also model for her regularly, posing patiently in the desired position; they pull a cloth over their head or do whatever is asked, not passively but interacting in a relaxed way. Katinka takes photos and only uses paint later, loosely basing her work on the image. The paintings rely on those fragments of the real world in which intolerance is rife and too many created beings ask the question: 'Do you like me now?'

'It is never narrative, and it is not about me,' says Katinka in the interview programme *Kunst is Lang (Art is Long)*, 'it's more that I'm trying to paint myself out of the work.' Katinka deliberately slips out of the way in order to make space for the viewer, for the truth that they may absorb from behind the mask of the model, from inside.

> Proust learned from the art critic Ruskin that it is only through paying extensive attention to how things look that you can discover the essence that lies concealed beneath it. The depth below the surface.

The depth below the surface

Katinka Lampe, *4050134*, 2013, 50 × 40 cm, oil on linen

Then, like a lonely star in Katinka's oeuvre, there is the portrait of an ideal, kind mother, giving her all and cherishing her baby, carefully supporting its head with misty white hands.

'I painted my mother with one of her eight children: my mother in her younger years, as I never knew her, because she was forty when she had me. Immediately after her death, I felt the need to write a book about her life because it was a veritable novel. But unfortunately I can't write, so I made a painting, as a ritual to paint away my profound grief', Katinka wrote in an email.

The portrait is strongly reminiscent of *Mother Louise Holding up her Blue-Eyed Child* (1899) by Mary Cassatt (1844–1926). This heroic woman already decided at an early age that she wanted to be an artist and that a marriage would not help her career. She remained unmarried and triumphed despite all the limitations women faced in those days. She specialised in sweet-as-candy mother-and-child scenes that are still hugely popular, and can be ordered online, both as posters and as copies painted in China.

Katinka placed her mother back in time, at a time when the family was still together and she tells me the story that in fact begins with her father, that annoying story, as she calls it, that has to come up briefly now. When she was a young girl, her mother fell head over heels in love with this handsome, charming man and the result was eight children. The norms of the church were firmly impressed upon women: in the Catholic south of the Netherlands, contraceptives were taboo and the pastor used to call by regularly to enquire whether another baby was already on the way.

The father decided that this life with this family, with all those children, couldn't make him happy, so he took off and left his wife behind without concerning himself about what she actually wanted to do with her life. Or how she would survive now. A cowardly retreat, without looking back. It also turned out that his imagination had made him live in a different reality, full of imagined events and lies, a dream life in stark contrast with the reality of the large family.

Then, the mother took her apron off, rolled up her sleeves and set to work to support the family, taking no notice of the great taboo of single motherhood, a situation that—even though it was not a choice—went very much against the grain of the period.

The portrait shows a classic mother-with-child scene and yet her mother was not a mother-mother. The situation forced her to go out to work, but that secretly suited her better than the housewife-and-cleaner existence of clearing up the children's mess every day, making all those beds, the merry-go-round of the laundry, and cooking meals every day. Now the tasks were simply divided up and she had help. Katinka's mother was a doer and also somewhat distant. 'My father's departure benefited all of us', she explains. But despite this, her mother had difficulty getting over her grief. She did not want to talk about it, she could not share it because that would affect the feeling of independence that was indispensable to her. But by keeping all those feelings inside, she may have come across as rather cool because that hidden-away grief also pushed other feelings aside. 'Do your best' is one of the sentences she liked to use. That irritated me, her persistence in keeping on going. 'Come on!' was also one of her favourites. She resolutely buried all her emotions away, deep down in her large handbag, and then snapped it shut. Spending a week crying in bed can be so beneficial. I would have been happy for her to do that. It is only by putting all your grief through the wringer that you can process it and create space for all feelings. 'I think your children suffer as a result,' says Katinka, 'yet I as the youngest had a very strong bond with her—I really had to tear myself away from her.'

The rigid shield with which the mother armed herself disappears on the portrait, leaving the way wide open for her gentle side. Katinka is in fact moulding the image of her mother to the spirit of that time, the mother who immerses herself fully in her child. She is honouring the glorious aspect of her mother, who goes out to work, swimming against the current, and saves her family. Perhaps the portrait is intended to nip any criticism in the bud, yes, this what motherly love looks like, according to the norms—holding tight, fulfilment—motherly love of the kitchen sink and the washing-up, but this mother's love was great too, even though it may have taken a different form.

Proust's statement—'Art is a perpetual sacrifice of sentiment to truth'—could serve as a motto for Katinka's work, but here, in this particular case, sentiment has crept in front of truth. Katinka's ode is absolutely sincere; sentiment is also concealing a truth here, quite possibly one that is deeper.

The depth below the surface

And although their father's departure pushed destiny in a better direction, Katinka felt intensely abandoned, she yearned for fatherly love. 'I wanted him to see that I was a nice person.' That longing continued to spread rampantly below the surface until the moment when he phoned her out of the blue. 'Do you know who you're speaking to? Your father.' He wanted to come to stay for a night, he wanted to see her work, but Katinka didn't want to let him into the studio just like that. The paintings passed by on her computer screen at home and then there was finally the appreciation that she had always craved: 'He thought I was amazing to the superlative degree, my success, my fame, he couldn't stop talking about it.'

She had been waiting and hoping for this moment all her life and when it finally came, the recognition lost all its importance. In one fell swoop, the case with all that yearning fell out of her hands, flew open immediately, leaving only dust and grit lying there. Evidently, a different truth lay hidden beneath her longing. She did not need his appreciation; happiness was already there.

'The facts of life do not penetrate to the sphere in which our beliefs are cherished', wrote Proust as the beginning of a very long sentence in which both God and doubt about a family are mentioned, in his book *Swann's Way*.

> 'In reality, every reader when he is reading,
> is the reader of his own self.'
> – Proust [28]

Love is All Alone. Together All Alone.

Love is All Alone. Together All Alone.

Bas Kosters, *Love is All Alone. Together All Alone.*, 2016

When your body is cold, you yearn for a fluffy duvet that you can cosily wrap yourself in. The death of a parent also sends a shiver, a chill, through your whole body. Bas Kosters lies here, seeking comfort and warmth in a big coat sewn onto a rug that stretches out on both sides, like the rectangular wings of an old-fashioned aeroplane. The artwork consists of his father's entire wardrobe, with the exception of an ugly jacket, his socks and underwear, and has nice thick padding. The clothes still smell of heavy tobacco and hospital, Bas left it like that. The scent of his father.

Love is All Alone. Together All Alone.

Apart from items such as books, records and some antiques, his father left behind a modest wardrobe. As an inheritance it was sober. 'It was beautiful and sad at the same time', says Bas. 'And also characteristic of this humble man who barely took up any space. He simply went along with life in the family. When I used to call, he would immediately say: "Here comes your mother."'

'My mother had been ill for years and everything revolved around her. My father was also able to hide away in that caring role, Bas muses thoughtfully. Unexpectedly, his father died first.

'I was overwhelmed; who was he really? We talked while he was in hospital and got to know each other better after all. In response to my criticism about the unhealthy smoking and greasy food at home, he calmly said: "We did our best, we didn't know any better", and that's the way it is.'

His father wore Bas's brightly coloured T-shirts and exuberantly printed tops with pride. His parents were always present at his fashion shows. His father would accompany the models onto the catwalk, wearing a waistcoat that the whole family had embroidered with angelic patience full of glitter and sequins.

In the photo, Bas is lying with outstretched arms in total surrender in that big coat, sinking peacefully into the fabric. Even as an adult, you seek warmth from your parents. The rug was assembled with the help of interns 'but despite the fact that someone else is participating, it still feels real', says Bas. It's a good thing that several hands were working on it, because the collective effort also brought stories and insights. *Together All Alone.*

The rug had a transformative effect. It made him think about his childhood and upbringing. 'I realised that I am more than I thought: I am also like my father. I gained more insight into myself. It makes me a more complete person. Sometimes my father visits me in my dreams. This textile collage gave me a new hopeful starting point which I took with me. I focus more on joy and pleasure now.'

His mother died soon afterwards. And now, six years later, Bas is working on a small rug, using one of her quilts as the basis. A quilt involves a rigid process in which pieces of fabric are sewn together very precisely. Stitch by stitch, Bas sews small, embellished patches onto this organised base. It is rather like a sampler, where you try out all kinds of different techniques. There is a portrait of his mother in her youthful glory, there are flowers, fawns, teddy bears, hearts. Childhood and mother meet each other again.

    The collage is being created from small pieces of fabric that are sewn onto it with obvious stitches. It is untidy and no effort has been made to make it extra beautiful. 'In this project for my mother, it is especially important that I am doing it myself, using different fabrics that all have a connection with her.'

    And perhaps his mother's care is continuing after her death: embroidering this rug by hand is a diversion for Bas from the digital world, a better way of coming into the here and now.

Love is All Alone. Together All Alone is a huge, monumental piece of art, a museum exhibit. As if the father is being given the space after his death that he didn't take up in life. The collage for his mother is smaller, chaotic, lovingly assembled from mini remnants of fabric. In this way, each parent is receiving a tribute that complements their earthly presence.

Reviving the word

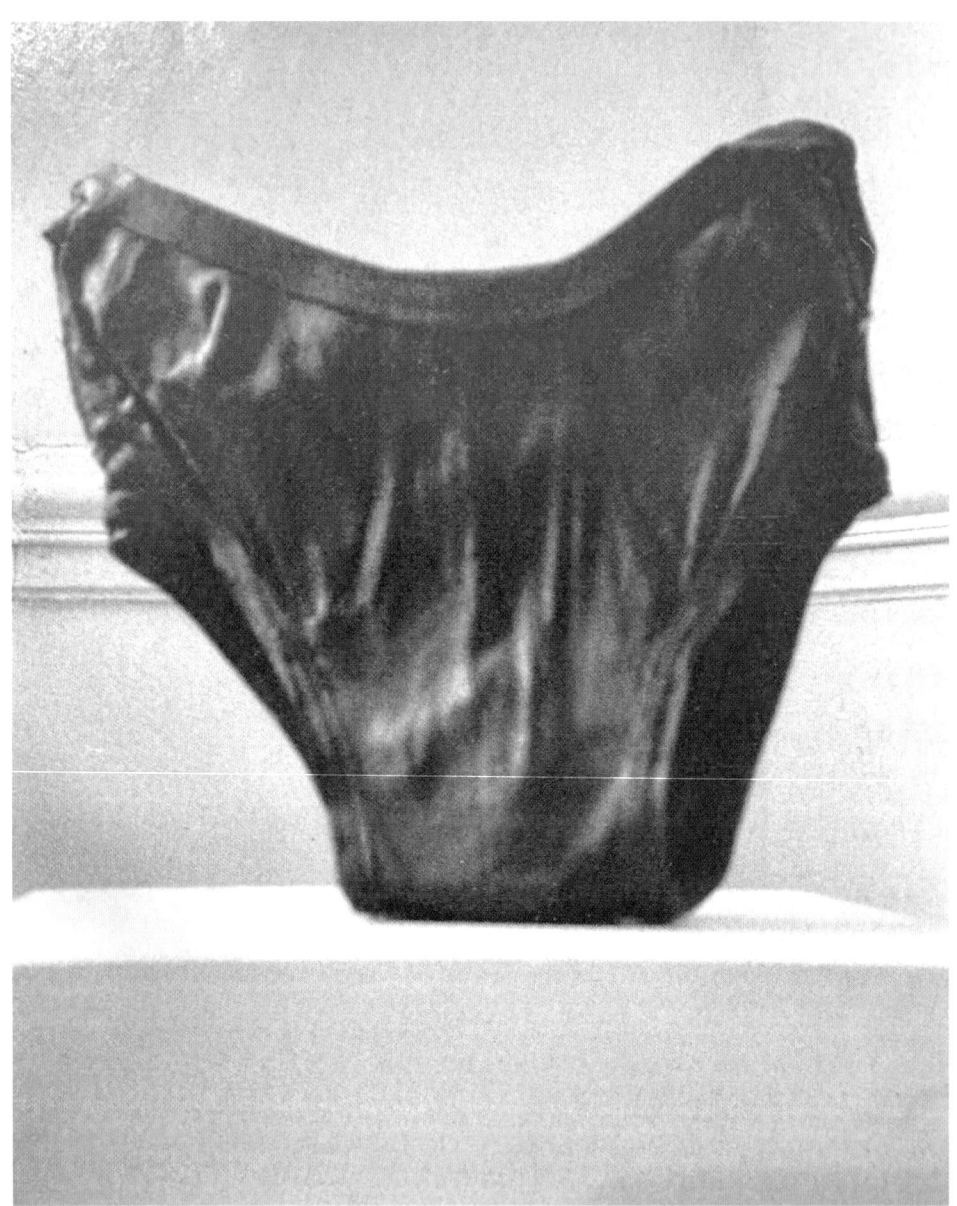

Job Koelewijn, *My Father's Underpants, 1929–1992*, 1994

It is 1997. At the exhibition *What is finished, is not done* in Utrecht, I see a pair of underpants on a plinth. The side is a bit torn. This old-fashioned pair of men's underpants has been dyed a grey-brown colour and has been placed upright using starch, although the word 'upright' is inadequate to describe such a ghostly apparition. It seems as if the article of clothing is being worn by an invisible being. 'They are underpants to commemorate someone, it can't be anything else', I wrote at the time regarding the encounter with these underpants of Job Koelewijn, entitled *Monument to temporality*.

Twenty-four years later, I speak to the artist and by now the work is called *My Father's Underpants, 1929–1992* (1994) and I know that his father was wearing them at the time of his death. The underpants are of the conservative type, rather unflattering white loose-fitting underpants with high-cut legs like you still see on washing lines in the countryside, hanging next to the blue overalls. Job does indeed come from a no-nonsense family from Spakenburg, where his father worked as a builder, and starch powder was an everyday product that was used to stiffen the flowered fabric of the *kraplap* of the traditional Spakenburg costume. 'That black is really too literal, an unnecessary intervention; white would have been better', Job says about his work. He likes to keep art close to reality.

While the deceased father was being laid out, the body was washed carefully and then dressed in a smart Sunday suit. Afterwards, the clothes that had been taken off were left lying in a heap in a corner of the bedroom. Job took the underpants, and the sculpture came about almost by itself, based on the everyday reality surrounding his father's death.

A year earlier, Job made the work *Kids Walk Away With My Thoughts* (1993): a touching photo of a rather untidy row of children wearing folded paper hats on their heads and leaving the school across a paved school playground that is covered with chalk drawings. The paper for the hats consists of pages from Job's notebooks and the pupils from his old primary school are walking towards the world with his poems and notes close to their own thoughts. The last blond boy is looking back timidly. Perhaps Job's thoughts are lighting a spark and give some elasticity to the beliefs taught at home.

Job's way of thinking is spreading through the village and will probably end up on the ground as a crumpled ball of paper or in the wastepaper basket. But perhaps there will be a child who will read their hat or will keep it with their collection of stones and a dried frog. Bye bye Spakenburg, there is still so much to discover! *My Father's Underpants* fits into this process of saying goodbye and coming to terms with loss. Bye, father. No bronze sculpture that will last for eternity, or a portrait that would capture his face, but a humble piece of clothing that was there when his father died, that was touching his skin. The direct contact with death and the genitals via the son's hands and the fabric is almost unbearably intimate.

    The sculpture no longer exists and the single murky photo that I took at the time is included in a booklet, though the original photo was lost after that. And yet the work lives on because I, and no doubt other visitors, haven't forgotten it.

Job tells me about his father in a stream of not particularly flattering anecdotes—'but of course you have to love the man', he suddenly says passionately and goes on to sum up his positive characteristics. 'My father was also super cool. His sharp humour was peppered with quotes from the Bible. He had a strict work ethic and if he promised something, he would certainly do it. My oldest brother Jan helped out in the building trade when he was fourteen and had to spend a week pulling nails out of wooden planks. My father thought that was rather stupid and the following week he went along to help Jan and simply set fire to everything so that only the nails were left. I learned a lot from him.'

    'But my parents weren't a happy combination together. My father lived like a bachelor in our family and didn't show consideration for my mother. For example, a leather sofa was once delivered and she looked at it in surprise and said, "I didn't order anything." That rankles of course, and as a child you take your mother's side. When they went to a birthday party, my mother would leave first and my father ten minutes later. When I saw friends' parents sitting holding hands on the sofa, I couldn't believe it. But my father wasn't a bad person and his temper was primarily due to helplessness.'

This view of his father is very 'Spinoza', who gives both a positive and a negative explanation for every human emotion, without moralising or involving religious belief.

Spinoza equates God with Nature.*29 By this, Spinoza meant that God resides in Nature, where Nature has a capital letter because this encompasses the entire cosmos. In nature, you can't really speak of good and evil. Is a sparrowhawk that uses its talons to kill a coal tit a bad creature? Is a black widow spider that eats her partner after mating a murderer? In nature, everything is connected in a yin and yang equilibrium. Seen from the bigger perspective, there are no thoughts about good and evil. Spinoza's Nature encompasses everything. Everything IS. People think up (belief)systems that lead to judgements and an unbeliever can thus be rejected as a bad person, or adultery and swearing can be regarded as sins. But the cosmos knows no judgements and the highest good is more like water, which fills every space without differentiation.

Farewell Spakenburg (1994) implies that you can leave the past behind you. A washing line with clothes hung out to dry has been drawn on the wall with soft green soap. On the ground is a laundry basket that seems to have been made out of starched white underpants and shirts, as if a strange hocus-pocus-trick has drawn everything out of its usual train of events: in an unguarded moment the washing has flown down from the line in order to become a laundry basket. The shadows stayed behind. The white-shirts-and-underpants-laundry-basket does not contain any washing but clean Spakenburg air, or stuffy reformed air. The shadows materialise the way your upbringing lingers in who you are: the smell of green soap hangs around in your nose for a long time. I saw this laundry basket again online at a sale by Christie's auction house, but this time with a lid; it looked more like an urn now. Nothing is definitive.

Wat af is, is niet gemaakt, the title of the exhibition in 1997, was borrowed from a collection of essays by Paul Valéry, in which he explains how he creates his poems. Writing was not an up-hill struggle for him but more like walking round in a flower garden with a butterfly net, catching thoughts, images, phrases, and rhythms that blend together to form poetry. Effortlessly.

Just like that butterfly net, Job Koelewijn's head is a gathering place for poetry and aphorisms, and during our conversation quotes, aphorisms and one-liners are flying around my ears. Job Koelewijn is especially fond of poems, which he likes to learn by heart and recites with love. 'A poem in the right form can contain a thousand truths. But it does not *say* a single one of them', is how Ursula Le Guin refers to the *Tao Te Ching* by Lao Tzu. According to Koelewijn, this book contains at least a hundred words for 'doing nothing'. That is an assertion I can't really check, but the importance of doing nothing certainly meanders through the entire book.*30

```
The Way never does anything,
and everything gets done.
If those in power could hold to the Way,
the ten thousand things
would look after themselves.
If even so they tried to act,
I'd quiet them with the nameless,
the natural.

In the unnamed, in the unshapen,
is not wanting.
In not wanting is stillness.
In stillness all under heaven rests.
```

Life is simply breathing in harmony with the rhythm of the earth. 'Doing something' is on an equal footing with 'not doing something' and because we as humans are accustomed to action, the book places the emphasis on not doing and on allowing yourself to drift along with the stream of events. Ursula Le Guin speaks about the water soul of the Tao that is mobile and follows and fills. 'Flowing water never disappoints', says Job at one point during our conversation.

The Tao sees wisdom in what is not there, just as a rounded vase is useable because of its hollow space. 'The root of the noble is in the common, the high stands on what's below.' His father's starched underpants are also one of those things that emphasise absence more than anything else: the man is no longer there, he is now awaiting the end times of the reformed church, or is a part of Nature with a capital 'N'.

The *Wei Wu Wei* principle (not doing something) resonates in Job's artistic practice, and in his life too, because in the end you can't distinguish between the two. 'Effortless' is a word he uses several times. 'Effortless', otherwise making art becomes more work, and it needs to simply be life. Intense life, of course.

'I have an ideal, I'm trying to make something of my life' and 'It's about refreshing and focusing the human mind. You should never take something for granted.'

In order to make something of life, Job integrates a strict discipline into his life. Since 1 February 2006, his morning has a set ritual: put on tracksuit trousers, have breakfast, and then read aloud for 45 minutes from a (usually) philosophical book. A touch on the red button starts the recording. Job reads with the intention of understanding the meaning of the text as well as possible, so there are sometimes silences, sentences are repeated, and there are slips of the tongue. 'It's difficult to read aloud and understand at the same time. I've got quite used to it now and I read very slowly. It is a sort of exercise in concentration and reading aloud clearly; it doesn't matter if you don't understand everything.' The beautiful thing about discipline is that in the end it becomes effortless, or worse, you can no longer do without the habit you've learned.

Of course, we all wonder about the meaning of life now and then, usually without attaching any conclusions to this. For Job, this is different. When he was 21, he had a serious car accident and at first the outlook didn't look good for him at all: life in a vegetative state in a wheelchair. While he lay motionless in bed with a broken neck, a stream of intense experiences began. In that scaled-down, flat life, each change was dramatic, such as being able to breathe without a machine again, the smell of coffee and the rattling of metal trolleys. Job speaks about a border-experience through which he experienced the wonder of reality in its essential form. Hallucinations and vivid dreams dealt a blow to his concept of time which shot out of its usual rhythm. In the images that were evoked, he was back in the classroom or kept experiencing a holiday again and again.

It turned out that all those experiences happened within a ten-minute timespan but nevertheless they felt eerily real. In life, time is an unreliable partner in crime. We understand time as a straight line and hope the (life)line will be as long as possible. But perhaps we are dashing to and fro in time; we do that in our thoughts and dreams in any case, and perhaps a short life is in fact more desirable than a long life. 'The experience that you can evoke images and memories in your mind that are so realistic, irrespective of your physical limitations—that has never let me go.' He enrolled at the Rietveld Academy in Amsterdam. It fascinates me that Job of all people, who has experienced something irrational, ends up reading philosophical books that deal with truth, God, and our existence in a rational way. Perhaps he is following Spinoza: 'Humans come to true knowledge through their intellect, and not through faith, and philosophy is the perfection of intellect.' Perhaps he has taken Paul Valéry's words seriously: 'I confess that I have made of my mind an idol, but I have found no other.'

'I can sharpen my mind on great masters. A person should not take their own stupidity as the norm', says Job. Staying alert, not slipping into the TikTok swamp, Netflix, or other forms of passive entertainment. Job doesn't want to spend his days and hours watching such futile forms of amusement. The art he subsequently makes smells of green soap, talcum powder or broth, or reflects and shines and gleams. Sensory, and fleeting.

Job's mother died in 2020, 28 years after her husband, and in that period she was able to do things in her own way after all. A small headstone was placed on her grave, next to her husband's large stone. This may reflect the reality of this marriage but not the love that her children and the villagers felt for this woman, who lived with God's word in her ears. Her faith was her comfort and truth; cleaning was her therapy. She was always ready to turn the other cheek. To forgive.
At her funeral, Job read out a poem by Willem M. Roggeman:

```
What matters
is what you keep silent
when all has been said,
is what remains of you
if you are still there.

Just as I'm no longer here
when you say nothing more to me,
or when you stop calling my name
As I stay silent in what I recognise,
that's how it is.

The silence of your words.
The sounds of your silence.
That's what matters.
Nothing else,
Believe me. On my word.
```

A short memoriam like this, hanging in the air for just a moment, can be more intense than a gravestone. And encompasses all that is not mentioned. Endlessly much. Endlessly much love. That remains. A short life, a long life, one cheek, the other cheek. As humans, we're no more than that, a fragment of ignorance in the yin and yang of the universe. We just have to make the best of it.

'As long as you continue to push death away, you are not embracing life. I say: embrace death. That experience with death when I was 21 made me wise about life. I looked it in the eyes. The limitation on life, which death is, sharpens us. Imagine imposing the following limitation on men: you may only have a relationship with three women. Or an artist: you may only make a hundred artworks during your lifetime. You can bet that this will force them to take things seriously. That's how it works with death too. Imagine if we all knew it would end on our 70th birthday—what would our life look like then?'

Lotte van Lieshout, *Couzijn*, 2019, 207 × 120 cm, oil on marbled paper on packaging cardboard and cotton

Blue

Caren van Herwaarden, *Blue*, 2015,
Caren made a number of small cuddly dolls from old sheets, towels and cleaning cloths from her mother.

I wouldn't have missed his death for the world

I wouldn't have missed his death for the world

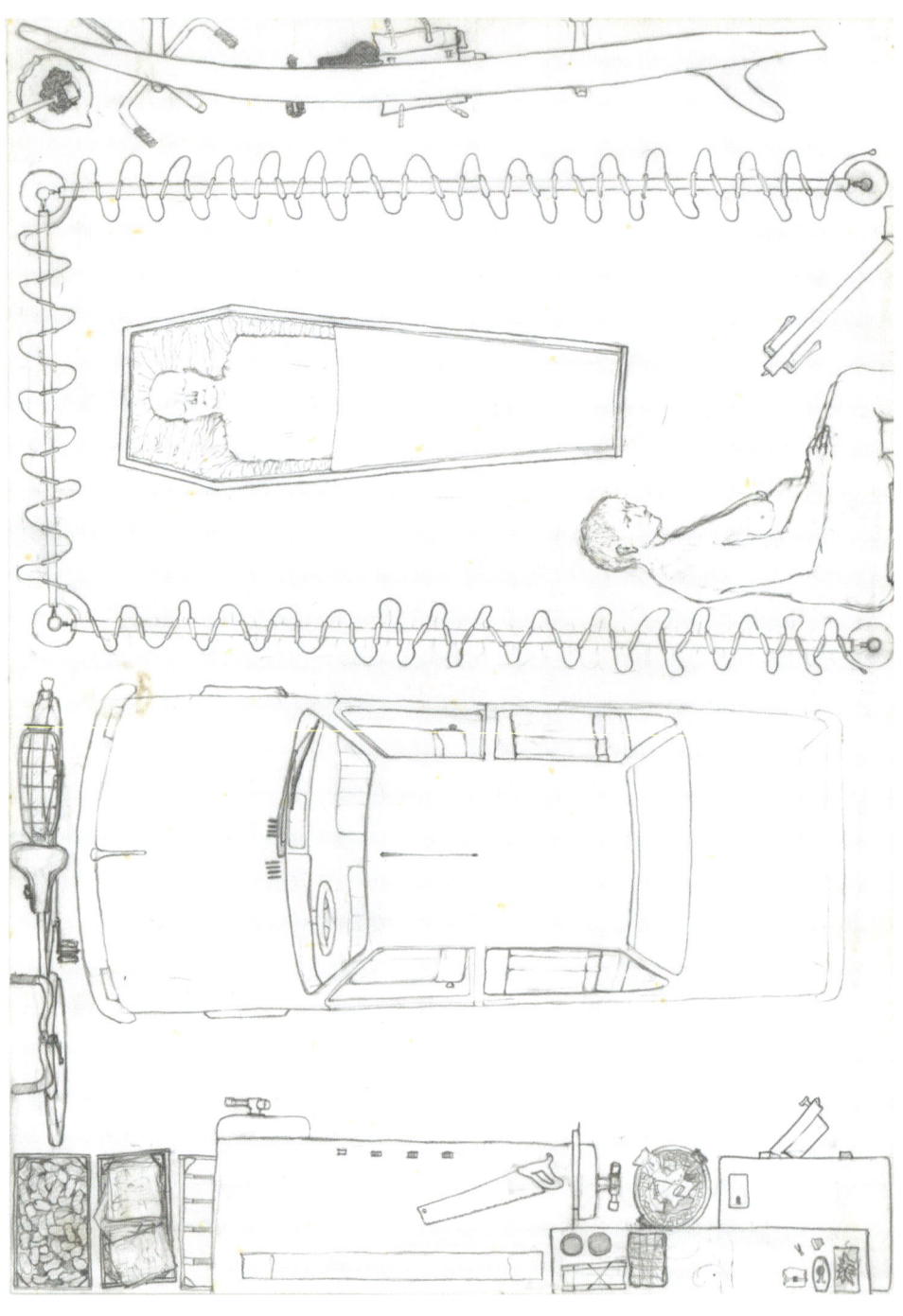

Arnoud Holleman, *Car and coffin*, 1993

Anyone who has seen *The Big Lebowski* by the Coen Brothers will never forget the scene: the two friends, Walter and The Dude, are walking towards the Pacific Ocean to scatter their friend Donny's ashes, which they're carrying in a coffee tin. When they arrive, Walter embarks on a eulogy to their friend and, as always, this turns into a tirade about the Vietnam War, his favourite and in fact only subject. While they're staring at the flowing water, Walter opens the coffee tin in order to cast the ashes into the river but the strong headwind decides otherwise and blows the ashes over them. They stand there like two zombies, covered with grey-white powder. Solemn words and laudatory phrases are often spoken surrounding death, in the context of seriousness and gravity. But mundane blunders also happen surrounding death, it's just that no one likes talking about them because this detracts somewhat from the dignity of the deceased person. That's why my archive of 'funny misunderstandings' contains only one single item about death. Arnoud Holleman's drawing of his father lying in repose is funny and absurd although it records the reality in quite a matter-of-fact way. You are looking from above into the garage, where a car is parked on the left, and on the right his dead father is lying in a half-open coffin, surrounded by bicycles, apples in a box, and a mop to clean the floor. The funeral director has put a black curtain around the coffin. Death in an everyday situation seems rather improper; the solemnity falls away and the potatoes appear. And in the shielded-off area, a woman is sitting on a chair, a rigid-looking, naked woman who is keeping watch. An angel? His mother. Naked, how awkward. It's a clear drawing, nothing airy-fairy about it, rather too down to earth for a subject like death. Relieved of all his gravity, like a car, his father lay in repose there for a few days, in the cool of the garage.

When I enter Arnoud Holleman's studio, I almost stumble over a round table and four chairs. They come from his parental home and are still in use. Yes, that furniture. 'There was often an oppressive silence at mealtimes,' says Arnoud, 'we just didn't really know what to say. My parents didn't have a bad marriage, but the atmosphere was always strained. When I was an adolescent, black clouds were hanging above my head all the time and my father usually bore the brunt of it, so I was also to blame for that vacuum. We were conflict-averse and invisible heaps piled up under the table.'

Arnoud smiles his generous round smile that takes all the sharpness out of his remarks. But I still feel a stab of emotion because of that gentle meeting of table, chairs, and trauma. The furniture is standing there in spite of this. It's not been chopped into pieces, circles haven't been sawn out of it, one leg hasn't been made a bit shorter to give it a nice shaky balance. No, the table is there as a silent witness and is used and cherished.

Such a quiet father, who was present in the house like a ghost and was okay with everything. 'I lacked the boundaries I needed.' Arnoud mentions a lack of example and direction so that he never fell hard in everything he did but always landed in a soft bed of marshmallows. 'I drank beer like lemonade and when I was completely drunk and fell into the hedge, vomiting, that was also fine. What I'm missing in that example is discipline; it made me feel unseen, left to my own devices. My decision to become an artist didn't arouse a millimetre of resistance either.' Within the family, the father pretty much lived his own life that took place at the Academy for Industrial Design, where he was a lecturer, and in his study, where he conscientiously prepared the lessons for the following day. Presence in absence. The extent to which a quiet, an almost invisible father can also have an oppressive influence only became apparent after his death. His death, the real absence, suddenly gave all the family members breathing space.

 His father died in 1993; Arnoud was 28 years old. A few months after his death, the mother and her two sons began clearing up his sanctuary together: the study with Heugaveld tiles where the cigar smoke had remained hanging in the air pervasively, even though he'd not smoked for twenty years. The process of sorting things out drew them closer together; they came across various surprises, such as geometric drawings from his school days and cassette tapes with recordings of him playing piano.

 Things already began to move during the mourning period: fresh air mingled with the cigar air. The family rearranged itself: 'The relationship with my mother changed, she was taking us into her confidence now. And my mother was good at being alone, she was enterprising and enjoyed her rowing trips across Europe.'

After his retirement, the father had begun studying piano again, and he did that thoroughly and precisely too, just like everything in his life. He used to record his playing on a cassette tape, and he listened to the recordings to check whether he had played the music correctly so that he could continue to study. A rather mathematical approach, certainly if you compare it to their neighbour, a jazz pianist who threw caution to the winds and improvised to his heart's content. 'We are used to hearing the music of the world's very best piano players in our homes, but in my father's playing you can also hear him toiling away, and the not-quite-perfect elements. That restrained piano music is so much my father, that inhibited inner world which meant you could never make out what was going on inside him. That music, that's so typical of him.'

The CD *Stars from Heaven* by Wim Holleman is on the table and a photo from the time of his engagement adorns the cover, a balding man with a small wreath of hair, dark glasses, and an intensely satisfied smile. Arnoud made three copies as presents for his family. He subsequently had a CD produced in 2003, eight years later, as a giveaway artwork because he wanted to share the memory of his father with more people. This time in a modest white sleeve with the sentence 'My Dad Playing Piano'. Arnoud added silences so that the music keeps starting afresh and attracting your attention. That silence lifts the sounds out of reality for a moment.

The death of his father caused a change in direction within the family. For Arnoud, questions were triggered about artistic practice; he always wanted to spread his wings and go for eternity. That fantasy of greatness undoubtedly had to do with his black-cloud-world and his father's unpretentiousness. '"Me and Rodin" has been my mantra for quite a long time. I literally link my work to Rodin's, our great artistic forefather, and wonder how I can still make a meaningful gesture, in view of all the baggage of art history.'

'The hero is he who is immovably centred', is the motto of the book that Rainer Maria Rilke wrote in poetic words about the sculptor Auguste Rodin. In his letters, Rilke is consistent in his use of 'master', 'great master', 'dear master', and only later on 'my dear friend'. 'One day men will understand what made this great artist so great: He was a worker whose only desire was to penetrate with all his forces into the humble and difficult significance of his tools', writes Rilke in his introduction.*³¹ His flattering words must have pleased Rodin because the Rodin-phenomenon was also a vain man who did everything in his power to immortalise his fame. Despite the fact that he had dozens of people working for him, he cultivated the myth of the solitary genius. During the world exhibition in 1900, Rodin opened his own retrospective exhibition, with 170 works in bronze, marble, and plaster. He personally created the Musée Rodin by gifting all his work to the state, on condition that it would be displayed in a museum, for which he made his own house and studio available.

The artist Arnoud Holleman gave the sculptor Rodin the role of a substitute father in his oeuvre, the egocentric, great genius as a counterpart to the modest father. Rodin embodied the desire to excel yourself, to surpass your father. At the same time, the urge for fame is diametrically opposed to the fear of failure, and the need to keep yourself small and unseen.

In time, his view of his father changed and Arnoud reviewed his own role in the family too. And that again influenced his artistic practice. *Immovably centred* is the title of a series of performances in which Arnoud examines the relationship between delusions of grandeur and fear of failure by letting a contemporary artist with a Rodin-complex do the talking. The text is spoken by a number of different people. 'Arnoud Holleman cuts up the artist', writes the NRC.

The silence in the music of the CD *My Dad Playing Piano* led me to one of the performances in three movements of the 1953 composition *4', 33"* by John Cage, in which the piano remains silent, and the surroundings determine the way the silence is filled with coughing, shuffling of shoes, creaking articles of clothing, bags that open and close. How do you perform silence? That can also be done with a lot of actions, apparently: 'Please welcome our soloist, William Marx.'*³² The man bows deeply to the audience, sits down at the Steinway grand piano, throws back his coattails and puts his glasses on. Then he closes the lid of the piano and raises a fist in the air dramatically, clutching the stopwatch, as if he is controlling the silence single-handedly. The same ritual takes place for the second movement; there he is again with his raised hand. And then a third time. Instead of allowing the silence to do the work, he draws all the attention to himself, towards him, the great artist. It is André Rieu-like. Rodin-like. As if the silence cannot exist without *him,* without his hand. What I see is a gigantic ego, with none of the modesty that John Cage was alluding to. Simply opening the window and listening, that's possible too.

```
Debussy: The music is not in the notes,
but in the spaces between them.
Cage: I got ya, mate.
```

And that's what it is. The space in between the notes. Fortunately, Arnoud has not put on the great maestro's tail-coat; he is opening the window to allow the silence to be heard. Arnoud approaches the great Rodin with his own modesty: a study, a small change in the context, the sculpture *Balzac* that rotates slowly, the *Adam* in Zwolle is given a voice, an article in the magazine *De Groene Amsterdammer.* On the wooden desktop in Arnoud's studio, beside my cup of tea, is the book *Zo doe je dat (How to do it)* by J.J. Beljon, the bible of making things for students, from around the eighties. The subtitle is *Basic Principles of Design.*

'Shapes have an influence on our feelings', is how the first sentence goes. 'There are reassuring shapes, terrifying, intelligent, or stupid shapes. A shape does something to us.' The dryness of design language, simply: hierarchy, composition, repetition, contrast, addition—and this simplicity characterises Arnoud's work. The added silence in his father's piano playing.

In *Jeugdfoto* (Childhood Photo), Arnoud is holding two photos next to each other. His mother came across the boxes of her husband's slides while having a clear-out: 'Papa's slides—don't you want to have a look?' His father photographed land-scapes in well-balanced compositions, but perhaps rather boring and unnecessary. But in the procession of images that passes by, a family photo suddenly lights up. 'I'm standing there as a child beside my mother and I'm pointing my camera at Aunt Greet. So my father must have taken that photo. I suddenly understood my father's presence; he was looking at me through the lens of the camera. I suddenly saw myself in his field of vision, a child wearing clogs, holding a camera.' Being seen. Being recognised. 'I was seen, but didn't see it.'

> 'While we as mere mortals sometimes wonder in desperation whether any part of us will ever come into the picture, when an angel looks into the mirror, weary of simply being a spirit, they secretly make a list of touching moments in which we play the leading role.'

'While processing his death, I have gained a father I never had in reality, because I have come to look at our family differently and with a greater realisation of reality. I wouldn't have missed his death for the world, especially because it has brought me so much self-awareness.'

The concept of 'not being seen' had to be adjusted to 'two generations who can't reach each other'. 'A feeling for which you are jointly responsible. Giving the other person the blame is a blind alley. What do you actually need in order to change? That whole process started after the death of my father. That complicated father was also a projection of how complex I was myself. In that sense, it was mainly after his death that I found my father and that battle I fought when I was 28 disappeared completely after a long process of mourning. 'And so I landed with my feet on the ground again, was able to let go of Rodin as my great example and was able to give my position as an artist the scale that suited it.'

The sculpture *The Thinker* by Rodin was stolen from the Singer Museum and was later found, covered with deep cuts: the thieves had tried to saw the sculpture into pieces using an angle grinder so they could sell the bronze. It is precisely because of those thick cuts that the sculpture has gained a human dimension. Arnoud developed a project together with Gert Jan Kocken about the damaged *Thinker* that consists of research, text, and a photo.

This sculpture, the dented thinker, is the only sculpture by Rodin that really moves me; nothing is more beautiful than someone who bares their soul, their scars, their grazes. This is the sculpture I like most. And Arnoud's contribution was merely seeing how intense that sculpture was. So modest.

I wouldn't have missed his death for the world

Arnoud Holleman, *My Dad Playing Piano*, 2002

p. 194-195: Arnoud Holleman, *Childhood photo*, 2018

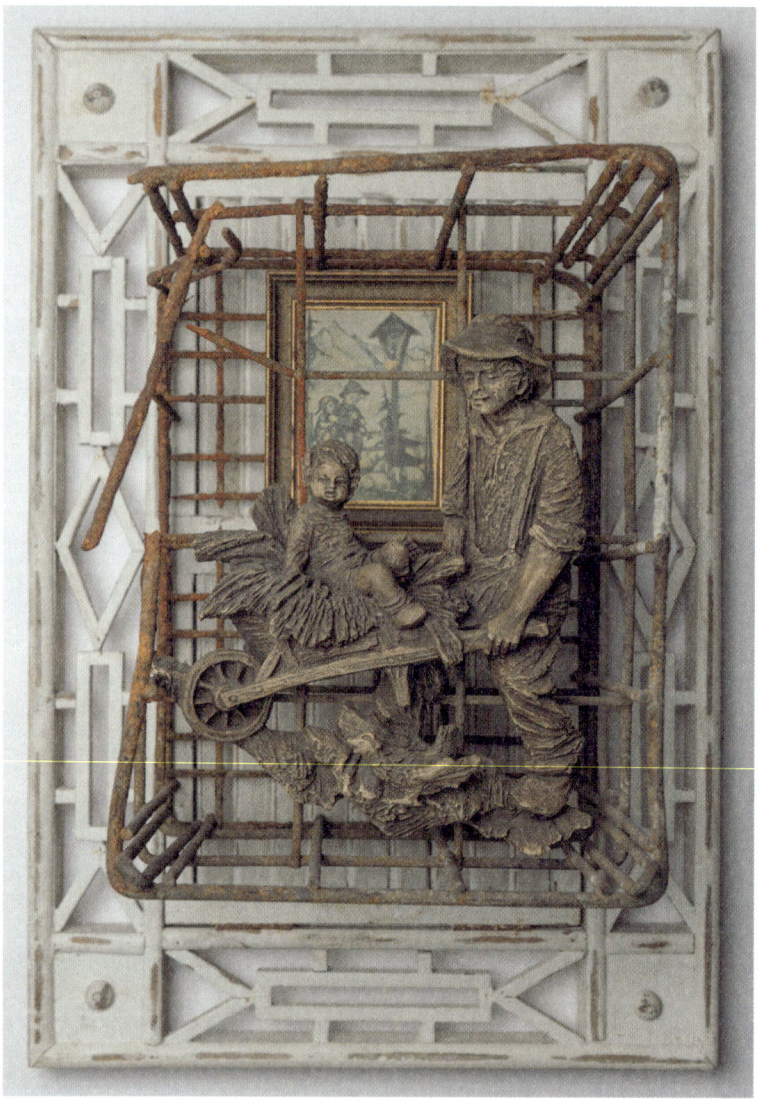

Vincent van Oss:

This work is a farewell to my father. Lots of people had the figurine in their homes, but we didn't. My parents thought it was kitschy. The framed print in the background was something my parents did have, though. Nice and sweet. The intention was that we children would become sweet little angels. My father was Catholic and believed in the hereafter. I don't believe anything.

Vincent van Oss, *Father's wheelbarrow,* 2021, ceramic figurine, Hummel-print in frame, a rusty rack and a closed decorative mirror

Object for Opa

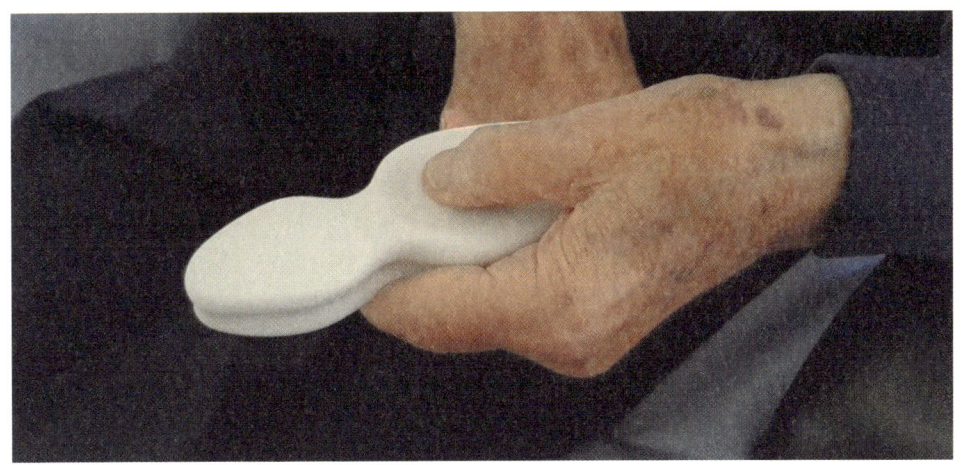

Sijben Rosa:

This is W.C. Reij, a retired professor and engineer, and also my grandfather. We've always been close. He was taking me to museums, drawing together with me, and meticulously following my art career for as long as he was able to.

During the last few years of his life he had to deal with aphasia, an impairment causing him to slowly lose his linguistic and other cognitive abilities. When he could barely speak any longer, Covid-19 robbed us of the only way of communication we had left: touch.

That's when I decided to make an art experience that was tailored to his specific condition; one that was to be experienced somewhat through sight, but predominantly through touch. The shape of *Object voor Opa* (Object for Grandpa) is based on movements I remembered him doing with my hands, on ways of touching and holding on that he seemed to enjoy. He had been nearly constantly holding it during what turned out to be the last two months of his life.

Sijben Rosa, *Object for Grandpa*, 2020, sculpture, tangible experience, epoxy clay 16 × 6 × 3 cm, private exhibition for my grandfather

A house without a key

> We journey towards a home not of our flesh.
> Its chestnut trees are not of our bones.
> Its rocks are not like goats in the mountain hymn.
> The pebbles' eyes are not lilies.
> We journey towards a home that does not halo
> our heads with a special sun.
> Mythical women applaud us. A sea for us,
> a sea against us.
> When water and wheat are not at hand,
> eat our love and drink our tears…
> — Mahmoud Darwish *33

Time and time again, Mahmoud Darwish's poems lay bare the harrowing situation of the Palestinian people and the pain in their soul; it is, after all, his own history. To the present day, the injustice of their circumstances has not been resolved. In 1948, which is now 74 years ago, following the proclamation of the state of Israel, the Palestinians were driven out of their homes, hearths and their own land. The Nakba, or catastrophe. History. The diaspora that resulted from this has an unprecedented impact on families and their children, and it remains outside the field of view of many people. A sad, inextricable knot.

Lack of understanding is what Susanne Khalil Yusef (Germany, 1984) regularly comes up against: 'What are you going on about? Palestine! You were born in Germany, Europe! Far away from Palestine in time and space. What business of yours is that history?' In her studio in Arnhem, I encounter an abundant quantity of work, colourful and unrestrained. You sense her enthusiasm and also something cheerful, with a zest for life.
A large pot is encircled by a green glazed snake that is spiralling upwards. Perhaps it is the Palestinian adder, the most dangerous of all seven venomous snakes that live in Israel. I see a dromedary, a lighthouse, a jar with Haribo frogs. A green heart. Three copies of sentimental orientalist paintings of women with jars and children are hanging on the wall. White rifles are dangling on chains in front of them. Unfinished pots with flames licking at them stand on massive blue potter's wheels on castors. A glass cabin outside turns out to be the Yusef's Schwärmer exhibition space and it is full of ceramic pots with shiny white beads hanging on them, colourful glazed rifles are stuck to them, and spiky cacti are growing painfully slowly while mega-palms are rocketing up.

A mysterious totem. It is as if all the works are written in a language I don't speak, full of references that I don't fully understand.

> – Where are you taking me, Father?
> – In the direction of the wind, my son…
> He touches his key, like it is part
> Of his body and he relaxes.
> While they pass through a thorn fence, he told him:
> Remember, my son,
> Here, the English crucified your father
> On cactus thorns
> For two nights
> and he never confessed.
> When you grow older, my son
> And recite to those who inherit rifles
> An epic of blood on iron.
> – Mahmoud Darwish

The long foothills of history extend from the Nakbar towards Susanne. Susanne's grandparents fled from Jaffa and since that time the family has lived in diaspora. Her parents were born in the refugee camps of Sabra and Shatila in Lebanon. Even though the camps have been transformed into a kind of city neighbourhoods, the situation of the inhabitants hasn't improved because they have hardly any rights and also the 'right of return' (as formulated in UN Resolution 194) has not been implemented. Since 1948, almost a million Palestinians have been displaced and it seems like no one in this world really cares. 'We want to live with dignity', was the cry from the heart of the Lebanese population for a long time but in the meantime, out of desperation, this has been shortened to 'We want to live'. This sentence is even more urgent for the Palestinians.

    Susanne's parents both fled to Germany and met in a centre for asylum seekers. They were allowed to stay but without refugee status, with the associated permanent residence permit, because Lebanon was regarded as a safe country. Her mother wanted a safe situation for her children and she did everything to achieve this. She set off regularly with a car full of children without informing the father, to yet another new destination in the hope of asylum. In the studio, I unravel the transfers on the ceramic minaret of Jaffa with its shining golden crescent moon: family photos and history overlap each other around it. A photo of her father being embraced by his three children. 'That was in the asylum seekers centre in Sweden: my father stood outside and called our names. I recognised his voice. We hadn't seen each other for at least a year.' There is also a photo on which her father is grinning broadly with his children close around him, swaying on a ship.

Her mother wanted papers so badly that she finally married an Iraqi refugee with a residence permit. Who knows? Perhaps they were in love. The family drove by car to his flat in Arnhem-South. When she was fourteen, Susanne left home and wandered around without papers because she had not completed the requisite three years with her stepfather. She did finally get a passport via a lawyer when she was 25 years old and this enabled her to go to art academy.

A passport is the lifebuoy in the turbulent water of a refugee's life. A resident permit correlates with identity, origin, and nationality. After that, a swampy area of 'source documents', evidentiary functions, verification inspections, and a 'dubious debtors' fund for vital medical care is what determines the life of a girl without papers. And if you are deprived of a passport for so long, who are you, do you really exist? Little remains now of the fertile Palestine of the past:

> 'Now we find ourselves on a dung-heap', is how the poet Nizar Qabbani described the situation. 'In our hands they left a sardine can called Gaza and a dry bone called Jericho.' *34

Nowadays, that dung-heap is surrounded by high fences and the Palestinians can't go anywhere because of all the Israeli security checks. They live in a permanent lockdown.

Because Palestinians in diaspora are cut off from their homeland and are surrounded by ignorance in their new country, artists collect facts, stories, and personal histories. The Palestinian artist Emily Jacir is able to travel to Israel, the West Bank and Gaza, thanks to her American passport, and she takes with her the requests of all those who are not permitted to visit their homeland. 'Go to my mother's grave in Jerusalem and lay flowers there on her birthday.' 'Drink the water in my parents' village.' 'Go to Jaffa, find our house and take a photo.'

The privilege of travel determined her artistic practice. Almost every work of a Palestinian artist in diaspora is a memorial that attempts to tie together the broken threads of their heritage. Loss and longing. Since 2004, the freedom of movement of Palestinians with a foreign passport has also been restricted. Israel does not like Palestinians returning to their homeland.

We want to live and move around, with or without papers! We want to live, that must surely be possible. But Israeli politics scarcely seem to allow this for the inhabitants of the sardine-like Gaza and the dry bones of Jericho.

At the art academy too, Susanne kept getting those questions: 'Why do you have a thing about Palestine? Why do you keep bringing up that past?' A lecturer encouraged her to follow a course at the academy of Ramallah to give substance to that connection. Susanne: 'I didn't know that it was possible and was certainly not sure whether it would work. Negative travel advice had been issued and the academy wasn't very responsive, but I persisted.' Susanne got on the plane cheerfully in 2014 with a stack of official documents, but the Israeli border control turned out to be a nightmare. 'The soldiers were suspicious. I sat in the cold for fourteen hours, without food, I was shouted at, sweet-talked, and yelled at again. Soldiers with rifles were walking around me.' She finally got a visa for 30 days, for Ramallah only. 'Watch out, we're keeping an eye on you', were their parting words. In the middle of the night, she walked towards the warmth of Jericho, in shock, and also very relieved. Since then, she has used a different name as an artist so that she is free to make her art and to keep the possibility of returning. 'I've delved into why we as Palestinians find it so difficult to live in diaspora, but in Palestine it is even more hopeless, and it seems as if that has greater urgency than my own existence. It was a happy and intense experience, full of friendships. I feel an obligation to speak about *there*. Perhaps I can set something in motion, who knows, perhaps my work has an influence, that's all I can do.'

Her work is a witness. A protest. For example, Susanne followed the news for eight weeks via Arabic media and counted thirty deaths in Palestinian territory, for the most part young men between 14 and 22 years old. The faces of these thirty boys look at you from a cluster of helium balloons, smiling and full of hope. They are no longer there.

She also began to collect everything about her Palestinian background: the *Handala Archives,* interviews of her own, the book *All That Remains* by Walid Khalidi, every card or film she could get hold of and even Israeli propaganda films. She saw a reproduction of a painting by William Halewijn offered for free on an online selling site, *Palestine refugee mother, a last glance.* A Madonna-like mother is fleeing with a child in her arms. 'It made a deep impression, yes, it is sweet and romanticised, as if the woman is leaving in her best dress, but it is nevertheless an artwork that documents the Nakba at the time it took place.' With her characteristic perseverance, Susanne took the telephone book and began phoning everyone called Halewijn. A man in Ede turned out to be a nephew of the artist.

The ceramic vases have faces, or put the other way, heads became vases. 'It started with a small vase with a rose by Joseph Beuys, it was left over from an installation where he called upon residents to come together to discuss the problems in the area. I decided to turn the heads into vases too, in order to open up the conversation.' Susanne conducts that conversation in the nomadic *Café Disorient:* she serves good strong Arabic coffee and talks with visitors about all her experiences, topics that have an impact on people's lives, but don't make it into the news. The Palestinian 'question' is an explosive topic that many people have an opinion about and the conversations are often difficult and emotional. She approaches people's ignorance in a velvety gentle and straightforward way. With that wonderful name, *Café Disorient,* Susanne Khalil Yusef presented an installation in the Valkhof Museum, where she transformed the entire space and installed a neon sign: we want to live.

Almost like an altar, an original painting by William Halewijn is hanging between two panels with a neon pattern that looks like crocheted wool or the loops of a chain-link fence. The floor and walls are covered with a mega enlargement of the Arafat scarf. This shawl from the past seems to be a symbol for hope because during Arafat's time peace talks were at least taking place. During a meeting of the United Nations, Arafat declared:

> 'I come bearing an olive branch in one hand, and the freedom fighter's gun in the other. Do not let the olive branch fall from my hand…' *[35]

A bunch of keys is hanging on the wall, in a frame, which gives them even more importance. During the Nakba, Palestinians took their house keys with them as a symbol of their return. Older women still wear their door key around their neck like a precious piece of jewellery. On the carpet, there are busts of young men, standing or lying down, created in ceramic, bronze, and aluminium. 'Justice' is glazed on the inside. The installation is one big cry from the heart, drawing attention to the Palestinian question. It is impossible not to be deeply affected by it.

The work is a witness and an attempt to open up the discussion. 'Getting to the raw material behind hard convictions and making people think about issues from a different perspective is precisely what art does', I read in a text accompanying a work by Sandi Hilal and Alessandro Petti. Then I listen to *The Ramallah Syndrome,* a fragmentary audio work. Like a circling and incantatory formula, I keep hearing *You need to understand, It is important to understand* between the fragments of text. The incomplete and fragmentary nature of this reminds me again of how little I actually knew about the diaspora of the Palestinians, the gaps in my own memory, but also the realisation that the situation is still going on, the hope of improvement is crumbling.

One of the big busts lying on the ground has been given the facial features of Susanne's father. Her mother and sisters recognised his portrait immediately. Her father died in Germany in 2010 and his death gave Susanne mixed feelings more than anything else. 'My family is always asking me to go with them to the grave or to commemorate him. I don't actually really dare to focus on his death. I thought that I didn't care about it much but last week I walked into the studio of a fellow-student and saw her painting of a sick father in bed, being fed via a tube, and children who were crying. I was suddenly overcome with heart-wrenching grief and was extremely upset. The violence of the emotion took me by surprise. The scene made me think of my father, who often needed to be on oxygen during the last years of his life.'

Perhaps Susanne's grief is being held in check by an unjustified feeling of inadequacy. In the tragic final years of her father's life, she did not manage to go to Germany very often, she tells me softly.

But perhaps there is also a limit to how much care you can give your father. There is still much to investigate.

Her father was a kind man who lived for his children. As a fourteen-year-old child soldier, he fought with the Palestinian resistance based in Lebanon but never spoke of it later on. Susanne understood from a friend of her father's that they had spent a year together imprisoned under the ground. Susanne describes her father as an honest, gentle, but very depressed man. He would do anything for his children. 'When we were still living together as a family, my mother was often away and he looked after us, in his way. In the morning, we would find four small piles of money, the same amount for each child. We could use this to buy lunch. He gave us a crazy amount of sweets: for example, he'd buy a batch of Haribo Frogs, Gold-bears and Bananas that were almost expired, and the kitchen cupboards were overflowing with all kinds of sweets. It wasn't responsible, but I felt a lot of love in it. He had a short fuse but always said sorry.' After the move to the Netherlands, they saw each other less and less, although her father phoned every day and she could hear the coins jingling down in the payphone. But he became addicted because he had nothing else to live for. 'He dried up like a plant without water.'

'Through these sculptures, I am giving him the recognition and the respect that he deserved. When I made the *Yusef Boys*, the balloons with the faces of the murdered Palestinian boys, I had to think about him so much. He had also joined the resistance at that young age. I based his portrait on his registration photo, showing him from three sides with a number underneath. Life had beaten him down and had gradually made him stooped. I am showing him as a proud, upright man. As a strong person. The person he was deep inside. His body was worn out, but I have seen his soul and his love.'

Susanne's heart-breaking past won't let me go. Being dragged from pillar to post gave her a deep feeling of not being rooted, a feeling of being unwanted, fear of the outside world, of other people, fear of everything. 'You think that Western people are better; it's an inferiority complex that becomes integral to your thinking', is how Susanne describes it. A mother who is always on the run with her children, yes, that is no doubt harmful for those children, but at the same time you see a mother who wants to make life better for her children. Susanne is keen to make her art more personal but fears the lion's den of public opinion. What do you want to bring out into the open? Your parents, your past, it hasn't all been flawless, but you certainly don't want to be judged by the outside world.

No. We need to understand.

p. 200: Susanne Khalil Yusef, detail of *Yusef Boys*, 2022, bronze, aluminium, (photo: Liza Wolters)

p. 206: Susanne Khalil Yusef, *Yusef Boys*, 2019, ceramic, exhibition at GoMulan Gallery in 2021, (photo: Jonathan de Waart)

p. 210-211: Susanne Khalil Yusef, *Yusef Boys,* Foam 3h, 2022, (photo: Christian van der Kooy)

Her hand

Lisa Couwenberg, *Mom,* 2021, 110 × 49 cm, acrylic on panel

Lisa Couwenbergh:

My mother and I fought a lot. There was a huge generation gap and our characters frequently clashed. I was a rebellious adolescent and ran away from home. When I was a child and came home in tears because the boy next door had hit me with a rake, there was no comfort to be found from my mother. Crying was a weakness. She ran the household with four children and took good care of us, but you had to deal with your own problems, heartache, and fears. The older my mother grew, the mellower she became. But I also came to view her more gently with the passing of the years. She had a lot of ailments, but never complained. I saw how tough she really was and that she was able to take pleasure in very small things. When I took her to a café terrace in her wheelchair and we drank a glass of wine together in the sun, she said: 'It's just like being in Italy.' She was still living independently when she was 97 and coped very well, in her wheelchair, with the help of carers. When her physical health deteriorated even further, she very bravely and resolutely opted for euthanasia.

During the last week, my brother, two sisters and I stayed with her day and night. When I sat beside her bed and helped her to eat an ice cream, a feeling of warmth came over me that I had never felt as strongly before: 'This is my mother and I love her.' Friday 13 August approached. She would no longer be there at half past three in the afternoon. When the time had come, I asked her if I should hold her hand. 'You don't need to do that', she replied. But I held her hand anyway while the doctor administered the euthanasia drug. And now I miss the mother I had in those last years. All the annoyances, disappointment and mutual lack of understanding had suddenly vanished. Those last years were a tiny piece of our life together, but they were crucial.

I made this painting a few weeks after her death. Her emaciated hand, weak, but also powerful. That hand was the last contact I had to let go of, wistfully.

The future is built with fragments from the past

No parent brings their child into the world with the intention of traumatising this tiny new being; a miserable and bleak childhood, no, that is never a parent's intention. Despite this, growing up is a minefield for countless children. Some parents embark on this adventure in total ignorance, without knowledge of themselves and their shortcomings, and they fail miserably from the outset; drugs—drink—violence—incest—neglect—it's all there. A dysfunctional family living together in a house inhales toxic air, as if there is an old stove in the sitting room, releasing small puffs of carbon monoxide. The family members gradually have difficulty breathing and even die a little because of it. God created man by blowing the breath of life into his nose, and the man became a living being (Genesis 2:7). Breathe my breath, feel what I feel, and the family will be doomed—his breath smells of drink or unbrushed teeth, lots of men stink.

The artist Eva Spierenburg grew up in a house like this with a leaking gas heater; perhaps it was still sometimes warm and soft and full of oxygen until her parents' divorce, but it definitely wasn't afterwards. Eva and her sister remained with their father because their mother did not want custody due to her illness, MS. 'My mother thought she had nothing to give us,' explains Eva, 'but from what I knew of her, she surrendered herself completely to her disease, becoming a victim through and through. I resent the fact that she left us in that situation, for not doing everything she could for us, her children.'

When her mother died, Eva was sitting beside her bed and followed the process intensively. 'I found the moment when her last breath left her body so profound, you literally see life slipping away out of the body, that suddenly becomes soulless and cold. Amazing.' Eva does not believe in a life after death, but she did make contact with her dying mother by talking to her. And she kept on speaking, even after her death. Afterwards, the air seemed fresher, purer. As an artist, she performed a ritual in *Recreating My Mother, Attempt 4* (2015) that begins with modelling a rib out of clay, on a thin birchwood board. Very tenderly, the fingers sculpt a small head and then a snake-like body, like a sperm cell. She draws around it and moulds a mother with two legs who she then picks up carefully and rocks to and fro: dangling legs, a limp body. Soothing hands of an adult child that are assuming the care of the mother. Then she pulls off the head, that shortly afterwards is remarkably peacefully attached again, resting on a flowered handkerchief while the mother doll's little clay hand lies on the heart briefly, in an apologetic gesture. Later, the hands of the artist make a round hole in the belly, in the place where the second chakra is located, the energy flow of emotions, and cover up the clay doll with the handkerchief. She purifies the body with powder, makes peace and, as she draws, takes up her own role, that of the artist. Gently and lovingly, she concludes by chopping the body into fine rubble, using a tiny hammer.

Recreating My Mother is a healing process: my mother, my origin, yes, there is something lacking, is there still love? rehabilitation? and can I detach myself from it?

After her father's death, Eva tries to carry out this ritual once again, but it doesn't work. 'I didn't even want to touch the clay doll, my body resisted.' Eva hadn't had any contact with her father for eight years, because always holding out hope mainly meant that she kept on flying against the glass with a crash again and again, like a bird that knows no better, and then had to lie on the ground to recover, dented and dazed. That hope was always there: perhaps there would be a moment of real contact, a question that showed interest in his daughter, a glimmer of love in his eyes. Perhaps a conversation, a different point of view. But as a chronic alcoholic, her father lived in his own bubble of oblivion and suspicion.

Eva got hold of her father's diary and those pages unleashed an unpleasant picture of a narcissistic man who made everyone dance to his tune. Misogynistic, racist. 'I find it hard to call him my father,' says Eva. 'I have little understanding and respect for him as a person. My father always ruined everything. And however messed-up he was, he always managed to speak like a pastor and that was even more confusing.' In the aftermath of his death, the past keeps coming up in her dreams and thoughts, and the tension creeps into her body like an invisible paralysing venom. Because she wants to destroy this terror from the past, she starts to meditate on the memories by precisely observing what can be felt in her body. After the meditation, she notes in small schematic drawings all the sensations she has encountered in her body. In this way, an index is created of non-visible bodily feelings, of a physical undercurrent.

On the first days, she draws on small sheets of pink paper, but she soon realises that these notes could lead to a work of art and she sticks the drawings into a leporello book that has been awaiting a purpose for ages. Each meditation begins by noticing the breath. In-out, in-out. Simple. It becomes clear that the movement of the breath can take many forms. Sometimes her chest is squeezed and the breath slips through it quickly and expands at the bottom. A chest cavity can feel clenched as if there is no room for air. Or the breath fills the space in the ribcage and only goes a bit lower, like a small trunk, so that the drawing looks like an ancient fertility figurine. She draws the upper and lower jaw using diagonal lines because they are so tense that she can feel pressure on her teeth. But the jaw can also look like a sort of bow. The leporello becomes filled with body parts that move in response to the stress and emotions, with words beside them that clarify the sensation, such as 'pain points floating around' or 'cold tingling'. 'Sticking tongue out from oval into depth, flapping.' The jawbones, upper legs and chest remain the champions of sensitivity to stress and react by shrinking, expanding, becoming rigid, drooping, or beating.

A biology textbook has crystal-clear images of our insides, such as the respiratory system: the route that the air takes from the mouth via the windpipe to the bronchial tubes, where the alveoli absorb oxygen from the air and release carbon dioxide. That's fascinating, you think, so that's what a human looks like from inside, that's what a liver looks like, and that's how the circulatory and respiratory systems work. Eva's little sketches give a very different picture of our insides, showing how the body, as a pumping and living network, takes and drives forward its own decisions. How it can thwart its own functioning. The body refuses to join in that pretence of nothing-is-the-matter even if you would love to use your reason to make all the misery go away by no longer thinking about it.

    But the body has stored up the information, like in a safe, and it has an impact. In the process of meditation, the artist feels her organs, everything within her, and that produces a reality that you never come across in a biology book: the fact that anger can make your body tense up, that stress can hamper your breathing. A sour taste in your mouth, a burning sensation in your liver, hot and unsettled intestines, a dripping mass coming from the skull. A chest that is inclined to double over if emotions are running high. For Eva Spierenburg this is the all-determining reality.

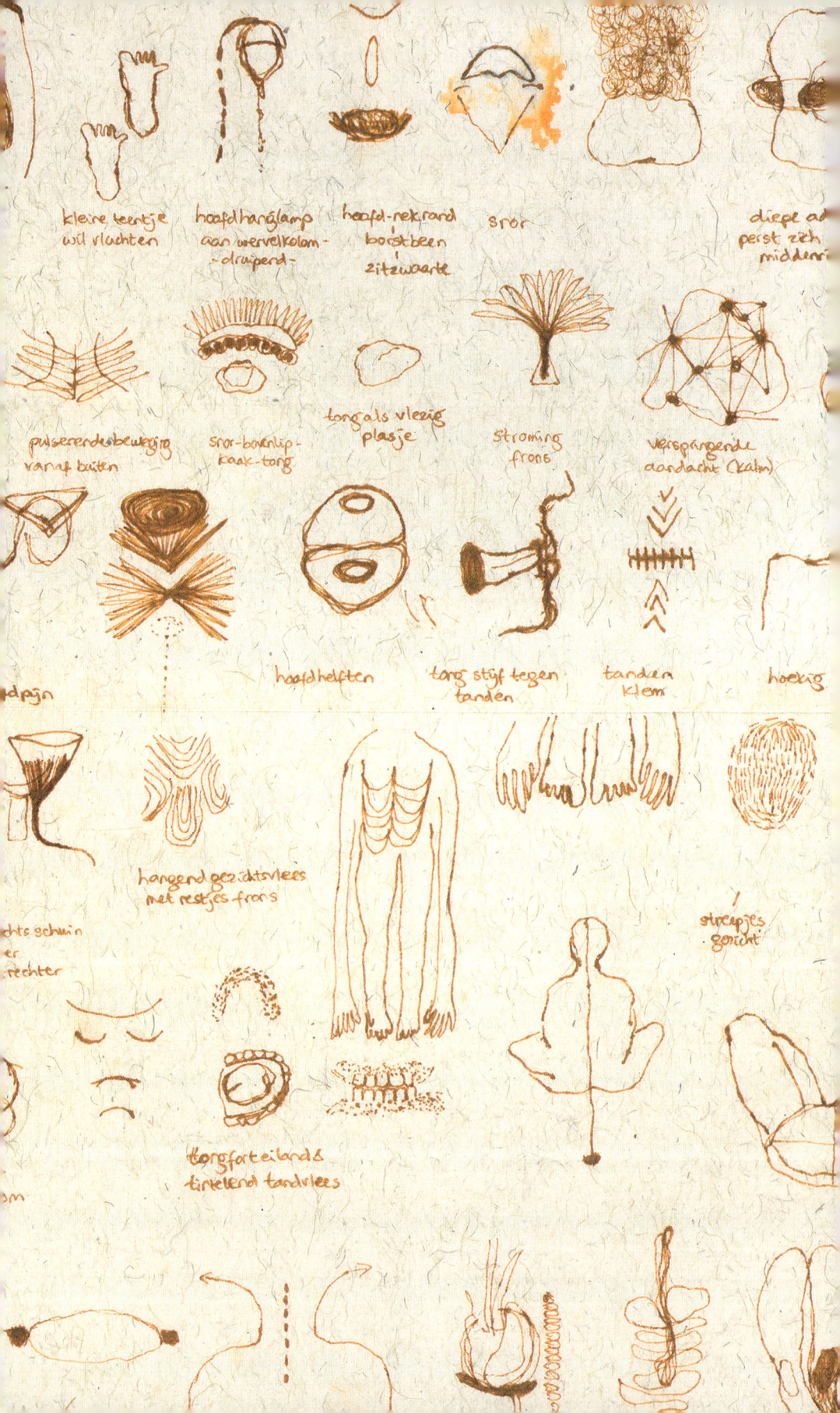

During a meditation session, all the attention is focused on the here and now, on 'being in the moment'. You learn to see thoughts as clouds that come and go, floating by, and you can therefore gradually let go of them. In the drawings, she is reaching out towards the small child of the past but does this from the perspective of her adult self, which has more power than the child.

Writers, too, who tell stories about a painful past often leave space between the child—the I of the past—and the independent I of the present.

Philip Huff wrote the book *What you know about blood* about his violent childhood in the you-form. 'I don't like literary novels that are written entirely from a child's perspective. I chose to take the long line, not only considering how it feels for a child but also how it still has an influence on my life. I wanted to say something about life as I know it, to tell my truth.' *36

Manon Uphoff sought words to look back towards the abuse she experienced in the past and wrote about it from the perspective of the present. 'You didn't want to surrender your younger self too?' people ask her. 'No. You know more than your past self. And it might seem as if you are reproaching your younger self for something. Which is in any case the difficult thing if you deal with this topic. That you always tend to look at it from a perspective with more knowledge. And you describe and consider things. Finding words for everything.' *37

Eva's little sketches have a certain impassivity, the body as a container that holds the feelings but does not depict them. And that is what is special about the leporello, a sobering quest in which the father remains out of the picture, where only the impact of his influence is visible, in those doodle-like notes.

The leporello seems to be putting a case for the book *The Body Keeps the Score* in which the psychiatrist Bessel van der Kolk explains how a traumatic event seizes a child's body by the short hairs. *38 In a family where the tension is quivering in the air, the child's body is always braced for possible danger. These children live in a state of constant watchfulness. 'This has attached itself in non-verbal parts of the brain and expresses itself via the body. That is why attention must be primarily directed to what is happening in the body. Do you know what you are feeling?' 'You don't leave the past behind you, it resides in you', says Philip Huff in an interview. And that's what you have to deal with in a society that doesn't have much idea of how to handle emotions and where the norm is that you should be strong and good company. Trauma sounds dramatic but for a child an unsafe situation without protective love is shattering. Sometimes friends and therapists think it can't be too bad if there's no sign of blood, but this lack of recognition of the depth of the trauma only makes you doubt yourself more. Aren't you just exaggerating?'

'Powerlessness is anti-life. Life wants to go in a direction, life wants to be able to do something. If you are held back in this, you blame yourself. And now I had run up against the most difficult part, against that door. I had to dare to go back to the moment of complete loss of your own autonomy. Loss of who you are,' says Manon Uphoff in an interview. 'In the meantime, I have learned that the way my body freezes up is linked to the insecurity, and to the love that was missing,' says Eva.

The drawings turn into sculptures: bodily sensations dangle from threads in the room. The jaw and mouth are given a teardrop shape that is leaning on a stack of stones, as if they need extra support. A hanging breath is shaped like a kidney or an inverted heart. The tongue continually changes shape. During the meditation, Eva notices how her tongue curls up stiffly against her teeth or lies on the floor of the mouth like a fleshy pool. The tongue slowly gets its mobility back, then you can stick it out—get lost—and ally yourself with the gargoyles who show their power like this and protect the cathedral. The tongue opens the way to the outside once the lump in the throat has gone and the tongue has regained its strength. That sweet pink tongue that would like to scream from the mouth, together with the vocal cords, so loud and shrill that the windows would rattle. 'Yes, anger, of course there is anger, for that small innocent child. But I can't do anything with it anymore, it would be screaming at a dead man, and besides, there was nothing to be gained by that. So you end up with yourself.' Saying farewell to her father is a movement towards herself. And all the power gathers there like a deafening scream that finally blows the father away.

The title is borrowed from *The Future Is Invented with Fragments from the Past,* a title of an exhibition by Maria Lassnig that she in turn got from a poem by Mayröcker.

The future is built with fragments from the past

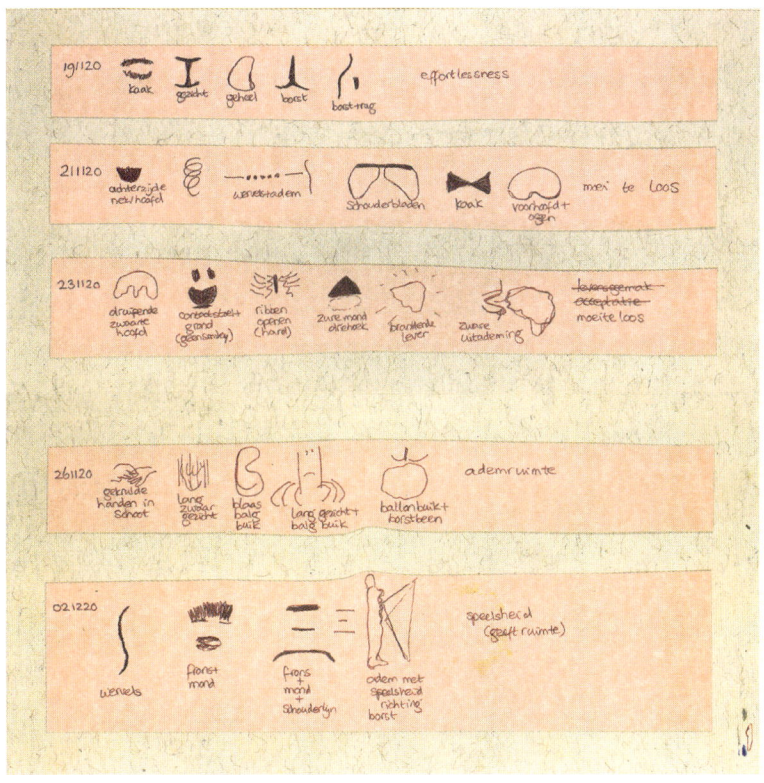

Eva Spierenburg, *Documenting the Body*, 2020–2021,
(photo: Erik Fliek)

p. 216: Eva Spierenburg, *Drifting Stones and a Broken Bird*, 2021,
(photo: Aalt van de Glind)

p. 220: Eva Spierenburg, *Documenting the Body*, 2020–2021,
(photo: Erik Fliek)

The future is built with fragments from the past

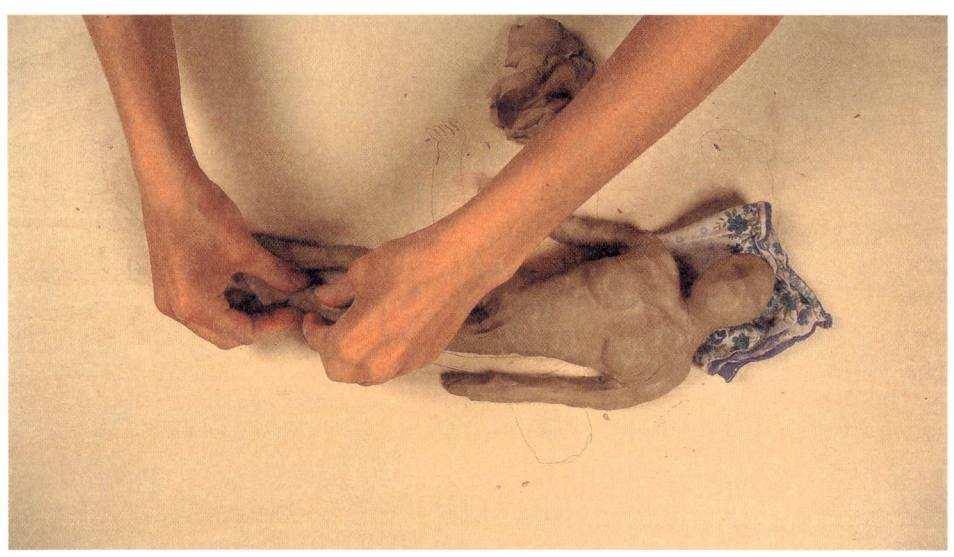

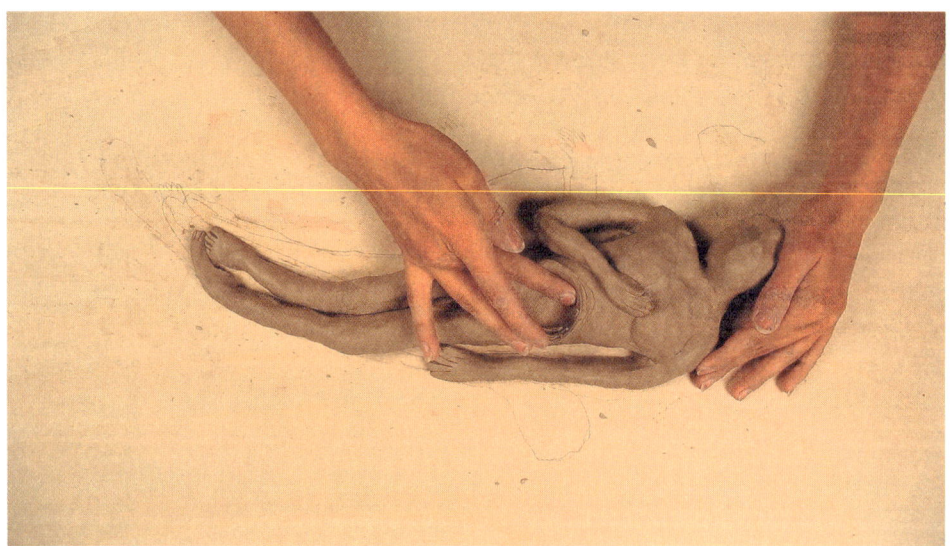

The future is built with fragments from the past

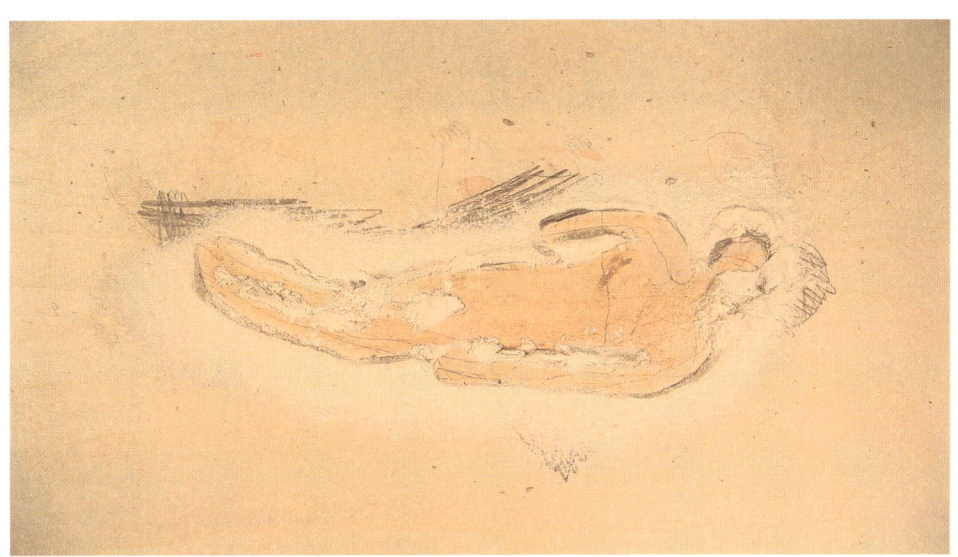

Eva Spierenburg, *Recreating my Mother, attempt 4,* 2015, video projection, 47.35 min.

Missing feels like a hollowing-out

Missing feels like a hollowing-out

Narges Mohammadi, *The Making of Passing Traces,* 2020, 19:07 min video and installation with halva as seen during *Best of Graduates exhibition,* Ron Mandos Gallery, Amsterdam, courtesy of Ron Mandos Young Blood Foundation 2020, all rights reserved

'I make works that embody long-lost memories', says Narges Mohammadi. Long-lost memories, where have they found a place to stay? We carry along within us everything we experience; it all leaves an impression somewhere in our body, perhaps in our heart, or the experiences hide themselves away in the kidneys or liver (making us thirsty). We have lost memories along the way, so it seems, but yet they are still sticking to or within us. Remembering is sometimes desperately grasping a wave that is gradually retreating. Mohammadi makes artworks to discover where the red button is that can bring back something of the lost memories; a play on smell, touch, colour, embedded in a cultural field.

Narges Mohammadi won the Young Blood Award for the best work in the exhibition *The Best of Graduates* at Galerie Ron Mandos in 2020. I saw her graduation project *Passing Traces* earlier at the Royal Academy of Art in The Hague: she made a narrow passageway by constructing two walls in a room and then she stuck halva all over them, the handprints still visible and spreading a sweet scent. For everyone who comes from Iran or Afghanistan, halva brings back memories: it is the taste of loss, of saying farewell. After the death of a family member, a friend or a loved one, flour is bought, butter, sugar, and cardamom. This is stirred together endlessly to produce a smooth-textured round cake, that is cut into slices and served to all the guests at the funeral. The passageway that suddenly appeared there in the room and led from nothing to nowhere but that you had to go through anyway, that passageway triggered an explosion of memories, thoughts, and reflections for me.
 Recesses were visible in the cladding of the passageway— the negative shape of a lamp, a table, a bed, a pillow—an echo of a bedroom, a room in which a head was laid on a pillow, the light was switched off to go to sleep. Until the light stayed off. The room is still present, albeit in an absence, as part of the passageway of halva, the tunnel that brings living and dying together. But how death and life are to be reconciled is still a great mystery to me. 'How very much quieter death is than sleep', has been there to read on my sister's gravestone for more than twenty years. Perhaps life is the bump in a universe that otherwise stretches out endlessly. Here in the Netherlands, the majority of people have lost belief in God and then the

great nothing awaits after death; that's certainly scary. I have trouble believing in this nothing. For believers, death is not an end point but more of an in-between state, an in-between life, which also implies a spiritual life, a continued existence or resurrection. There is only a slight boundary between living and no longer living, life as a ribbon that is unrolling itself, it just meanders on after death.

Missing feels like a hollowing-out, an absence, a negative space that is left behind. And although you can't do anything but accept death, because it is inextricably bound up with life, the feeling of missing remains. But the sweet passageway of halva also presents me with other thoughts. Halva is embedded in a culture of rituals that give warmth to the collective farewell. Even the language has incorporated the ritual in sayings such as 'I have already handed out my halva', which means something like 'I'm ready for the next phase'.

The ingredients for halva are simple, but it has to be made with precision and that takes dedication. The flour is toasted in a pan for a short time but it must not stick to the bottom, and the butter and sugar are added at the right moment. The mixture becomes stiffer and heavier to stir. The collective effort is comforting; at such a time, it is just good to have something to do that is also meaningful. The individual pain of the loss is embedded in a sharing, a collective lifting up of the loss. Stirring a bowl of dough together gets the conversation going and provides a moment to exchange memories. It allows this person to live on in words. Rituals are comforting like poetry.

> 'Like poetry, the experience of grief is universal; it crosses eras and cultures. Like poems, the experience of grief is unique in every form it takes.'

The rituals around saying farewell, this is what we, the majority of Dutch people, can learn from other cultures, for we have lost more than just our loved ones. We have outsourced all the rituals, to a funeral director, a funeral home, to viewing rooms. At my father's funeral, how very Dutch, slices of cheap cake were served, directly from their plastic packaging, without smell, without structure, without flavour. The memory of that cake only evokes shame in me, a soulless slice of yellow stuff with a brown edge. I had no say in it. The halva passageway is a monument that evokes and binds together memories and that houses the precious rituals of a community. A monument through which loss gently blows its breath and where togetherness becomes visible. But even more than these essential questions about death and life, where each person and each belief has to go their own way, it is infused with a desire to call back memories, to connect then and now, to reconcile life and death with each other. Love for a person, a country, a cherishing.

> ```
> Do not question love as it is the inspiration
> of your pen
> My loving words had in mind death.
> – Nadia Anjuman, 'Strands of Steel' *39
> ```

In order to be able to show her graduation project in Galerie Ron Mandos, Mohammadi made a translation of the original piece (in collaboration with artist Julia Sterre Schmitz). In this new work, a touching film shows not only the process of making halva, but above all also the culture in which it is rooted. Around the screen, the halva is plastered against the wall. While the oil is spattering in the video, you hear the ringtone of a telephone. Her grandfather is on the line. Delightful pleasantries are exchanged, and Mohammadi tries to break through his kind words about five times to tell him that she is busy making 700 kilos of halva. 'God bless you', grandfather then says, 'are you giving alms?' They say goodbye: 'I wish you all the best in this life, and in the afterlife.'

We see how Mohammadi and her friends mix and stir with full dedication. Meanwhile, they get talking. One of her friends remembers the last time that she tasted halva, on the day an uncle died. How does it feel for her to be making halva now? 'Yes, it's hard when someone dies', she says, but she also remembers the warmth, the togetherness:

> ```
> 'There is also this nurturing, caring and feeling
> of being home. So for me it is not hard to see but
> it makes me emotional to see it, also good emotions
> of being at home, close to home. […]
> In the same way it represents life, it is part of
> a process, in every culture.'
> ```

Her mother phones and Mohammadi carefully explains that she is making the halva slightly differently, using ordinary flour instead of rice flour. It's no problem, of course, but the words are surrounded by so much love that I blink my eyes a little extra for a moment. The switching between languages, Dutch and Farsi (Dari), and later the search for the word for 'pillow' in Farsi (balesjt), and lamp (cherogh), reveals something about the position of families who are forced to move to another country, that in-between position that makes something crumble off on all sides. But once again the warmth glows through the words.

Then her mother and grandfather come by to view the artwork at the academy and Mohammadi is nervous, she admits, their opinion is very important to her. Yes, in a personal work the reaction of those involved counts more than that of any reviewer: a deeply felt work is not something you make for the art world but for yourself or for that other person, or to make a connection between then and now before it crumbles away and an unbridgeable distance has opened up. The grandfather explains what happens at a funeral in Afghanistan, and how the spirit of the person who has died returns home in the days after the funeral, until the moment when the sun sets on the third day. He speaks of the importance of giving (alms), but he says that in the end it's all about being happy in this world, making the people around you happy, and donating money, as much as you can and pressing it respectfully into the other person's hand. Beautiful lessons for us all. What a kind, wise grandfather. 'You are making an interesting work', he says. 'You left a footprint.' 'Art for me is a means—for connection and sharing long lost memories. I see it as a tool enabling emotional understanding, a tool that doesn't require you to speak but kindly asks you to feel. Asks to allow yourself to be immersed in an experience, to get lost in memories', writes Mohammadi. *40

```
Do not ask of my blooms great looks
On hands, feet, and tongue strands of steel
on the tablet of time, this will be my mark.
– Nadia Anjuman, 'Strands of Steel' *41
```

Missing feels like a hollowing-out

p. 233-235: Narges Mohammadi, *Passing Traces,* 2020, 2,15 m × 4,78 m × 0,80 m, 700 kg Persian halva (flour, sugar, butter and cardemom) and two wooden constructions, (photo: Io Sivertsen)

Memory of a certain time – a marker on the timeline

Memory of a certain time – a marker on the timeline

Iqra Tanveer, *Fall*, 2017, inkjet print transfer on wall, LED lighting

Around me, the debate about Islam keeps on erupting. Friends who grew up in Iran and fled to the Netherlands can't bear to see another head covering and only have negative things to say. I seldom manage to make the conversation more nuanced. 'Understanding, understanding', a Dutch friend recently said to me bitterly, 'I've really had it with that understanding.' But no other way, no other way!

I would love to believe in a God, but I've not yet managed to do so. For example, I find it difficult to accept that sometimes a faith only reserves a space in heaven for its own followers. They alone, after all, have earned eternal life. Sometimes heaven is open to anyone who believes in a God, but then again not to unbelievers. But perhaps I can put this aside and start looking for genuine criteria for believing. Give me something to work with, God!

Perhaps I can follow Stephan Sanders' example. I read in an article that he had begun his conversion to the Catholic faith by 'a trial form of believing'. When he realised that this half-hearted decision was leading nowhere, he decided to change tack and to join in fully as a believer, for example by going to the church service, taking part in the rituals, and waiting to see where it would lead. A rational decision. Looking back, he wrote, his main conclusion was that he had become a better person through faith, more empathetic, warmer and with more sensitivity towards others. And that struck me: this is a delightful argument. I can embrace everything that makes someone a better person.

 In his view, faith is a feeling you can't explain, a transcendental experience: a personal covenant with God that is supported and sustained by church attendance. He hears the gospel there, which preaches love, and he meets people there who remained outside his field of vision before. 'Before', that is the time when he still voted VVD and thought that people should look after themselves. Now he realises that some people are simply unable to do that. 'The deficit', writes Sanders, 'peculiar to humans, to not only know good, but also evil'. Yes, good and evil, that's what it's all about. *[42]

After the death of my father, I sent an email to the deacon of the Basilica of Saint Nicholas (Sanders' church) asking if he would talk with me about good and evil. The idea of a heaven and a hell seemed unacceptable to me, but it is part of religious belief and I wondered how people with black marks on their soul could still end up well. No one should have to burn in hell for ever. I don't believe we figured it out together, or that he had an answer to my question, but the deliberations were comforting. The universe is vast and absorbs a lot. Perhaps we can take heaven and hell less literally, and it's more about the essence, the acceptance of good and evil and how we can relate to it. Of all churches, the Roman Catholic church is the dearest to me because I partly grew up with it and, despite the fact that I have few good memories of it (for example a pastor who would ask me on Monday what had been preached on Sunday, because he knew that our family didn't go to services), it is familiar to me. Everything that can't be put into words happens there in gestures, in rites, in bowing, kneeling, and standing up again. 'Kneeling is the hardest thing there is, but also the most beautiful, you take leave of your pride by doing so. I love the gestures that precede words,' writes Sanders. Kneeling, yes, that evokes reluctance; but humility, that's something we as humans can certainly use. That also makes us better people.

Iqra Tanveer comes from Pakistan. In a way, the death of her parents became an opening to delve more deeply into religion. In her work, we encounter a vision about being human that is rooted in Islam. She portrays humankind as a humble speck compared to God. During the Kochi Muziris Biennale in 2014, Iqra made a veil of dust dance in a beam of light in a darkened room. Indeed: when I think about life, I think about time, about dust, about moments, about the path the sun follows around the earth. The essence of our existence is so intangible that I have to fall back on immaterial elements and vague words, to ultimately acknowledge that I have no idea, only that we greatly overestimate ourselves, as the centre point of the cosmos. Like the thought that there was a time when you did not yet exist and then the thought that we fear so greatly, that you will no longer be there. It's all about that tiny marker on the timeline: life. Dust is life. It is matter which has fallen apart, and that's what I like about it. Because with a little imagination you meet other beings in the dust: tiny shreds of plants, skin flakes from other people, ash remains or decayed bones of loved ones who have died, animals that you may or may not be afraid of.

Pollen, desert, spores, fungi. It's all swirling through the air. Also, asbestos residue, exhaust fumes, and for example nicotine. At the same time, the artwork was a portrayal of infinity, the cosmos, as if the beam of light were revealing a galaxy. In this way, through the swirling of the dust, the visitor was able to discover that life is just as temporary as a shadow and as intangible as oxygen. The work is called *Paradise of Paradox*. It is a title that catches your attention because the pronunciation seems strange, not easy to understand.

We are our body (our life, is what I think of), and possibly, perhaps, a further life of the soul as an incorporeal element. I know this life; life after death is a great mystery. Like God, whom I just cannot comprehend. But when I talk further with Iqra, I understand the paradisical aspect of this contradiction better because she sees it as an apparent contradiction. 'The world around us is a mental projection of the human mind. Our reality is what fits into our limited intellect and its imagination. And as humans we are continually judging what happens to us in life but our senses limit what we can perceive. As far as death is concerned, it is considered to be a very important experience in the heart because death is a constant reminder that this world is temporal and an illusion, it is not the reality.' *Paradise of Paradox* was the first work that Iqra made after the passing of her mother, as a reflection on her death. 'Our faith teaches that the soul transcends and leaves the body behind on earth with its bones, skin and tendons. True life only begins after death, that is the true reality. These religious insights about human destiny helped me to deal with the death of my mother. It gave me peace.'

'During my mother's illness, I tried to help her by praying and requested people who went on pilgrimage to ask God for her healing. Most of all, I felt the fear of losing her, but at a certain moment I had to let her go anyway. 'I remember that it looked as if she would die. My sister, my aunt and I discussed who would sleep with her for the last time and I was able to lie down beside her. I prayed that she might die peacefully and because I accepted her passing at that moment, all fear had vanished. I fell asleep and awoke 15 minutes later; she had died.' Not that Iqra had peace with her death immediately: she was young and felt a deep sense of grief. 'Soon after her death I began to distract myself and went to work and social gatherings.

Memory of a certain time – a marker on the timeline

Iqra Tanveer, *The Forgetting Curve,* 2017, transfer on a lithography stone

But our life is in the hands of God and that's why it's also so important to follow the path towards death peacefully.'

The Forgetting Curve is the first work by Iqra Tanveer that I see in reality. At a temporary attic exhibition of two artist friends, there are three lithography stones. It is as if the stones want to bring in memories of other locations. One stone bears an image of the parental house in Pakistan and she made this stone in memory of her father. This work about loss and grief bears, as part of the series, the name of a mathematical calculation. *The Forgetting Curve*. The forgetting curve originates from a study by the 19th century German psychologist Ebbinghaus about the speed of forgetting. The abundance of information that we receive at every moment of the day is so overwhelming that we cannot possibly retain everything. You forget most of it immediately but if you repeat information, the brain gets better and better at remembering it and it remains active knowledge. Just as you learn a new language more quickly by practising every day.

This stone bears a confusing image of her father's bedroom that is placed over a landscape, with a large, white, rectangular area pushing away all the other information. It takes a while before you understand the picture. The light that comes through the leaded-glass window puts the image under pressure while at the same time death is already announcing itself in the room. You see the intimacy of the bed, the pillows, and the side table with medicines on it. 'I like how the light comes in through the window because for me that is what is 'transient', it marks a moment when you are simultaneously in the house and can see the outside. A lot of my works have a strong relationship with the laws of physics. The stone is also a memory of our house, the place where I was still together with my parents. Because we rented the house, of course we lost it. 'Our house' no longer exists, the room in which he lay, the house in which we lived.'

'You told me earlier that faith helped you to process the grief around the loss of your mother. How was that with your father?' I ask her. 'In Pakistan everyone is Muslim but not everyone is strictly religious. At home I learned the basis of the religion, the Koran, how to pray, to fast, but quite casually. When I grew up, I also resisted, like I didn't care.

But with the loss of my parents my faith became deeper, more intense. I'd always called myself Muslim, but now I am a practising Muslim.

Death is a transition, and that's why it is not only sad but also a celebration that the soul is entering another realm, that is drawing closer to the final destination. The soul is in a state of waiting, an in-between state (the barzakh) until the world comes to an end and all the souls gather, then the real judgement will take place.' 'As a Muslim you believe in that transition. I think that one of the most important aspects of religion is that it makes your heart humble. You really start to reflect, you are a human being, but faith reminds you that you are not the centre of the world, that is God, the supreme being. The human being is one of the superior creations, but the fact that it is a creation in itself induces a humble acceptance.

Like Stephan Sanders, Iqra Tanveer mentions the realisation of one's own smallness and insignificance as a human as a positive force of faith. Faith helps her to accept life as it comes, even death. 'The memory of my parents is all I have left and that gives value to many things in my life, such as the realisation that I form part of a larger group, that I stand in the line of my family. I want my children to know about my father and mother so that my parents can be a part of their lives too. I commemorate my parents as a part of everyday existence, I cook my father's favourite recipe, I listen to music that my father enjoyed hearing, sometimes I put on one of his jumpers, I wear my mother's perfume on special occasions. I also still use my father's wallet and the fact that it looks rather worn-out is of no importance. I commemorate my mother and my father by organising a gathering with friends and family on the anniversary of their death. I recite a prayer and cook for them and share the meal with my friends. Based on our religion, you share the food with the poor on such a day. I feel that loss also brings something beautiful, it teaches you something that you have to learn here in this world, in order to fulfil the purpose you have been created for. And once it's done, you move on.

My mother had to go, and I had to accept it. Once I was really able to accept it, I was thankful for it, because the acceptance helped me and it helped her.'

The images and memories fade but the rituals and actions that Iqra Tanveer carries out ensure that she keeps her father and mother close to her. You could interpret this as a Forgetting Curve in practice. Rituals in order to live on with those who have died. Indispensable.

> 'And if it were true, that God is love,
> then this would mean that we only existed
> in as far as we loved.'
> – Gerard Reve [*43]

Seven times around the earth

My sister Aldi was a professor of econometrics, she did research into poverty, and she knew how to hold her own among all her male colleagues. Aldi got cancer and died when she was 39 years old. It was hard for her to say goodbye to life, of course, and at the last moment we changed the text on her card: there was no question of a peaceful death, it was a battle.

My sister believed in science and in the end of life, and not in all kinds of vague spiritual possibilities that I like to keep open. But she was afraid of being forgotten, afraid that her name would no longer be spoken aloud. Ten years after her death, I wrote a letter to her colleagues and friends: please take a photo of a photo of Aldi that you still have at home, just wherever it is lying or hanging. Not everyone understood my request, but that made it all the more exciting: faxes arrived, zoomed-in photos, an audiotape, photos of a bike ride, most of them identified as clearly as possible. Each photo brought stories and memories with it. I compiled a book using everything I received and sent it on to the family and all her colleagues who were also her friends. Your name, Aldi, so loud and clear.

Carnival

Disappearing

Carnival

Berend Strik, *Prins Willem I,* 2005, embroidered photo

Prince Willem I poses gloomily in front of a velvety background, a brown cloth that makes the dazzling white cloak stand out extra well with its elegant fur trim and the pointed cap, on which three regal pheasant feathers are fluttering. He is holding the key to the city with both hands; for the duration of the carnival celebrations, he is the mayor of Iseldonk, which is called Ulft on ordinary days. 'As long as you have fun' is Iseldonk's carnival slogan in 2020.

The weight of this honorary function only really dawned on me when I watched the documentary *Nao't Zuuje (To the South)*. The television presenter Lex Uiting was chosen as the new Carnival Prince in his birthplace, Venlo. 'If your father falls into your arms crying when he has never done that in the past 30 years, then that shows just how much it means in Venlo to become the prince.' A function that every boy in the South of the Netherlands dreams of. The role fits Uiting like a glove, he is immediately in the midst of the throng and shakes everyone's hands with an irresistible smile. As the Carnival Prince, you need to be able to do a spontaneous little dance with a pretty girl, wipe a reveller's nose if necessary, and above all be the life and soul of the party, the broom that sweeps the atmosphere into the festivities.

Berend Strik found the small square photo in the biscuit tin full of family snapshots not long after the death of his father, for he is the one who is portrayed here. At first, Strik was fascinated by the dingy background but when he enlarged the photo he saw unmistakeable fear appearing on his father's face.

Another image looms up, a scene that Strik told me about: the moment when he looked from the hall towards the podium during his father's cremation ceremony. There he saw his deceased dad in the coffin in his Carnival Prince suit, suggesting that this role had been the high point of his life. 'Friends stood around the coffin in a semicircle, dressed as the traditional carnival figures of the 'Council of Eleven', wearing black costumes with wide blue revere collars, white caps from which a plume dangled and edged with a festive silver-blue trim, complemented by gloves, badges and medals and a blue bow tie. His dead father as Carnival Prince. Disconcerting. Crazy.

Strik sat in the room, 23 years old, and his body filled with an unspeakable, immense grief that didn't pound in his body but swelled up slowly and kept on spreading, although there was nowhere for it to go. At the same time, an overwhelming emptiness entered that weighed down on his spirits like a wet, far too heavy army blanket. How can you endure it in your own body? You're 23 and your father is lying there, dead, a death he had chosen himself, and it was as if the message was reverberating from every nook and cranny in the crematorium, that life is not worth living. That thought pressed on his ears, his spleen, his liver. It knocked on his head, throbbed inside his head.

It was his beloved but also strict father, who, when he brought a girl home for the first time, put on a James Last record and asked her to dance.

It is a rather sombre portrait, a black figure that is barely distinguishable from the dark background. The red embroidery stitches score and scratch the face. This rather melancholy man is chosen as Carnival Prince. A dream role. But on the photo his eyes are squinting a bit, he can't quite visualise it. Has he not lost his ability to whirl around somewhere, along the way? And then soon there'll be the carnival cabaret in the community centre, no turning back. As long as you have fun.

'As a child you were indeed a bit afraid of him', Strik tells me. He worked as a labour analyst in a factory where they made pans and stoves. Each year they checked to see whether the process could be organised more efficiently, which meant further redundancies. Until he himself had also become surplus to requirements. His wife left the family and went to live with the man from next door. And one day there was an envelope on the mantelpiece in his father's firm handwriting: 'I can't take it anymore'.

'Why couldn't he take better care of himself?' Strik wonders. 'As a child I had fantasies that I earned mountains of money and would make him happy by sending round a woman in a sexy outfit. After my mother had gone away, he looked after us; I can still see him with his winter coat on while he lifts the lid of a pan.' He remarried. But after his death Strik also found the copies of all the letters he had written to his runaway wife and in which he almost begged her to come back. Desperation packaged in envelopes. 'For', as Strik says, 'if you read those letters you sense from the imploring sentences that the chance of it succeeding was zero.' Continuing to hope against his better judgement. Why is it that one person is successful and the other ruins everything? Why is it that not everyone manages to come out of depression? Does God play dice or does God not play dice?

'My father ended his life on a Monday morning. It came unexpectedly but the tragedy was always palpable between the cracks.' I came home and had to sleep in my dad's study. There must have been 15 sorts of rope in a small cupboard; he had obviously been contemplating the idea for a long time. I read it as a sort of euthanasia, as unbearable mental pain.' From then on, the neighbours crossed the street so they didn't have to walk on the pavement beside the house.

To what extent is a person able to shape their life, to fend off gloominess, to draw happiness in? Perhaps you have to have it in you: 'I was born lucky', says the Lebanese artist Huguette Caland, who made her life a party full of infidelity and naughty art, who left her husband and children in order to be an artist in Paris where she walked around in kaftans on which breasts and a vagina were painted. No one fazed her. A Sunday child from a wealthy family. But you can also be born without shining stars. That happened to a large part of the reconstruction generation who had to bear the consequences of the war. The new moon was shining, the darkest night.

The trauma of the war pursued these young people. Their fathers (or mothers) were in the resistance, betrayed or not, or had joined the Germans instead; they came from families in which parents, little brothers and sisters had died in a bombardment. Or through reprisals by the Germans. Families with unsoothable sorrow. Fathers who had returned from Indonesia: behind their eyes, the harsh images of unprecedented violence. Come here with your plate, lad, take some potatoes and the biggest piece of meat is for you, and will you then just cut the grass, it's getting too long. This generation didn't lie on a psychiatrist's sofa, they worked and started a family. What else?

These boys and girls started their life together with high hopes, but they often had too little time to rock-'n-roll together or to dance the twist. Because, if the girl fell pregnant during that sparkling courtship, then the moralistic (Catholic) finger was immediately wagged. They couldn't marry in church (because it was sinful), the village wasn't allowed to know, the baby grew up with grandmother, and if you were able to marry in church after all, years later, then you couldn't have a white wedding, and yes, if you finally got your own house and you were able to live together, well, by then the fun has really gone out of it. Humiliated to the bone, you have to fan the flames of love so that you can forget those affronts. That doesn't work, it fails miserably: a generation of unhappy parents in struggling marriages.

'I think that you have to learn to play with the trauma', writes Arnon Grunberg.*44

As a five-year-old, Strik changed his name from Bernie to Berend: both names mean 'strong as a bear' but the suffix 'ie' acts as a diminutive and that makes the name less solid and serious than Berend. How does a child of five come up with the idea of changing his name? Strik sees it as a first act of resistance against his possible destiny, he is dreaming bigger, hoping to become a brave adventurer, like the ones in children's stories and songs. The fact that a five-year-old does something like this indicates that the world is makeable too; perhaps Strik was born to escape. As a ten-year-old, he made a scrapbook about his father, as someone else makes a scrapbook about a film star, about their football hero or *Star Wars*. It has a white ring binder and the punched holes have torn away in many places because of all the leafing to and fro. 'My father taught me photography and drumming, and when the neighbours came to complain he stood up for me. He was my hero, and it seems as if, with this scrapbook, I wanted to cast a spell that he was my hero and would remain so.' 'Look, this page gives a good picture of who he was, he loved football, canoeing, animals (a dog), and he worked in an office.' The process of organising the photos, sticking them in and looking at them again and again is like calling up forces that can steer fate, prevent, threaten, and preferably eliminate it. When all the incantations had stalled, the scrapbook, the fantasies, coins in a wishing well, then an acceptance came to the surface, a mildness that results from simply looking at the life of this man. Sometimes Strik as an artist still tries to steer something in his father's life as he stitches and embroiders. *The Man who went into a Flower* is another portrait of his father, this time sitting behind a desk, perhaps at the pot and stove factory. In delicate thin lines, a flower appears above the scene, like a fata morgana, a mirage.

Our life is determined by an unknown mix of genes, our background, such as where we were born, the family in which we grow up. You need certain characteristics in order to find your own way in life and a unique talent can help with this, such as Strik's drawing talent and great imagination. Arnon Grunberg calls thinking and culture the means by which you can take fate into your own hands, or at any rate help to steer it. 'In addition, I think that everyone will appreciate the idea that they are not completely at the mercy of circumstances. Every parent will burden children with something. Trauma does not only have to be something negative; it could also be something that makes you stronger. Someone's apparently weakest points can also be their strongest points.' Later, Grunberg answers the interviewer's question:

> 'What do you think you could do for me (through writing)?' 'As I already said: I think that you (one) need(s) to learn to play with trauma. I can teach you to play.'

Grunberg defines 'learn to play' here as part of his role as a writer. Indeed, he himself romps across the pages of his books with his traumas.

The person who plays creates a realm of freedom, like an escape clause in life, a temporary world where rationality withdraws and imagination takes over. In his book *Homo Ludens,* cultural historian Johan Huizinga describes play as a necessary condition for culture.

'You can deny almost everything that is abstract: justice, beauty, truth, goodness, mind, God. You can deny seriousness. Not play. But with play, you acknowledge the mind, whether you want to or not. For whatever its being may be, play is not matter. It breaks through the boundaries of what exists physically, even in the animal world. Compared to a determined thought-world solely made up of the effects of forces, it is a superabundance in the fullest sense of the word, a superfluity. Only through the influx of the mind, which eliminates absolute determinism, does the presence of play become possible, thinkable, understandable. The existence of play constantly confirms, and in the highest sense, the supra-logical character of our situation in the cosmos. Animals can play, so they are already more than mechanisms. We play, and know that we are playing, so we are more than just rational beings, because play is irrational.'

Our existence is often like a marble racing through a marble alley, but our mind is the only option for shooting out of that marble alley although more than logic is needed to take us humans further. The irrational, the non-logical, is the basis for creativity, through which unusual solutions can arise and new paths can appear. Play stands for freedom from obligation, except in the acceptance of self-chosen temporary rules. Play is how we leave behind the predictions that astrologers make according to the position of the stars, planets and the moon, in order to outplay the laws of nature. In order to escape from the labyrinth of the family we need to play, allowing the mind to blow a fresh breeze through familiar and constraining situations. Play, thought Huizinga, requires a certain looseness, a realisation of lightness and cheerfulness.

It is not for nothing that the portrait of his father is captured in the carnival, it contributes to the meaning. Carnival is a peculiar type of play in which the city of the everyday shuts up shop, everyone cuts the family ties for a while and lets themself go in a haze of music, drink and a fling. The festival of looseness and of fun and abandon. If you can't give yourself over to play and if life has not drawn up an escape route for you, then you're lost, then you're crushed by the superior forces. Play is the extra space that we get. When he enlarged the photo of his father as the Carnival Prince, Strik saw the glimmer of fear in his eyes: the fear that he might not succeed in being a charismatic prince, in playing, in letting everything go for a time.

Speaking about what an artwork could do for you, Strik says: 'The music of a James Last lets you down because it is a sugary sweet and isn't really absorbed. A good artwork helps you to discover feelings and to make them your own.' The beauty of a work embraces you, to subsequently plunge into the depths together with you. And yes, then it works, you let go of your resistance and you go with it.

People in mourning often reach for the Goldberg Variations by Bach to endlessly practise the notoriously difficult chords with iron discipline so that they don't have to think about anything else for a while. But somewhere along the way those sounds float inside, bring peace, memories and associations, they reach out to you and hopefully, somewhere, far away there is acquiescence. For that is often the highest point attainable: that you can go on living. The more we recognise that the possibilities to escape are limited, the more we accept the idea of a fate, the more space there is for compassion.

And hence this portrait is an inner investigation into the breath of this father, enabling the artist to finally look at this man with gentle eyes. Not leaving anything out or adding anything to who he is, just his father. A plea for compassion.

Berend Strik, *Diversion*, 2006, embroidered photo,
(photo: Gert Jan van Rooij)

Dear Berend,

Your mother, my mother, they come from the same period, the post-war generation. They also look quite alike, attractive with dark hair, a rather a narrow nose, and broad, dark eyebrows. In your studio, there's a photo on which your mother is 23 years old. A warm, round face with a bright look in her eyes; 'she looks at me, from the past to the here, and now there is contact.'

You made fifteen works about your mother and in all those works she is posing, and yes, she does it so well. She's a natural. And your father was a skilful photographer. A perfect couple, you'd think. Perhaps that's what they were in their days of young love. As a photographer it helps if you're a bit bewitched by your model and that's certainly what your father was, bewitched. She is holding an envelope bag elegantly in one hand; the other is touching the wall lightly. Or both hands in the air with a lit cigarette and a glass of wine; the full skirt fans out even more elegantly because of the lace that you've stitched over it. On your favourite photo, she is crouching in a bathing suit next to an open car door and she is playfully giving the photographer a kiss with puckered lips. At that time, there was romance, love. After that come five children in a life full of adversity. But that kiss, is it really there? Isn't she just holding a bottle top between her teeth?

   It is disastrous if you grow up in the putrid air of a bad marriage in which your parents barely tolerate each other. If you find photos later on from the period when the sparks of chemistry were still flying, that is comforting, it seems to me. The assurance that you were born out of love. That love felt like fertile ground for a life together, but the soil turned sour, not because they were bad people, not because they were unwilling, but because too much polluted rain fell. Along the way, they both got beaten down. Your mother left the house when you were ten; the bang of the slamming door is still reverberating. You asked your mother to write her life story in a notebook and gave it to me, you let me read it.

As an artist, you can make the world as you would like it for a while, and perhaps that's why you select photos in which your mother is so sexily and happily radiant. You also call it

Freudian, the name of Oedipus is mentioned, but I suggest that we leave Freud out of it; his theories are fascinating but more like a parchment document: he developed his ideas in a deeply patriarchal society, in which women barely had the right to exist.

His theory about the Oedipus complex whereby young boys apparently unconsciously want to go to bed with their mother and have to detach themselves because otherwise, once grown up, they remain too attached to their mother, is a malicious fabrication. A young boy should identify with the father (the aggressor!) and his mother's dedication only obstructs that process. Ascribing this and other strange sexual fantasies to a child hinders a flow of love because cuddles and other expressions of that love supposedly only stimulate the fantasies. I believe in love as the greatest good at each stage of development and I don't hear Freud speaking about this. The fantastic expression 'penis envy' can only occur in the brain of a man; women were, at most, justifiably jealous of men's opportunities and privileges. Freud's ideas about the inferior morality of women primarily reflect his own prejudices, which again contain the norms of his time.

But enough about Freud. It seems to me that it is a total bankruptcy for a family if a mother leaves the house and certainly for you because you are still so young then. Although her rather childish life story in the notebook with Goofy on the cover gives reasons enough to sympathise with her, as a child you are still left behind with that burning question of why your mother abandoned you. I have no answer to this; it is in a certain way unforgiveable. But, after reading her life story, then again maybe it isn't.

There's the work *Stiff City* in which she is posing in front of a stone wall and looking up, the road forms a graceful curve around her. There is a wonderful optimism in the picture because her gaze is focused on the photographer while the emptiness suggests that she can still go in any direction. The green stitching adds warmth to the bare, dry asphalt with the pool of water and she is enveloped in that warmth. She is the radiant centre of her own universe in that yellow-green embroidered dress. Yes, that's how it should have been. There are also photos full of mysteries. Photos with such strange details that you seem to have landed in a dream or a play instead of in a bourgeois living room in the south of the Netherlands. *Lemons and Mothers:* two women and a man are sitting at a table, your mother in the middle, spooning soup. Sparkling yellow embroidered stars stream down from her spoon via the tablecloth. The man on the left is wearing thick black leather gloves which makes the scene reminiscent of a still from a shady porn film in a typically '60s interior with a plant, curtains, a tablecloth and leatherette-upholstered chairs. An empty plate. A half-empty glass of Grolsch, probably the photographer's. The title *Lemons and Mothers* confirms the ambivalence towards your mother; citrus fruits may have been dedicated to Venus, but lemons also symbolise sour love and false friendship.

Then the work *Diversion* in which your grandmother, with a fag in her mouth, dumps a bag down on the table. A dominant woman who gives me the shivers. Your mother is sitting on the left on a chair, with her head resting on her left hand. Despondent. And on the right a hand is entering the picture, pulling at the tablecloth, as if your father, whose hand you think it is, wants to get rid of the whole situation in this way, like a magic trick by Hans Klok. The great vanishing trick, that will conjure up another life, a life without that grandma, without society with all its norms and constraining limitations. The stitched-on pieces of fabric all want to contribute to this disappearing trick, making that severe grandma dissolve. So that the picnic can still be fun. Or *Untitled* in which your mother is sitting on a bench next to a nun and is putting her hand underneath your little sister's skirt.

The first blow your mother had to bear was the German heritage of her father. He was required to serve in the *Wehrmacht,* but deserted and went into hiding. But there was little mercy after the war; he was convicted as a collaborator. After 18 months in prison, the man was released and in those months his wife and daughter had lived in a room with bedbugs in a hostile environment.

    Reports show that the past of these parents who were 'on the wrong side' hangs round the neck of their children like a rope. They are saddled with a misplaced feeling of guilt for life, according to these studies. Being blameless, and yet condemned, cuts deep into your soul. It seems as if that unjust guilt stuck to your mother because the mechanism does not seem to disappear in her life. And yes, she goes on to make questionable choices.

'I sometimes wonder if you children really love me', she writes. 'What I realise more and more is that when I am old, I will be lonely.' She lost real contact with you and died alone, leaving you behind, lonely. That beautiful young woman. Her story won't let me go. The tragedy of a life that is squeezed into a mould by the spirit of the age. Right on the first page, she indicates that she does not want to be like other women 'who only talk about their children', but what does she have at her disposal to make more of her life? The painter Alice Neel also wrote with disdain about a woman's existence and had ambivalent feelings about raising children. But she had that enormous talent, she lived to paint. And her children forgive her for everything.

There is a diptych of your mother with her oldest son, Wimmie. A homage to your mother with her first child. She brought him up, she cared for him, for all of you. Her skirt lights up because of the warm yellow that recurs in the garden border. That little boy with his short blond hair and a bow tie is smiling happily, with your mother's arm around him protectively. But on the right-hand part, the chilly blue has been added to the same photo and the little boy disappears behind stitched-on fabric. It is a desperate homage.
    You now have fifteen works about your mother, to acknowledge the loss, to live with it. You compared your stitching to a sampler, stitching as an organised structure that is laid over reality. A tribute, a treasure hunt, searching for something beautiful that you can love after all. I think that she is still receiving this spiritual tour de force, so she's perhaps less lonely, there, now. Just like you.

Berend Strik, *Untitled*, 2005, embroidered photo,
(photo: Ellen Page Wilson)

Portrait of my father Hans Breedveldt Boer

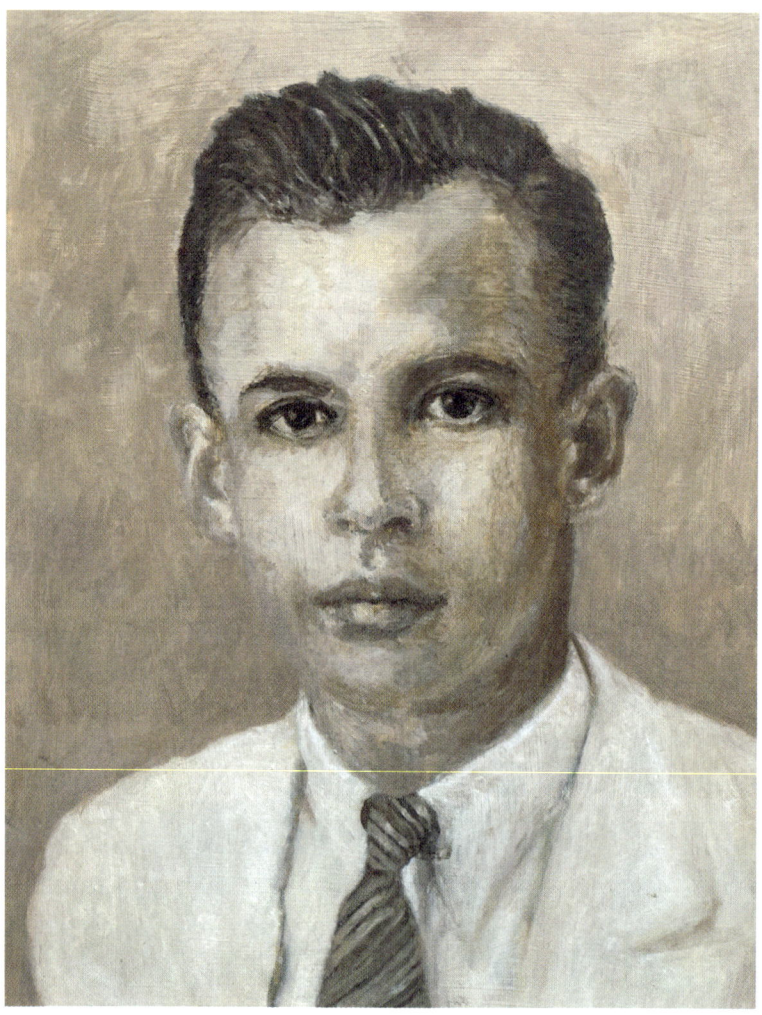

Inge Breedveldt Boer:

This is my father. To me, he always looked like this, whatever his age. When I was going through a late aunt's things, I found a small photo that exactly matched my memory of him. A photo that summarises his being.

I was a daddy's girl; there is not much difference in essence between my father and me. Even now, when I see this photo, it is as if we are converging. If I were able to meet him in a dream or in another life, I would ask him: Why didn't you reveal more of yourself?

Inge Breedveldt Boer, *Portrait of my father*, 2018

Untitled (Portrait of the Artist's Father)

Rosemarie Trockel's father was a taciturn man; communication never really got going. She was inspired by Freudian therapy, which encourages patients to draw images of family members as a way of releasing hidden emotions. Trockel allowed herself to be led by her intuition and finger-painted this portrait of him.

Rosemarie Trockel, *Untitled (Portrait of the Artist's Father)*, 1995

Was he not too lonely?

Monica Overdijk, *Cousin Sjaak, a few months before his death*, 1969 – 2017, (photo: Cassander Eeftinck Schattenkerk)

Was he not too lonely?

Monica Overdijk:

'Cousin Sjaak suffered brain damage due to a lack of oxygen during his birth. Communication was difficult. Despite this, Sjaak tried to lead a normal life. With the support of his parents, he lived independently in a flat and worked for the City Parks Department with great pleasure. He knew the plants and trees by their (Latin) names and knew how to care for them. I used to meet him on the street now and then. He was busy hoeing on those occasions. Seeing him at work like this gave me a feeling of pride and a sense of his specialness. How wonderful that he had that knowledge and skill! I always had a slight feeling of guilt, though. Wasn't he too much on his own? When Sjaak fell ill and it was clear that he would not recover, I wanted to do something for him: draw a portrait of him. I suggested it to him, his sister, and parents. His parents hesitated. He looked so ill. But I persisted.

I visited him in a hospice where he had already been for some time. My husband went with me. We went into the city first to buy a fish from his favourite stall. We also had a beer in a bar. When we got back, my husband left me alone with Sjaak. 'Now you can take the photos,' he said. 'Take your time. I'll wait outside.' I was nervous and felt uncomfortable. Was Sjaak really okay with this? How would his parents react? The few minutes it took to take the photos seemed to last an eternity. Sjaak was so quiet. Through the lens of the camera, I saw a grey face, a drooping eye, a turned-down mouth. He was a picture of sheer desolation, despair, and misery. Only… his limitations seemed to have disappeared.

I never got as far as drawing a portrait. I couldn't look at the photos without feeling ill. Five years later, I look at the photos again. The sorrowful, grey face is still there, but it doesn't bother me anymore. I also see what I had in mind back then, why I persisted; I wanted to meet his 'true self', without a mask, pure. That makes him so delicate, almost transparent. I spent three months drawing a copy of the photo. Dot by dot, I built the drawing up. The portrait gradually gained more colour, came to life. When I was rounding it off, I could see Sjaak himself before me again and I could hear his voice: M-O-N-I-C-A! His influence on the world seemed minimal, but it was not. His energy still permeates everything, still resonates. In his own inimitable way, he is continuing to live on after his death.'

E.I.G
Erik In Gedachten (Erik in our thoughts)

E.I.G
Erik In Gedachten (Erik in our thoughts)

> 'We are too limited to understand the infinite or infinity.'
> — Jane Goodall*45

The red of the amaryllis flower, the yellow of sunflowers, and sometimes the soft yellow with which Erik Andriesse coloured a crocodile—these are the colours that dominate his drawings.

Red and yellow is what Kees de Goede sees regularly when he looks out of the big window of his fourth-floor apartment—a sunset that lights up the sky with fiery hues. Maybe it's absurd, but I open the book *Sichtbare Welt* by Fischli and Weiss anyway, because I rarely see a sunset from my home in the city centre and I'm eager to look at the variations. There are six pages with a series of photos where the colours shift from vivid yellow to orange-red to the pale understated yellow of the sun sinking behind the mountains. The visible world here is not the world of the news or of newspaper photos, but that of the tourist gaze: city and nature, captured observantly and without much fuss as a continuous whole.

A sunset needs no explanation. In the same way, Kees de Goede also prefers not to explain his work; there is nothing to explain, at most you might destroy something with too many words. Even the work that is dedicated to his deceased friend Erik Andriesse doesn't get its title in full, but as the abbreviation: *E.I.G.*, his own version of *R.I.P. Erik In Gedachten*. He died unexpectedly, aged 35. Anyone who has Erik in their thoughts is visualising 'plenty', abundance, being exuberantly present, obsessive. The paper's edges can barely contain his drawings of nature but, in life too, Erik was 'a man of many houses, passionate in his love for many people', says Kees.

And Erik was just as economical about providing information about his work, because what is there to say about an amaryllis, except that it was his favourite flower because it bloomed so dashingly in the colour he loved most, red, the colour that unites life force and blood. 'Everyone understands it', he says, 'life and death.' Erik was a dear friend of the De Goede family, he was simply part of the family. He often strolled in just before mealtimes and sat down to eat with them.

On the Erik Andriesse online archive, I see an exhibition overview full of fiery red amaryllises and then, on the wall on the left, a shocking painting of a recently deceased baby hippo.

E.I.G
Erik In Gedachten (Erik in our thoughts)

The animal is lying on its back with the head hanging back as if it is uttering a final primal scream. The umbilical cord is hanging down like a red tendril. The belly was cut open during the autopsy, so you see a red pool of blood in a grey body. 'The subjects of visual artist Erik Andriesse will fill some people with disgust: skeletons with flesh still hanging from hem and a dead baby hippo', wrote Bianca Stiger in 1991.*[46] The baby hippo only lived for a single day; it was probably crushed to death by its mother. Instead of being covered by earth, the animal ended up in a freezer in Andriesse's studio. 'Of course I found this moving. I lifted the little hippo out of the freezer in my arms every day and laid it on the table. The umbilical cord always fell off. But I also get emotional if I paint a beautiful flower.' For Erik, dealing with dead animals was so self-evident.

Kees created the work *E.I.G.* as part of a series of circular paintings. 'When this painting was completed, it was bursting with yellow and during that period Erik was very much in our thoughts so that became the title. It happened in a very natural way.' Yellow is of course the colour of the sun, the gold of warmth, light and life. The painting is now on the wall of the entrance hall of ABN AMRO's head office in The Hague. I go to have a look. A sun that brings warmth and affection in this otherwise rather plain bank building.

It also resembles a face, four metres from the ground, two eyes, a snub nose, and the black circle like an open mouth, but that is too banal, and I prefer to forget that little man. In reality it turns out that the circles in the open holes look like three pieces of wood that differ in thickness. The round shapes in the work inevitably make you think of the cosmos, where planets are pulled into a spherical shape because of their mass. But then that deep blue underlayer; that makes the yellow flow. I see stones in a river, a shell, a skull. A watermelon. My friend sees a den with wolves. And it looks like an animal skin has been stretched out in that black circle on the top right. I see plant stems that have been cut through. A black potato with a shoot. The thinly drawn lines: a fossil. In the vastness of this cosmos, I can see the structure of a plant cell where it looks as if a tree is growing inside the cell structure. A round polished stone. Infinity has penetrated this circle like a too-powerful summary of the universe. We are being thrown into the universe. But also, still, a sun, which takes all organisms into its care.

E.I.G
Erik In Gedachten (Erik in our thoughts)

The sun in the ABN AMRO bank is a great consolation: numbers, calculations, profit and loss... all very important, but it is of course all about the sun.

Perhaps death is a return to the light, but not via one of those tunnels that lead you towards a wonderful unknown place, but instead towards the molecules of the sand and earth, water or the air, being absorbed once again into the realm that cannot exist without the sun. Where one substance merges into another and life continues to flow through all substances.

> 'Being happy, finding consolation, means that you become a part of a greater whole and feel that you are an element of it, an element that belongs to it in a natural way.'
> – Yehudi Menuhin*[47]

In a dream that follows the visit to the bank building, it's the numbers that pursue me first: they chase me out of the building and when I run faster and faster all those circles start moving; the yellow is flowing like desert sand and the sun transforms it into a big set of cogwheels that keep one another in motion. When I wake up and brush my teeth, I walk through my house, still under the spell of the dream, and stop in the hall, next to my son's height marks on the wall. I open the catalogue *Double Face, Split Level* and yes, Kees and his wife have also noted their children's growth on a section of wall—that lovely ritual where each year you lay a ruler on the child's head and then draw a line on the wall. Time marching on briskly without taking a break to catch breath. 'The days may all be the same for a clock, but not for people', wrote Clarice Lispector. It is of course a matter of living large and vivaciously, or small and attentively, that's possible too, to keep the lines on the wall up to date. Time strolls on, nothing is ever the same. This world in which we exist quivers and radiates and communicates at all levels. Trees have a secret language of scent, as has become apparent from observations in the savannah. As soon as giraffes start nibbling the leaves of an umbrella thorn acacia, the tree produces a toxic substance that it sends to its leaves. The giraffes then calmly move on to the next tree, but this one has been alerted by a scent in the meantime and is now also producing the toxic substance. The giraffes walk on a bit further still and this prevents a cluster of trees from being stripped bare.

Equilibrium.*48 A dog recognises its master, but it seems that hens also have a complex emotional life, even if they are less attached to whoever comes to bring them food. They experience fear, anger, and affection. People sometimes think that the universe can be understood rationally, that we can file it away as data, that hens are products rather than animals, but that means the essence is disregarded. It means we lose contact with that underlying stream, something invisible, that works.

In some parts of the world, the inhabitants take dead human bodies to the birds. The Zoroastrians allow the body to decompose in the sun and to be picked clean by vultures. It seems crude, even macabre, to feed people to the vultures but, if you take a step back and think about it, worms aren't very different. Birds are actually very suited to eating dead remains because their powerful digestive juices kill viruses and bacteria. Despite this, the ritual was forbidden in Iran, and it is only still permitted in India, but since 1980 the population of vultures there has declined by more than 97% because they ate the carcasses of livestock that had been treated with the anti-inflammatory drug diclofenac.

Vultures have a bad reputation; few are fond of this bird with its long bald neck and curved beak, but these are human sentiments, because vultures actually fulfill an important role in the ecosystem. And where humans believe they can help nature, it alarmingly often goes wrong. As with diclofenac. We'd do better to keep our mitts off the self-regulating living recycling system.*49 In five billion years the sun will die, explains astronaut André Kuipers, and then it will be all over for Earth too. That seems infinitely far away but, in the meantime, humans don't seem to care if that end is rapidly approaching because of their own actions.

Erik in our thoughts. Still. Kees shows small wooden ancestral figures from the Pacific that were intended to be carried with you, so that the deceased ancestor could travel with you in your pocket, for generations. 'That really is the essence. That's why the family sends round a photo of the deceased person. That's why there's a photo of Erik among our other photos on the dresser. His drawings are on the wall.' The yellow sun keeps Erik in our thoughts. Have faith in the sun. Have faith in Swallow Yellow, Primrose Yellow, Wax Yellow, Lemon Yellow,

E.I.G
Erik In Gedachten (Erik in our thoughts)

Saffron Yellow: all those yellows in nature, where they are present for a while and then discolour and turn brown—because they weren't intended to last for eternity. Or perhaps they were.

Gallery overview, *Hedge House* in Wijlre, 2009, (photo: Leon Gulikers)

p. 270: Kees de Goede, *E.I.G. 1992–1994*, diameter 190 cm, acrylic and charcoal on linen, 4 parts, ABN-AMRO collection, (photo: Rob Versluys)

Broken eyes

Broken eyes

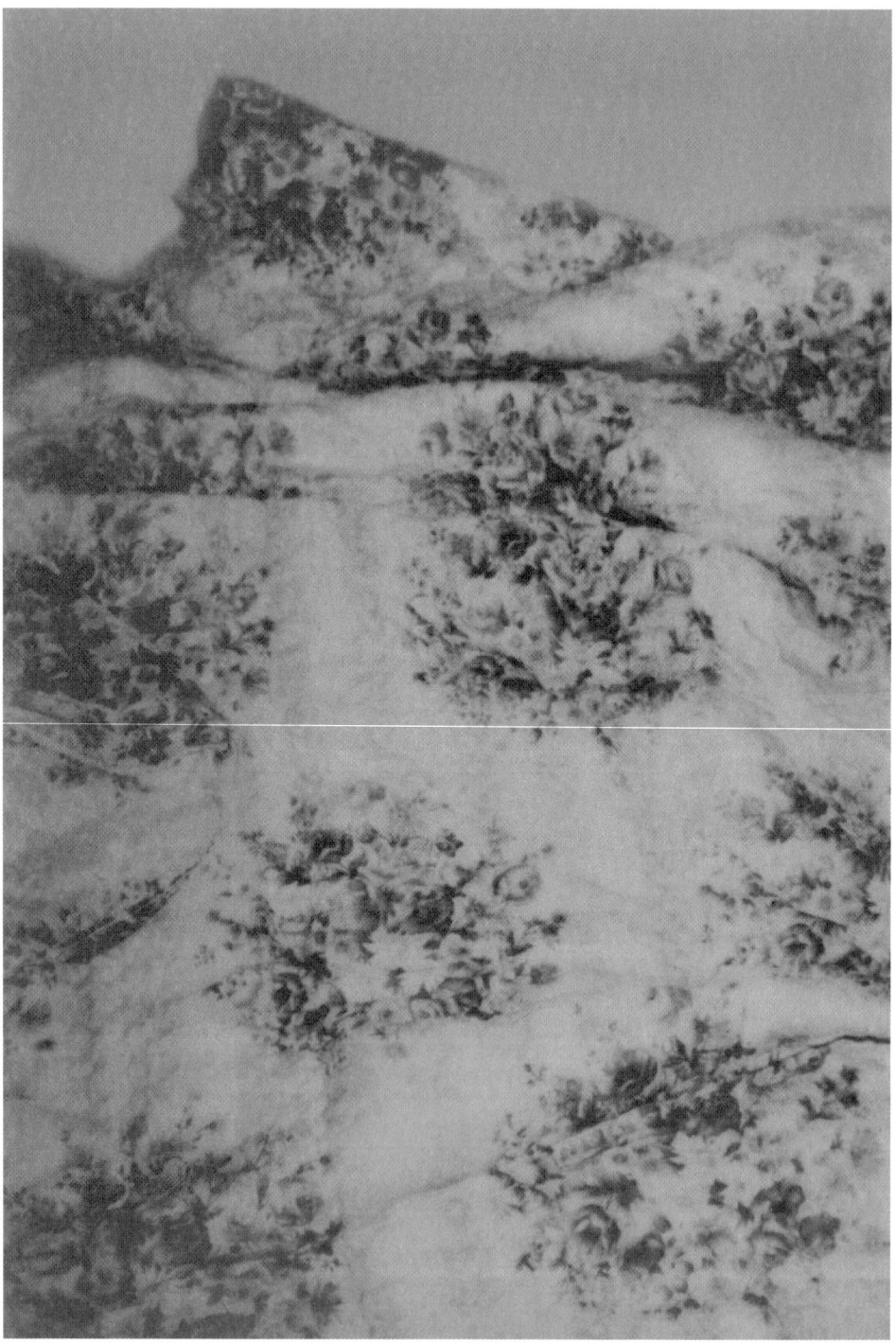

Dirk Braeckman, *B.D.-P.L.-95-01,* 2001, 180 × 120 cm, gelatin silver print on aluminium, Courtesy of Zeno X Gallery, Antwerp, Galerie Thomas Fischer, Berlin and Grimm Gallery, New York

Even if you don't believe in a God, sometimes you still have the feeling that some ends don't meet just like that. We can disregard it or we can call it coincidence, but in retrospect the connecting threads that you don't see in the moment often become visible. In this way, you could say that the tragically short life of his soulmate Willy has offshoots in the entire oeuvre of Dirk Braeckman.

In a village, you can see the stars twinkling in the dark night, you live close to the cabbage and the apples and purely by living there you are part of a community. But a village can sometimes also be a bit oppressive. Dirk Braeckman grew up in Waarschoot in Belgium: everything was good and safe but deep inside there was a longing for more, something unknown that is close to the soul. Willy looked quirky with his long hair and he was very gifted at drawing and painting. They got talking more and more about art and how to live, they saw each other every day. Until Willy died in a fire during a visit to his sister in Ghent. He wanted to run downstairs but the flames were already swallowing up the staircase and he was suffocated by the smoke. The police came to tell Braeckman at his home in Waarschoot.
    The death of the eighteen-year-old Willy hit him hard, and it took him at least half a year to get back to his daily life, to pack his school bag and to go outside. 'For the first weeks, I didn't dare to sleep alone in my room and after that I suffered from all sorts of fears for a long time.' In the year that followed, Braeckman took the decision to go to art school, in order to continue their conversations in this way. He was fascinated by drawing and really wanted to master it as well.

We are sitting silently opposite each other, in his studio. Such a young life. Such a loss. It seems so unjust because you simply want to spend more time with someone and at the same time the realisation dawns that time is like elastic. Someone who lives to be ninety is stretching the elastic quite a bit, but in retrospect each life is a flash. A person consists of flesh and bones, thoughts and, with any luck, a soul, but you could also say that a person consists of time, the time one occupies as long as the body is warm and moving. A short life, a long life. The importance of a human life cannot be measured in time.

What is the weight of a life? Perhaps that you have meant a lot to someone else, like that one teacher who showed you a glimpse of another life, a life full of books, art, and thoughts. Or a love that was so intense that you can't in fact go on living without that glow. A piercing loss. Willy.

Gebroken ogen, gebroken palet was the title of Willy's last painting. 'At first sight, a bit of a naive title for a self-portrait with white eyes', says Braeckman. 'But almost prescient.' Yes, scarily visionary. Shortly before death, the pupils no longer respond to light. The eyes turn cloudy, a phenomenon that you could call 'broken eyes' and it is often regarded as the moment of parting from life. Braeckman went to the academy in Ghent but abandoned drawing and painting in favour of photography. In his photos, Braeckman remains in dialogue with Willy as the profound experience of his early death seeps into the photos. Not in a direct way and certainly not as an anecdote but through the simple realisation that life is full of mysteries. 'We do not know who we are, it's about then, now, and afterwards. With my photos, I'm trying to say something that you can't express in words.' A story would press all those layers together whereas it's all about that multiplicity, and just as in literature it is the sentences themselves that are important, the suggestions evoked by those sentences, the scent you smell when you read about mushrooms.

'In which ways did Willy remain present in your life, how did those conversations continue, apart from choosing for art?', I ask him. 'Although I could not see or hear him, he has always stayed with me anyway. His spirit? His soul? Sometimes there is a vision. Delusions perhaps, or wishful thinking. My parents died soon after each other and despite the fact that I'm an atheist and don't believe in a life after death, I still speak with them. You know someone so well, you almost know what he or she will reply. So you ask them questions in your mind and you also hear their reaction. In this way, loved ones remain alive, in this way you keep them close to you.'

Where death is concerned, faith with its life-hereafter is often unexpectedly close by, as can be read in the lines that the not-so-religious writer Joseph Brodsky wrote down for his two-year-old daughter before he had to undergo a heart operation:

    'On the whole, bear in mind that I'll be around.' *[50]

'The Catholic faith with which I grew up has got under my skin after all, you can no longer unthink it. Perhaps that's where that fear came from, after Willy's death. Although my fears certainly also have something to do with my need for control; I am rather a control freak, and I had no influence on that event and those feelings. Faith determines what a life is and what happens afterwards, but I don't know what a life is. We can't rule anything out. Nor do I claim that science has an answer. Humans don't know everything, they are limited.'

'Love is essentially an attitude maintained by the infinite towards the finite', wrote Joseph Brodsky about the, for that time, unusually concrete poems of Anna Achmatova.*[51] 'The reversal constitutes either faith or poetry.' And that's how I also see Braeckman's photos: from the earthly temporality towards something much greater, which is possibly there or perhaps not. In the photos you see his attention for the defenceless and incidental, a love for everything that exists.

'We are all equally vulnerable. I try to show that through my work, the insignificant, which is precisely what has value in my opinion. My way of working arises from a social commitment. I focus on it actively and I need it in order to be able to make my photos. Not that it appears literally but it is certainly present. It gives a profound feeling, when you can really mean something to others. Standing up for the weaker has always been part of me; at school, I already took bullied children under my wing.'

His photos sometimes also make me think of my own house; I'm not someone who has their house plastered every five or ten years, I also hate painting, it's a bit of a mess. No perfect spaces, which would easily make me feel uncomfortable, because suppose you knock over a cup of coffee or make a scratch when carrying a chair up the staircase. Sometimes I take a photo of a bouquet of flowers, or an ex voto that I have placed somewhere. It strikes me that the background takes over the image, a corner where the plaster has been chipped off, gathered dust, a crack. Small blemishes. Imperfections. Braeckman's photos are what you might call purely background and wonderfully beautiful precisely because they carry those imperfections within them. They are vulnerability itself. During a residency in New York in the eighties, Braeckman got hold of the book *Evidence* by the photographer and writer Luc Sante and this set him on a different course. The book contained fifty-five photos of crime scenes in New York from the years 1914–1918. During his research in the municipal archives of New York, Sante was asked if he might be interested in old police photos. The director subsequently brought him fifteen thick ring binders in which about 1400 images, prints or old glass negatives were stored in manilla envelopes. Sometimes the emulsion of the negatives had been eaten away by moisture or it had stuck to the paper. It was a mishmash that had stood unobtrusively under a staircase and had thus survived the great clean-up operation of the sixties. Amidst the photos of driving licences, horses, jewels, and a hand with two thumbs, Sante came across those breathtaking photos of crime scenes. Sante calls his book 'A memorial to these dead, named and anonymous as well as to their now equally dead photographers'. An ode to forgotten people whose existence and history was not considered to be important, given the fact that the entire archive was heedlessly tipped into the river.

> 'Here was a true record of the texture and grain of a lost New York, laid bare by the circumstances of murder.' *52

A few photos can be found online. Two chairs stand next to an iron bed, a wood grain table, behind it a radiator and on the windowsill a clock in the form of a house. It is dark outside. Articles of clothing lie over the back of the armchair; men's clothing lies on the left and on the right pieces of frayed material from what was probably a sparkly party dress. A simple tableau but full of surfaces, the striped fabric, shiny painted wood, gleaming artificial wood, the mattress cover into which thin flower stems seem to be woven, a checked blanket, a woollen cushion, the metal of a power socket. It is precisely the black-and-white that gives so much information about the immaterial qualities, for you are not distracted by the colour that would directly link it with the banal reality, that would connect it to a story. Across the surface of the photo, white spots and specks.

Dirk Braeckman is blown away. Those silent scenes. Most of the photos show a person who has been murdered, very unsettling because it feels improper to look at them.

But those places in particular, where there is no one to be seen, yes, those are astonishing. 'That's it', he must have thought: a place, and the rest is up to the viewer, their fantasy, their imagination, their heart, their fear and defence. Their compassion. A photo like this penetrates your humanity, right into the marrow of your bones. Some crime scenes show a sort of square or oval aura, perhaps the police photographer in his darkroom wanted to draw attention to something, or it was the afterglow of the magnesium flash. It looks like a dead person is lying in a corridor, but it turns out to be a silhouette formed by the blood that has been left behind, and here too those strange white contours, as if the holy spirit is coming to investigate what is going on. The photos are pure mystery. Something cruel and irrevocable has taken place here although the circumstances are sometimes so incredibly domestic, with white cloths hanging to dry on a rack, a pan on the table, a chair by the window. If you take a photo like this out of its context then the mystery remains, the puzzle of what preceded it, and how things went on with the murder case and those involved. It is possible that little attention was paid to the case and time simply went on while the impact on the lives involved must have been immense. Guilt and penalty, crime and punishment.

```
The Hourglass

Do but consider this small dust
Here running in the glass,
By atoms moved;
Could you believe that this
The body was
Of one that loved?
And in his mistress' flame, playing like a fly,
Turned to cinders by her eye:
Yes; and in death, as life, unblessed,
To have it expressed,
Even ashes of lovers find no rest.
− Ben Jonson
```

Time always goes on, whatever we humans do. Time does not die. An hourglass making the ashes of a loved one run back and forth connects time and death to each other. Death is literally imprisoned in the continuation of time.

There are numerous interpretations of the poem, but I read in it that even when human time is up-ended, love continues to exist. Dirk Braeckman's photos capture the time that lingers in this materiality, in the fading of the colour, in a smell that remains in the fabric, in the worn-out places, in the injustices. In *Evidence* we see the sort of curtains that come back later in Braeckman's work and there they don't feel dated, but just as if they have remained hanging there quietly and will always continue doing so. The photos are immersed in darkness, or a veil of specks draws over them to make them more abstract. There is great sensitivity in that transience.

The photos are dark, black and grey, and grainy. Black is a colour that overflows with meanings. Black is the colour of gloominess and mourning but that is an obvious interpretation. More than that, and above all, black stands for the intangible, the lack of bright light, a lack of certainty. Malevich painted the *Black Square* because he wanted to liberate art from the dead weight of the real world. Something comparable happens in the photos. The ordinary objects like armchairs, a rug, a pane of patterned glass, a corner of a room or a painting withdraw from the mundane. The darkness of the photo is like a black night in which a galaxy can be seen somewhere on the horizon, perhaps it is only a conjecture, seeing one on the basis of thinking or knowing. Our ignorance. Eternity. Black is complicated and complex, and that means there are big questions lurking in it.

In the middle of our conversation Braeckman says, quite unexpectedly: 'I actually forget essential things—I was in fact stillborn, the doctor resuscitated me by shaking me and holding me upside down. That experience is stored inside me.'
 'My mother had two miscarriages; together, we buried the little brother in a tiny coffin in the garden. Now I'm once again living in the house where I grew up until I was twelve, that place plays on my mind. Not that there is pain, but there is certainly the memory.' I thought about death from a young age onwards. My father was a deep-sea diver and I often went with him and then waited on the open sea until he came up again. I buried him in my mind a hundred times because I was overcome by the fear that he wouldn't come up again. He seemed convinced of his immortality and calmly stayed under water on his own for two hours with those big bottles of compressed air.

When his head rose above the water again, I felt a mixture of hatred and happiness, but he didn't realise what he was doing to me. I saw my grandmother die: she was slipping away, and right on the threshold of dying I asked as a child: "Is she gone now or is she still with us?" That question has stayed with me.'

A graphic designer friend, who was almost blind because of an illness, tried to explain to me what being blind meant; you tend to think of a black world, of a deep dark night. 'But', he said, 'you don't see grey or black, it's the absence of something. You can't imagine that, it's like looking with your nose.' There is a lot in our world that we can't visualise. The scene of the crime, we can imagine what happened, but we only have suspicions about what led someone to do it, about the true nature of the person.

'Throughout one's life, time addresses man in a multitude of languages: in those of innocence, love, faith, experience, history, fatigue, cynicism, guilt, decay, etc. Of those, the language of love is clearly the lingua franca. Its vocabulary absorbs all the other tongues, and its utterance gratifies a subject, however inanimate it may be. Also, thus uttered, a subject acquires an ecclesiastical, almost sacred denomination, echoing both the way we perceive the objects of our passions and the biblical suggestion as to what God is.' writes Joseph Brodsky about the poems of Anna Achmatova.

> That love for a place, a surface, a chair,
> that little piece of reality, the inconspicuous, the places people walk past unobserved.
> A place.
> Being a witness.
> Occupying a space.
> A door, a window, a corridor?
> Furniture and curtains.
> Closing off opening up landing, passage
> Inside, indoors – immanent.
> Infix, outfix.

I'm in luck: when I go to De Pont Museum in Tilburg shortly after my conversation with Braeckman, I come across a room in which his large photos are displayed. I stand opposite a woman, a naked woman, and realise the immense difference compared with looking at the same photo in the thick yellow book that is on my desk at home. This confrontation is direct, as if I really am standing opposite her. Her pubic mound is unusually fat, I'm not too sure what I'm looking at, perhaps a sanitary towel, perhaps a non-binary person, or simply a pubic mound that has turned out rather fat. I only know that my gaze keeps on returning to that 'unusual' place, my eyes can't get away, which means that I myself am becoming ever more naked opposite her. Shameful. The woman is self-absorbed and my gaze is so impertinent. In the background is a mantelpiece on which nothing is standing straight, yes, the clock, it is five past two. A mattress, a rug. Why am I so inquisitive, why don't I leave her alone, why are we programmed to look in such a normative way? Why can I not simply accept that place for what it is, a part of a body, a spot on a photo?

A very narrow strip of light on a metal curtain rod, but I can't work out whether it is from a flash or light that is passing through a slit. A heater with a cloth over it. I am looking at a white house, but I cannot look inside through the window because the curtains are closed. Something isn't right, but what? Then I see that real nature and the painted tree branches run into each other in a not-quite-right way. It is one of those houses you used to make up ugly things about—a Dutroux house—but perhaps the residents are simply on holiday. In *Evidence* we see the photos, knowing that a murder has taken place; in Braeckman's photos we don't know that; probably nothing happened. Ultimately, I have to accept the 'not understanding'. Uninviting curtains, small flowers on the ceiling.

Braeckman tells me about the time a photo requires. 'Before I go into the darkroom, I already have a relationship with the image. It starts with a place that holds my attention and I explore it by simply spending a longer period of time there. I get to know that place. I prefer in-between-spaces, transit, spaces that others may walk past. Sometimes people stand next to you, whom you don't see or who are still to come. That is also the value. The relationship with that place is what I take into the darkroom where the mental dialogue continues.'

   The spaces are full of hissing tension, like a room where there's been an argument. At that moment it is quiet and empty but at the same time the atmosphere is charged. The energy of people who come and go leaves traces. That's what life is, then.

No more, no less. The question he asked as a child when his grandmother died—that question gets an 'answer in a stream of photos and shows that there is in fact no answer.'

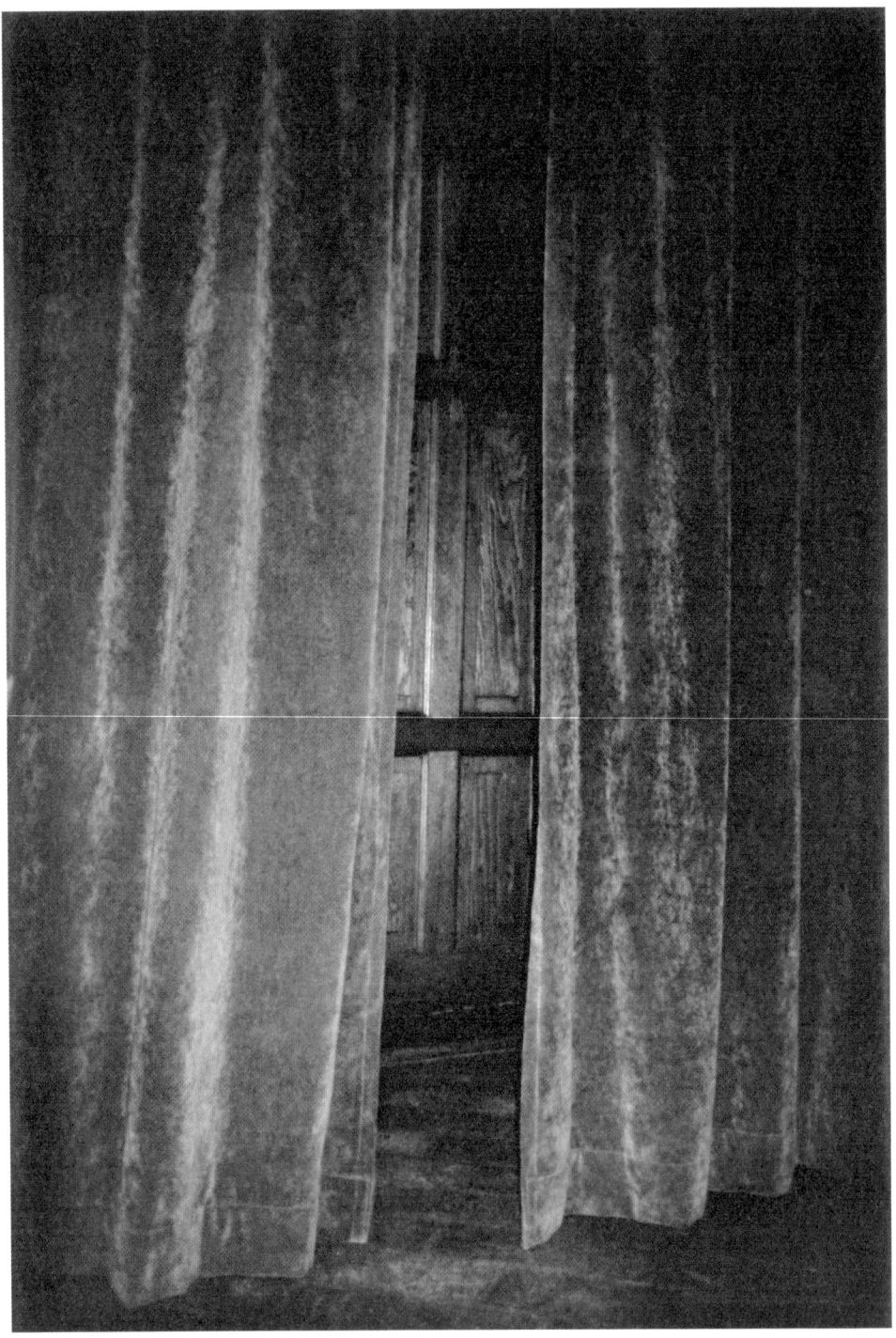

Dirk Braeckman, *A.D.F.-B.E.-03*, 2003, 180 × 120 cm, gelatin silver print, Courtesy of Zeno X Gallery, Antwerp, Galerie Thomas Fischer, Berlin and Grimm Gallery, New York

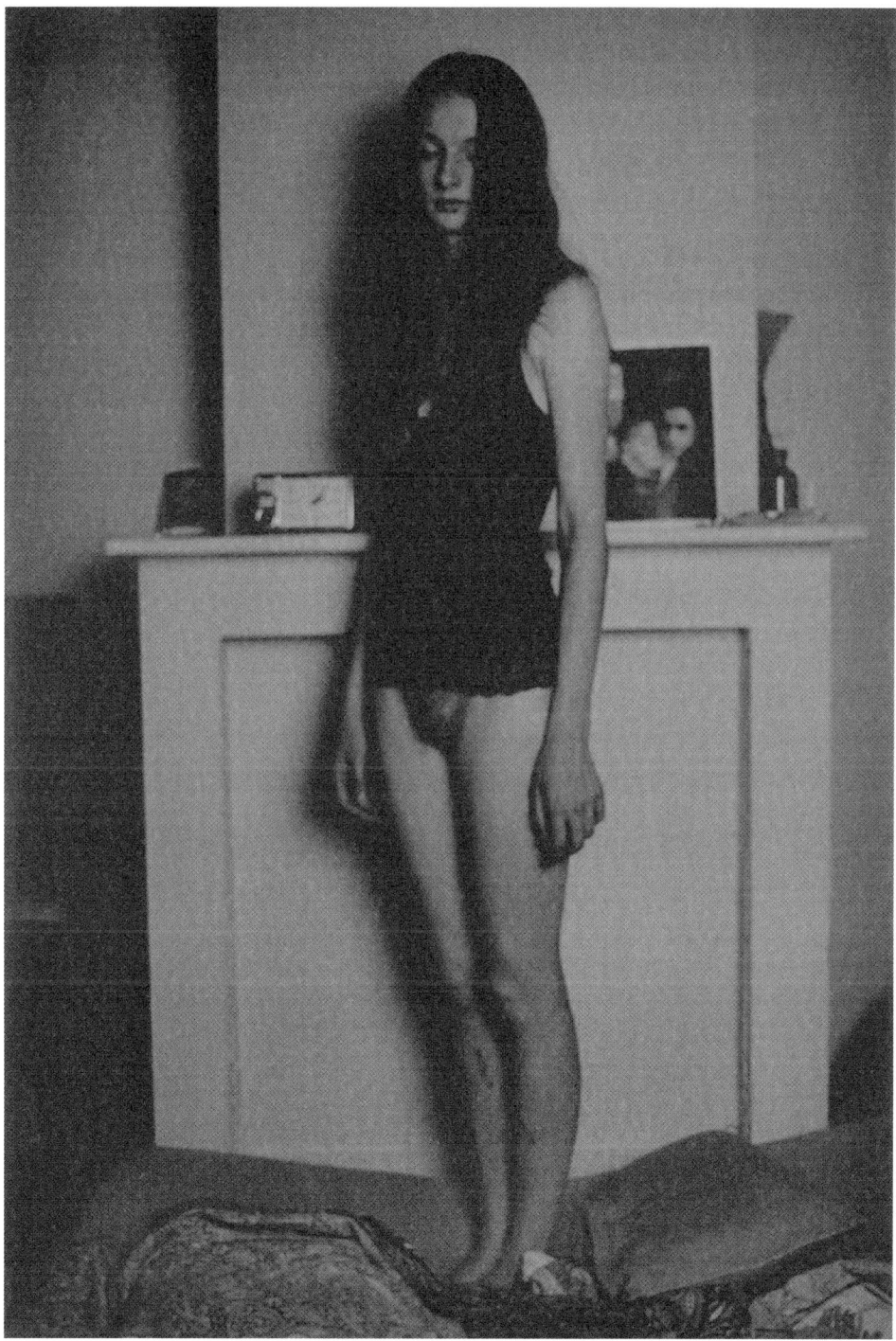

Dirk Braeckman, *A.D.F.-V.N.1-03,* 2003, 180 × 120 cm, gelatin silver print, Courtesy of Zeno X Gallery, Antwerp, Galerie Thomas Fischer, Berlin and Grimm Gallery, New York

Wim was my colleague at the Rietveld Academy in Amsterdam. Perhaps not even a friend but certainly enough of a buddy for me to feel intense grief when he died. He would sometimes ring the doorbell for a cup of tea after his yoga class, which was held just around the corner from here. The last time, I cycled with him to his house because he was frail and had only just enough puff to move the pedals. His short-cut route from the city centre to his house led along the back of the Hortus and the front of Artis. I still cycle this route when I need to be somewhere in the north-east of Amsterdam. And I never cycle there without thinking of him. The Wim-route.

Fatum

Rob Knijn, *Unknown title (Wibo van Rossum)*, 2017

On the print that accompanies the book *Fatum* by Rob Knijn, a wooden spear is pointing directly upwards, held by the hand of a man in a green robe. To the right of the lance, a hand with a raised forefinger is also gesturing upwards. The print is long and narrow, like a bookmark, and the cut-out originates from a crucifixion scene from the school of Duccio.*[53] The almost blind soldier Longinus*[54] brutally pierces Christ's side with the spear to ascertain whether he is already dead. A few drops of blood fall into his afflicted eyes and cure his illness in a miraculous way. Even on the cross, Christ is performing one more miracle, as the apotheosis of a life full of miracles. Through him, the blind were able to see again, the lame stood up and walked, and even broken hearts were healed. The Holy Lance of Longinus is referred to in esoteric circles as the spear of destiny. Fatum.

Miracles are rare but almost everyone with an incurable disease maintains hope, in a new medicine, science, the power of positive thinking, or in the promises of a dubious herbal therapist. This hope is desperately needed in order to get through that last bit of life in a good way, even if hope is shrinking a bit more all the time, from years to months to days. And when real hope has gone, there is still the possibility of a miracle. That's why I accompanied my sick friend Lucy to meetings of the weirdest healers who, for example, told corny jokes or had bad taste in shoes or wore loud shirts, and who all declared that everything is possible as long as you believe in it. That's quite hard to hear if you have cancer that has spread, and it was a bitter pill for Lucy to swallow, but we still kept going out in search of hope.

When it became clear that Wibo, the brother-in-law and friend of Rob Knijn, was terminally ill, they spent even more time together than before. Wibo agreed to intensive chemo in order to defer the definitive farewell somewhat and although it took a lot out of him, he retained enough joy in life to withstand the daily fatigue, pain, and discomfort. Wibo accepted that the end was in sight and resolved to spend most of his time with his four children, to have fun, and to then die with confidence, leaving them with precious memories as they continued with their lives. Wibo did not visit any obscure healers but did retain a spark of hope, somewhere in his heart.

Rob: 'I painted this portrait quite soon after the diagnosis, so that I could still give it to him, so that he would know that the portrait had been made. I thought, fully in the tradition of portrait painting, that I would make him less 'finite' and, as I was painting, would surround him with an aura of immortality. It gave me peace to work on this in the quiet of my studio, with thoughts coming and going like the rolling waves of a calm sea. At the end of the day, I sometimes cycled to the sea, close to my studio in Scheveningen, to absorb the endlessness of sky and water. That is how it will be: in my eyes, death is not different from the time before your birth. I am not afraid of death, I see something peaceful, a beautiful motion.'

Hanne: 'How was the work received?' Rob: 'Rather awkwardly, the gesture of giving it was rather a blunt moment too: I unwrapped the painting without much ado and showed it to him. Wibo was a bit taken aback and didn't really know how to react. It is of course rather an unusual portrait, so I completely understood how he felt.'

And so, years later, I am looking at Wibo, whose face is concealed behind lozenge shapes. There is an inside and an outside. The person and their surroundings. Stars? The hereafter? A dot can be all kinds of things—simply paint or paradise breaking through the darkness. Clouds are drifting over one side of the face and on the other an eye is just about breaking through the surface, above a pinkish cheek. Yet it is as if Wibo is making a withdrawing movement, using the lozenges as a screen to dodge behind. The chequered costume of a harlequin, that peculiar figure who has to make the audience laugh but for whom sadness always prevails nonetheless. Here, the diamonds look like facets of a gemstone, sparkling in all directions.

Wibo looks like a scholar, a bookish man, a renaissance figure. His hand and the book converge. He is standing a bit stiffly: his pose imitates that of the fifteenth century aristocracy. But despite the posture that has come from the past, the portrait points, as always, towards the future. Wibo was a colourful and nuanced person, a thinker. He liked the book *The man without qualities* by Robert Musil because the book makes an inventory of possibilities, does not state anything conclusively, but investigates what might be.

> 'Every true reader ought to read a few pages of *The man without qualities* once in their lifetime. Nowhere else in world literature do you find such condensed cerebral sentences that suggest so much and then go on to propel it in the opposite direction. Each sentence hits its mark and is added to the previous one as a new truth. Each observation (...) is exchanged a little later for an opposing statement that makes just as much sense.' *[55]

Looking without judgement and looking once again in this way suited Wibo who, in his thesis on the sociology of law, researched how judges interpret and assess the behaviour of suspects from different cultures. He provided each case with nuances of colour, like the facets of a stone.

Wibo is depicted as a rather rigid presence, but each possible interpretation is deflected by all those coloured planes. He is a colourful projection screen and his agility in 'thinking and being' is reflected in all those flat surfaces. 'This is what I have in mind, my portrayal of Wibo in paint. What I'm actually saying is: don't go away, stay, or I'm saying, yes, you're going away but at the same time you're staying with us.'

Painting a portrait of a friend who knows that he will die in the near future is pretty brave because with this realisation in mind a gesture of this kind becomes highly charged, like a lightning strike. Without words, an image like this mentions the reality that everyone is aware of, that you don't want to deny but that you don't find it easy to talk about either. 'Can you still wish someone who is terminally ill a happy new year?', wonders grief expert Manu Keirse and goes on to make an impassioned plea for openness, for acceptance and speaking about the end. Because if everyone looks the other way, the sick person, who is well aware of where they stand, is left out in the cold.

In an email, Rob writes to me: 'My work focuses on themes including appearing and disappearing. Life is short, make the most of it, is how I summarise the concept of *fatum*. Or better still, stretch your possibilities to the limits. Everything is futile in the face of eternity, of course, but it's good to wage a personal battle anyway. I think you see that too.'

Never is a very long time

Never is a very long time

Kim van Norren, *Could from the dead I bring back that one*, 2022

'A poem is all the better the less one notices its words', wrote the poet J.C. Bloem, and he later added that the 'voice of the heart' should speak in a poem.*56 But the reader has no false sentiment to fear because that heart must express itself in the perfect poem—and that is apparently a poem in which the reader meets themselves and perhaps their fellow human too. So his poetry contains no words that are too beautiful and artful, even though the word 'heart' does occur exceptionally often. Bloem also has a predilection for well-used sayings that he uses slightly differently so that something familiar springs up but the line of poetry still sounds fresh. In this exceptionally precise language, you hear more than is written, and a first reading is not sufficient to understand it; a poem is meant to be read and read again.

I'm sometimes alarmed by the sentences that Kim van Norren chooses for her paintings: when I look around at the *Ride the Wave* exhibition in Kampen, I read *Could from the dead I bring back that one, Stronger than death is love, We'll meet again, Imagine, I left so much behind* and *Leave me unloved.* Here, death is blowing its gentle breath over the living. *We'll Meet Again,* the Vera Lynn classic that even I can sing along to, expresses the uncertainty regarding the fate of the soldiers in the Second World War. Yes, we will meet again, perhaps in heaven. *We'll Meet Again* is a popular song at memorial services, it is number 21 in the top 50 of funeral music. *Imagine* is number 18. Precisely. To my dismay.

```
I came so far for beauty
I left so much behind
My patience and my family
My masterpiece unsigned
– Leonard Cohen
```

The poet Ida Gerhardt also loves simple language; as Komrij said, 'it contains no "poetic" words'.*57 *Could from the dead I bring back that one* is a line from her best-known poem, *The departed one.* Her verses are popular as street poetry and in anthologies, and this particular poem was turned into a song by Trijntje Oosterhuis. This line is also the title of a book of testimonies about the loss of a loved one. Precisely.

In Gerhardt's work, disappointment about life burst forth from every syllable, but also strength and concern and above all the hopeful vision of death as a passage towards life. Kim van Norren's paintings also move between life and death but are at the same time a sign of love to the sometimes cruel destiny of existence.

The poems that artist Eli Content wrote himself are still (for the time being) a well-kept secret; they express moments, sensations, and the web that is spun around sleep and death. At the exhibition *Ride the Wave,* the God of Ida Gerhardt, the God of Eli Content, and Kim van Norren's rather vaguer concept of God meet one another, the certainty and uncertainty of death. I see these three people one by one, standing on the bank of the IJssel, looking towards the opposite side or going with the flow into the distance, with the splashing of the water against the bank resonating in their heart. They store the rising mist in their organs. Ida Gerhardt lived there in solitude when she taught at the high school, the solitude that colours the words of the later poem *The departed one* like iodine. Eli Content was a lecturer at the academy in Kampen and Kim met him there. Kim continued her studies at De Ateliers in Amsterdam but later returned to Kampen, where she lives now.

    For all three, language is a place to take refuge. The language that rumbles through the streets of Kampen before moving into the countryside together with the mist from the Ijssel. Ida Gerhard's sometimes lofty, archaic words. Eli Content's lines. Kim picks them up one by one. Eli used to put his poems into an envelope to post to Kim. He would use a letter stamp to print poems onto a piece of paper to hang in the window of his house as a gift to passers-by. Words were indispensable for him, with a preference for Hebrew letters, because according to a Jewish story Creation was preceded by language. 'For without letters, there was no language with which God could speak the words of creation.' *58

During his funeral in De Duif (The Dove) in Amsterdam, the words of his beloved Karina filled the church, there were speeches by family members and by his friend Toon Verhoef; it was sober and loving. Eli lay in a cardboard coffin. His green handprints on paper were placed on top of it, and children and friends filled the rest of the coffin with drawings. Kim was also there because Eli was first her tutor, and later a friend. When Kim was going through a difficult period, Eli kept a close eye on her. His concern for the people around him was legendary. After her graduation from De Ateliers, Eli offered Kim the opportunity to work in the studio next to him. 'He showed how you can go on despite intense experiences in life, how you can continue to live if you are not supported by family (Eli lost many of his Jewish family members during the Second World War). I saw in him how you can link art with your own energy; he was an example. Sometimes you meet people who say that they are there for you, but some people are just there, without words, and Eli was like that. When Karina came into his life, he radiated happiness, their love was so deep.' Immediately after the funeral, she made a painting for him and Karina, based on a line of text from the funeral card: *Stronger than death is love*. Kim painted three pale yellow flames on it that reach to the sun. The letters have run together as if they are shrinking because of his death, but the black is changing into red, into love. In the exhibition *Lust for Life*, we see how Eli Content continued to make cheerful cardboard figures until the last moment and he lived life sparkling with joy, even though he could barely speak anymore. His approaching death was met with an unbelievable vital energy.

'Making something, a poem, or a painting, is a form of survival. The work survives people, time, and it also remains outside of time. A poem or a painting does not die. That is what I find beautiful about these art forms, that their power remains constant, or increases. By painting this, I hoped to commemorate Eli. From him, I learned how you can live life well as an artist. Life is in first place and art is a part of it. Not the other way around. In the best case, someone's actions are motivated by love, and for me that was the essence of what I feel when I remember Eli', Kim writes to me in an email.

```
Corinthians 13: Without love, everything is
meaningless.
```

A painting with text is all the better the more the words leap off the canvas, towards the viewer. Taking a sentence from a poem and finding a home for it with colours and shapes, this gives the sentence space and breath. The sentence breaks free.

In this way, Imagine becomes a wonderful, strong piece of advice. In *Could from the dead I bring back that one,* the I is leaping up in a flame, emphasising the unusual position of the 'I' as if you could still accomplish something after death. *Stronger than death is love* comes from the book *Song of Solomon* in the Bible and, in its most original form, death and love are placed on an equal footing.*[59] Yet you hardly ever come across this version now, perhaps because humans secretly hope to be able to conquer death, in any shape or form.
We'll meet again.

> Set me as a seal upon your heart,
> as a seal upon your arm,
> for love is strong as death,
> jealousy is fierce as the grave.
> Its flashes are flashes of fire,
> the very flame of the Lord.
> Many waters cannot quench love,
> neither can floods drown it.
> If a man offered for love
> all the wealth of his house,
> he would be utterly despised.*[60]

The Song of Solomon is not about death but, on the contrary, about life and love. Love that gives oxygen to the pain of missing. Death is inevitable for each person; love's heartbeat keeps life awake.

Making something is a form of survival and the studio is the happy place. 'Painting is a thread of life, it brings me back to the feeling that everything will be fine, that feeling that I sometimes lose.' While I stroll through Kampen with Kim, we talk about the despondency that can sometimes come over you. The wickedness of the world. The nonchalance of humans for the earth. The fear of missing. 'I have world pain', is how Kim's son described that depressed feeling, yet it sounds different in his words. Yes, world pain, but we are still there, with each another. 'Your children, your loved one; when you're with them, you feel an overflowing of love. The studio is the place where this feeling can be nurtured, where I am happy.' 'You will be with your loved ones again. That is what I need sometimes, especially now that my husband is ill.' Because never is inconceivable.

Never is a very long time

Kim van Norren, *Stronger than death is love*, 2022

A voice that glimmers in the light

A voice that glimmers in the light

Cici Wu, *Upon Leaving the White Dust,* 2017–2018, ceramic, clay, handmade glass, silicone, plaster, rice paper, ink, plastic drop cloth, sponge, floor cloth, Lehmann Gross Bahn train tracks, white LED, enamelled wire, video, varying dimensions. Light data from the unfinished film *White Dust from Mongolia* by Theresa Hak Kyung Cha. Courtesy of the artist

New York, 2018. I take the stairs to the exhibition space of 47 Canal. The room is darkened and the light is flickering like an elusive poltergeist. In a square area, objects are arranged in rows, such as little cube-shaped houses, an angel, two hands folded over each other, a small aeroplane, and a miniature train on a short section of track. Most of the objects are made of clay and reflect the light, making them glow bright white; in between them are square cubes with little straws sticking out of them and round LED lights that emit soft light. This translucent installation by Cici Wu is called *Upon Leaving the White Dust* (2017–2018) and it is a reconstruction, or a response, to the unfinished film *White Dust from Mongolia* made in 1980 by Theresa Hak Kyung Cha.

So this story begins with Theresa Cha (Busan, 1951). No, it actually begins before that, with the history of Korea, the peninsula that was once an impressive empire, and where a printing press was being used long before the 'invention' of printing in Europe. The Koreans call their country Han-guk, the land of Han, or Uri Nara, which means 'our country'. Their Korea, with its unique language and traditions, like those of female shamans, was occupied in 1910 by the Japanese, who attempted to turn it into one of their own provinces. The population was forced to speak Japanese and to change their Korean names into a Japanese version (sōshi-kaimei). On paper, this happened voluntarily but in practice it was impossible to refuse to do so because you would, for example, no longer receive any food rations. Many Koreans, including Cha's family, fled to the Chinese region of Manchuria in the north. Until Japan annexed this area of land as well and once again forbade them from speaking their mother tongue.

> 'The tongue that is forbidden is your own mother tongue.' – Dictee

For almost a century, Korea was the plaything of the major powers: Japan was able to remain in power thanks to an agreement with the Americans and, once liberated from Japanese oppression, the country became the punch bag of the communist Soviet Union and capitalist America. What followed was the 'Korean' war, an absurd name for a conflict that the great powers fought in an innocent country.

The Netherlands also sent troops, under the threat that the United States would withhold Marshall Plan aid. It is often called the silent war, the forgotten war. But for the Koreans the hubbub of unprecedented violence and the aggressive domination never goes away. And their side of the story is seldom told. The population was repressed, silenced, and remains dispersed to the present day: instead of giving the citizens in Korea their own country back, it was brutally divided into the communist north and the capitalist south. One wonders whether this cruel division can ever be healed.

'Language is the only homeland', declares the writer Czeslaw Milosz while in exile.*61 Language begins with the sounds that you slowly absorb while you are still in a relaxed slumber in your mother's belly: the rhythm, the tones, the love. Language is not only the alphabet that forms words that make sentences by means of grammar; language is the wool with which a sweater is knitted, in which thought obtains colour and form, and which keeps everyone warm. Centuries-old knowledge and thought systems are woven into language. Take the Korean word 'nunchi' that cannot be translated into Dutch or English. Taken literally, you end up with 'eye measure' and that means something like being good at gauging someone else's thoughts and feelings. It fits into a sensitive and nuanced system of interacting with one another. Language expresses who we are, as a people and as a person. A ban on speaking one's own language is like making small notches in your eye; it will heal but your sight will keep getting worse.

> 'You speak in the dark. In the secret. The one that is yours. Your own. You speak very softly, you speak in a whisper. In the dark. In the secret.'
> – Dictee

For Theresa Hak Kyung Cha, no language was self-evident anymore: she was born in Busan during the Korean war and when she is twelve her family leaves for the United States, where she quickly picks up English and later learns French out of interest. She studied art and experimented intensively, the effects of the oppression always looming up in language and images. In the book *Dictee,* she casually mixes the two languages, as the title already suggests. 'Dictée' is a French word (dictation, an exercise in writing flawlessly) but the accent is missing here so that it looks like an English word. The English 'dictation' (of following, complying, submissively adopting) also lies implicit in it. In this way, the word accumulates all the mental confusion arising from the ban on one's own language and from learning a foreign language.

> 'She mimicks the speaking. That might resemble speech (anything at all).' – Dictee

In spite of Cha knowing her way around in the United States and soon having an excellent command of the language, she also feels like a foreigner, her soul is wandering. In the book, she summarises the pain that she describes in short, incisive sentences; she disregards existing rules and, in doing so, arrives at her own authoritative, rhythmic language and her own grammar by, for example, omitting full stops and commas.

> 'It murmurs inside. It murmurs. Inside is the pain of speech the pain to say. Larger still. Greater than is the pain to speak. It festers inside.'

> 'The wound, liquid, dust. Must break. Must Void.'
> – Dictee

The discomfort of a foreign language that infiltrates daily life, as many immigrants experience, resonates through the book like the sound of a drum. In the chapter Calliope (named after one of the nine muses and whose name means 'with the beautiful voice') she speaks directly to her mother: 'You are not Chinese. You are Korean. You suffer the knowledge of having to leave. Of having left. But your Mah-UHM, spirit has not left. Never shall have and never shall will. Not now. Not even now.'

In 1979 Cha visits Korea but returns disappointed because, instead of recognition and connection, there too she is seen as an outsider.

> 'Born in Korea yet a foreigner.' – Dictee

In 1980 she sets off for Korea again to film together with her brother, but the work remains unfinished. Theresa Hak Kyung

Cha is murdered on the fifth of November 1982. She is going to the empty Puck Building in Manhattan to meet her husband, a photographer, who is documenting the renovation there. She is attacked there by the guard, Joey Sanza, and her body is found two days later in a car park. She is 31 years old at the time; it is a few days after the publication of her book *Dictee*.

The film that could not be finished is in the BAMPFA (the Berkeley Art Museum and Pacific Film Archive) collection, together with accompanying notes. The 85 shots that Cha drew on pieces of paper are also kept there, as well as a typewritten text in which she outlines the plot: A young Korean woman flees to China because her own country is occupied and she is no longer permitted to speak her own language, but when that part of China is also occupied, she gradually loses her memory and stops speaking. In this plot, we recognise the history of her mother. The decision not to talk anymore may be typified as an individual, desperate act of resistance.

The interest shown by Cici Wu (born Beijing, 1989, Hong Kong) in Theresa's work is not a coincidence. Both are artists in diaspora and are concerned with their position as Asian women in the world. Cha grew up as a Korean refugee in the United States and Wu left for New York after her studies in Hong Kong. For both, language, memory and awareness lead to a poetry of displacement, but their approach is essentially different. Cici Wu makes a sculptural version of the unfinished film and commemorates the life and work of Theresa Cha in this way. In the exhibition space, the articles that Cha had drawn as objects on small pieces of paper in the storyboard were brought to life. Almost every object contains an imaginable movement, such as the boat, the angel, or the locomotive. Each object is trying to bridge a distance and thus refers to the diaspora. The articles are lit by a fluctuating light reflection that is based on the intensity of light in the film *White Dust from Mongolia*.

Cici Wu's interest for this project lies primarily in cinema and especially in the traditional forms of 'film language' such as the shadow play, the tradition of the wayang or hand shadow images. In traditional shadow theatre a candle was used as the light source and the flickering of the flame produces softly fading, then resurgent shadow images. The performances were based on old legends and I read that the puppets were given a special status; they were thought to be in contact with the gods and spirits and therefore able to protect people from disasters. In each play, the shadow artist plays and sings all the roles and each time the old story turns out a bit differently. Wayang Kulit from Indonesia uses the beautifully made wayang puppets, that we all know in the Netherlands because of our colonial past, and is therefore rod puppetry and shadow play at the same time. It tells of humans as imperfect and failing beings. The shadow play is dynamic, interactive and breaks through the omnipotent perspective of the narrator. Everyone who watches is aware of the illusion of the play that is being performed. Cici Wu takes the projection of film as we currently know it as a symbol of the imposed colonial perspective.

> 'Cinema, deconstructed and stripped of its national and industrial apparatuses, is at its essence the experience of light.' *[62]

In the accompanying text, Cici Wu describes how she is wandering in a field of white dust: in the light of the projector that is still on its way to the screen, with the dust dancing in it, and that does not yet form a clear image, a field of being on one's way. It is also the white dust in which Cha's generation lost its way due to the aftermath of the domination, due to the alienation and not being seen and heard as equals. In *Upon Leaving the White Dust,* Wu arrives at a film language that fluctuates, that contains different perspectives and is more diffuse and more abstract. More open. She counterposes the scenario of Theresa Cha, in which a woman ceases to speak, with a voice from the present, a voice that, by contrast, sounds self-assured and powerful. The abandoning of the omnipotent perspective means that, as a viewer, you wander through the installation in a flickering light, looking at the disorientating shadows. *Upon Leaving the White Dust* departs from that anonymous area in which Asian immigrants seemed to find themselves for a long time, first dominated by the West and then marginalised as immigrants in the United States. That is over; Cici Wu is reclaiming the voice. Here, instead of the tragic feeling of being lost, there is the poetic strength of being present. The strength of several voices.

Wu describes how cinema can bring you to tears, purely by the flickering of light. The succession of fragments invites viewers to complement it from within themselves. The emotion flows through the spaces in between and in doing so also connects them; that is what she calls the 'movement of the soul'.

> 'A Bolex camera is like a spiritual tool, just like how paper lanterns had a similar purpose in the past. Both are technologies related to a spiritual way of searching for things.' *63

Spiritual searching is interwoven with an essentially different view of life than the cold western view, a life where there is space for female shamans, for mysterious powers, for the presence of a soul in people, stones, water and light. All these concepts have been pushed aside by western domination, silenced.

In *Upon Leaving the White Dust* the shadows of the objects appear as if in a procession on the plinth; perhaps they may be understood as the spirits of the people who haunt the world in diaspora and who have vanished from the writing of history. Everything moves and changes as you walk through the room, a fluid world, in which each person benefits from porous borders of identity. Each person carries many identities in their being.

The installation is a tribute to Theresa Hak Kyung Cha, a *memento mori*, but not so much an individual homage; rather an installation that 'shows the wounds that have been left behind by memory and time' and that celebrates the strength of this generation.

> 'The wound, liquid, dust. Must break. Must Void.'

A voice that glimmers in the light

The mother of Theresa Hak Kyung Cha, photo from the book *Dictee*, 1982

p. 316-317: Cici Wu, *Upon Leaving the White Dust*, 2017–2018

with her voice, penetrate earth's floor

with her voice penetrate earth's floor, Eli Klein Gallery, New York, 13 April – 5 June 2022

> Out of its futility life breeds countless illusions
> Even in the face of death and gloomy failures
> I'm full of resplendent respect for life
> It's life that allows me to witness the strangest scenes on earth
> – Quote from poem by Zheng Xiaoqiong*64

If a life ends young, there is an overriding sentiment of futility. All those lost years. The landscape looks like the deep freeze compartment of the fridge. A mentally disturbed man stalked the artist Christina Yuna Lee, and stabbed her to death in her own home. The makeshift memorial where friends and strangers left flowers for her was subsequently vandalised multiple times. Incomprehensible. So needless and cruel. Her gallerist Eli Klein wanted to pay tribute to her life and talent and to detach her name from the violence committed against her that was all over the newspapers. He organised an exhibition in his gallery, entitled *with her voice, penetrate earth's floor* (borrowed from the book *Dictee* (1982) by Theresa Hak Kyung Cha.)

The exhibition became a declaration of love to Lee. Can we do something to give the dying a better future? *65 In Chinese culture, *66 the repose of the deceased person's soul is of central importance and offerings help to grant the soul this peace. The deceased passes seven gates on their way towards total harmony. Family and friends offer food, money and clothing to accompany the soul on this journey, sometimes symbolically in paper form. In this exhibition, a simple white cupboard served as an altar and friends brought precious things as offerings: a seven-year-old girl gave a pinecone, there was also a jade bracelet, a prayer bell, mugwort incense, a shell collection, and cherry blossoms. Each gift tugged at little at the heart of the giver; giving something away is only meaningful if it hurts a bit.

The curator Stephanie Mei Huang wanted to create a space for them to mourn together. 'A space of mourning doesn't necessarily have to be a space of pain', she says. This place was also there to celebrate her life. *67

> Her voice penetrates the earth: don't let this voice disappear now that this young woman is no longer there.

From one thing to another

Every Tuesday, the bin bags wait outside, black and tied at the top. A man on a bike comes by, opens them up and checks the contents carefully. He takes a small damaged enamel plate away with him. The next man sets about it more crudely. He stabs the bags open with a knife, making the contents roll out onto the street. He doesn't take anything. I hope that Sara Bjarland will come along and take a photo of the half of a grilled chicken that has fallen out. I think the partly eaten chicken deserves the soft glance of her camera. I take the neighbours' plant indoors again. Who knows, some magical love and a little water every day may bring the plant back to life. Sara Bjarland hunts through the rubbish and takes the broken, wilted and stained things into her care, to her studio. She is the mantle Madonna for all that is discarded. Her eyes touch it and her gaze, through the camera, brings it to life. She transforms indifference into a healing picture and gives renewed value to things that are broken and banished.

'Photography converts the whole world into a cemetery. Photographers are the connoisseurs of beauty but they are also, wittingly or unwittingly, the recording-angels of death,' wrote Susan Sontag, *68 the grand old lady of photography. Everything is halted, frozen, for eternity, or no, until time turns the paper yellow, makes the colour fade from the photo, makes digital files unusable. Sontag who saw so clearly that death lurks everywhere, travels with you from the time of your birth and simply waits for you, did everything, absolutely everything, to stay alive.

 Katie Roiphe wrote an astonishing report about Sontag's last years; how she seized upon each treatment, against her better judgement. A bone marrow transplant destroyed her immune system and her body developed sores everywhere such that even swallowing was painful. It is inconceivable that a 71-year-old woman, against doctor's advice, still chooses this. Her loved ones looked on sorrowfully, but going against it was not an option. 'Continuing with life, perhaps that was her way of dying.' Extraordinarily intelligent, Sontag had made exceptionality her myth and it seemed as if she had somehow begun to believe that she could escape death.

Perhaps this is what disturbs our relationship with death so much; we humans have come to regard ourselves as too exceptional.

We think we can evade death, perhaps not with the dogged conviction of Susan Sontag, but we don't give up easily in trying to win the fight with death, even if the struggle is already lost, and we know it. Nothing can go wrong, after all: death is inevitable. Yet fear has taken hold of us. Katie Roiphe did not want to understand death, but to 'see' it. Speaking about death put her off and instead she dived into piles of books to form a picture for herself. Sara Bjarland also wants to see death, and this began with the insects in the summerhouse. She grew up in Finland and the summerhouse was the hub of her existence; a small wooden house with lots of windows, the doors to the terrace always open. In the arms of nature for an entire season, both inside and outdoors. Summertime is insect-time, certainly in Finland, where it is full of mosquitoes, midges, crickets, leaf beetles, bark beetles and horseflies. As a child, she tried to rescue insects in distress. Very carefully they were laid in a glass jar on a small bed of leaves, and they were fed. Honey, plant sap, her own blood if necessary.

Bjarland feasted her eyes: that body divided into three small parts, those transparent, ethereal wings, the almost invisible eyes, and then all those legs. She films the death of a bee, full of admiration for its striped body, its attempts to stand up, only to finally give up, a last movement, and then, rest. No, it is not cruel, but rather, intimate. Watching the death of a bee seems like a homeopathic remedy to already get used to death. In Sontag's view, a photo captures something that is going to disappear, but Bjarland's photos are forward-looking. Her bee-film and photos allow us to get used to the inevitable end before it comes. She leads us into a twilight zone where our ideas about death slowly shift. Bjarland sees death everywhere around her and at the same time also the life shining through it. A discarded sponge, a dead mouse, Venetian blinds hanging apathetically. She changes the appearance of the things around us, not by touching them with her hands, but just by looking at them, via the camera. And then we see it too. The dilapidated umbrella looks like a bat with a tail. The yellow leaf of a wilted Swiss cheese plant looks at you reproachfully, asking, begging. The nearly dead birch tree looks spider-like. A duck diving under water is like a floating plastic bag. We see in-between beings with human traits. Loose Venetian blinds, lounging lazily. And thus our understanding changes. Perhaps death is not the red line running through life. The similarities in shape gnaw away at the existing categories, of left-right, black-white, man-woman, human-animal. Of death and life. The strict division is removed. Bjarland creates a landscape in which the boundaries blur, in which an almost dead plant calls out to us. 'I look at small dead things a lot,' wrote Bjarland, 'and then I somehow connect them with living things. I sometimes find that lifeless things (such as a melted plastic crate) seem 'dead', and I find this beautiful because it suggests that they may in fact have lived. A piece of plastic flapping in the wind is just as alive to me as a bird in flight. I try to focus in a subtle way on dead, nearly dead, lifeless and living things.'

'After life comes death, and then it's over,' says man arrogantly. How do you mean, over? And above all, why are we so sure about that? In 'The Hidden Life of Trees', I read that trees can communicate with each other, that they can even feel.*69 If nature is one great cycle, of seasons, of ants, rotten wood and mushrooms, are we humans so exceptional that we stand outside of this? Dust you are, to dust you will return. The Christian faith introduced the idea of a beginning and an end, thereby giving rise to the concept of linear time. Enlightenment thinking added the idea of progress. But time could also be a rhythm that keeps repeating itself, like the Canto Ostinato, but always sounds just a bit different. Or perhaps time circles, so that it can go forwards but also backwards, without an end. Then there is no enemy who must be fought because death brings you back to something that you already know, you were already there at some point. Any idea about time is a concept in our mind. Perhaps as humans we consist not only of dust but also of the intangible form of energy that the Chinese call *qi*. The Chinese philosopher Zhuang Zi was intensely sad after the death of his wife, until he became open to another idea about her passing.

> 'In all that chaos and confusion, something changed and there was *qi*. And the *qi* changed and took shape. The shape changed and she came to life. And now something else has changed and she is dead. It is like the cycle of the four seasons: spring, summer, autumn and winter.' *70

Susan Sontag died on 28 December 2004. Through her books we remain in contact with her, as in this text. And, who knows, perhaps her son still speaks with her, or one of her ex-lovers. Nick Cave lives forever with his son who died at the age of fifteen.

> 'I feel the presence of my son, all around, but he may not be there. I hear him talk to me, parent me, guide me, though he may not be there. He visits Susie in her sleep regularly, speaks to her, comforts her, but he may not be there. Dread grief trails bright phantoms in its wake. These spirits are ideas, essentially. They are our stunned imaginations reawakening after the calamity. Like ideas, these spirits speak of possibility. Follow your ideas, because on the other side of the idea is change and growth and redemption. Create your spirits. Call to them. Will them alive. Speak to them. It is their impossible and ghostly hands that draw us back to the world from which we were jettisoned; better now and unimaginably changed.' *71

Perhaps the dead float around us like ghosts, perhaps they sit on a shoulder and watch, or perhaps that white bird is their mouthpiece. Perhaps the talking dead are shadows of our minds. With her shifting and overlapping images, Sara Bjarland suggests something about an in-between area, she puzzles with death, she puts possibilities forward. It is an open space which we are allowed to look into.

p. 322, 324: Photos from the book *Groundwork* by Sara Bjarland, 2019

Violence is a language.
To craft is to care.

Violence is a language.
To craft is to care.

Teresa Margolles, *Tela Bordada Sao Paulo*, 2019, film stills, courtesy of the artist and mor charpentier

Violence is a language.
To craft is to care.

The indifference is the worst thing, says a mother whose daughter disappeared and was later found murdered near the city of Ciudad Juárez in Mexico. 'The worst thing, the most horrific, is to know that nobody gives a damn about what happened to your child.'

    Teresa Margolles worked in the mortuary of this city and saw a phenomenal number of corpses of murdered men and women end up on the dissecting table. The bodies of the men often remained unidentified for fear of the ruthless drugs gangs. But the murdered women. One evening, or the morning after a night shift, they didn't come home from work. Their bodies were found days or months later, murdered but sometimes also abused or hideously maimed in a blatant expression of contempt for women. Women there live in constant fear, for since 2008 girls have been regularly disappearing in Mexico. 'Murder is always dreadful, whoever the victim is', says Margolles. 'But men are murdered because of what they do, women because they are women. That's a big difference.' *[72]

The murder of women goes on and on. People speculate on the cause, inevitably arriving at femicide. Multinationals have established huge assembly factories (maquiladoras) along the northern border of Mexico, attracted by cheap labour and tax exemptions. Even Philips has a factory there. Most of the women workers come to work in this city from the south; underpaid, doing long and arduous shifts, but at least they can support their families this way. And the men? They wait for a chance to slip over the border and see enviously that the women have the upper hand, and that gnaws at their macho hearts. It could be that the murders are intended as an urgent warning to women: stay at home, know your place. Or that they spring from a profound frustration at their own male uselessness. Juárez is notorious and is known as 'the most dangerous city, excluding war zones' and 'The City of the Dead Girls".

    Last December many of my friends and acquaintances travelled to Mexico; my son, my hairdresser, the daughter of my best friend and I all took a plane to go and celebrate Christmas there. We all came back unharmed, with pleasant memories of friendly encounters and full of admiration for the brave inhabitants, ever resourceful in keeping their heads above water. We were safe and sound, far from drugs-related violence, but the inhabitants have to struggle to survive in this country, especially the women.

Violence is a language.
To craft is to care.

I was walking down the street when a front door opened and a young girl in sports clothes stepped out. An unbelievable whistling and catcalling broke out, it was astonishing. I looked at the girl and said: 'Is this normal?' A strange question because what is normal? She shrugged and said: 'I'm used to it.' Mexico does not have a reputation as a woman-friendly country. Every kiosk displays newspapers with a photo of a gruesome murder and a sexy half-naked girl on the front page.

Gradually Margolles extended her studio from the mortuary to the streets, for what she encounters in the mortuary naturally reflects what is going on in society. Every murder has a devastating effect on the family, which is damaged forever. Not knowing what has happened to your child is a never-ending sorrow. The knowledge that your child has been tortured is unbearable and yet you must go on. Murders are rarely solved and the dead end up as a mere number in a set of statistics, surrounded by indifference. How do you make that vanished life visible, how do you save the dead from anonymity?

When Margolles was invited to take part in the Biennale of São Paulo in 2019 she focused her attention on the many murders of transgender women. The previous year had seen the murder of 125 transgenders in Brazil.
    Perhaps she was tired of all of those years of acceptance, so close to the violence, tired of the mortuary and the repulsive evil. Margolles introduced beauty and teamwork to her oeuvre by embroidering with the community, as homage to a dead woman. White cloths were dragged over the scene of the crime so that they could absorb the mud and possible remaining traces of the bloody murder. 'The textile is a microphone,'*[73] explains Margolles. 'It triggers conversation because of its power of having been in contact with the dead body.'
    The film *Tela Bordada São Paulo* shows her working process. Slowly and with dignity, two transgender women walk along a street, dragging a length of cloth like an animal skin between them through the mud and pools of water. One woman wears a top and skirt in a fleece-like fabric with black spots, and the other wears a hair band with little black ears. The white cloth thus comes in contact with the ground where the transgender girl Priscilla was murdered, and this is how they wish to preserve the presence of Priscilla.

Violence is a language.
To craft is to care.

Then we see a large table where the women are embroidering the cloth; first of all a figure is drawn, such as a naked woman on a horse galloping towards freedom with hair streaming in the wind. A small naked figure gradually emerges from the thick red woollen threads that mark her outline. Flowers in every colour of the rainbow. It is one great mass of moving hands pulling up the long threads, then drawing them down again through the fabric. A voice-over in lilting Portuguese talks about Priscilla: 'I knew her for a short time. She lived in the house where I still live. The house goes by the name of Florecer (blossoming). My impression of her was of a gentle, fragile person. Someone who was always racked with fear. She was always afraid that something like this would happen. During the regime of President Temer she felt unsafe. She was frightened, we were all frightened. Temer was a rough and ready soldier, full of machismo and bluster. He wanted to close down houses like ours. I tried to reassure Priscilla—*Acalmar-se* —(calm down), the house won't be closed down just like that. Sometimes I'd sit with Priscilla in the communal garden, she didn't even dare to hang her washing on the line. *Ficar em paz, ficar em paz,* (stay in peace).' 'She used to work at night. A week later the tragedy happened.'

And so more memories of Priscilla come to the surface, and gradually the conversation switches to how her murder has aroused fear in the transgender community. Her murder is not the only one and little investigation is done into these crimes. More voices talk of the brutality of Brazilians towards the transgender community, not only in words but also in physical violence, which can break out at any minute. 'We're talking about Priscilla, but we're all in the same boat.' For them Priscilla represents the body that is ignored, that is terrorised from the very beginning because the dividing line between the sexes is so strictly enforced. The body that is not understood. 'Why do you want to see us dead?', asks one of the women. And that is a question that stays in my mind. Being opposed to something, that's acceptable, objections for religious reasons, all right, but what causes opinions to be translated into violence? Why does someone kill because of their convictions? 'That's the problem with transphobics, while they scare us and want to kill us, we're not preoccupied with them. We like performing, embroidering, making music.' That is all very fine and brave but I sense despair beneath the wish to be strong.

'We have a different sort of body, but we don't belong to the mediocre mass, we question it but we stand outside it, we're proud of our bodies, of being different.' A voice relates how a transgender woman was violently 'cured'. She no longer recognised her own body. 'At the same time she is alive she is also dead.' 'Too many people talk about the transgender body as if it's public property, but it's ours, it's private.'

Meanwhile it all looks very homelike; the thick and thin threads grow into a splendid depiction of hope, grief and interconnection. While yet another horrific story is related, the flowers grow under their hands. Embroidering is a healing process. Teresa Margolles speaks on behalf of the victims by means of these and other embroideries, for in this way she can let their lives speak for themselves, lift them out of anonymity and prevent them from simply vanishing, as if those lives were worthless.

The feminist art historian Janis Jefferies wrote the now famous sentence: 'To craft is to care.' And this particular embroidery 'cares' for Priscilla and her fellow victims. Embroidering together is a healing activity because there is consolation in the conversation that takes place during this ritual, and in the connection that this creates. The time that they spend on embroidering is a gift for the deceased, this portion of time is for her. The cloth full of evil-averting motifs is a memorial to Priscilla and her fellow victims with the emphasis on life itself, and the beauty of every life. *74

Violence is a language.
To craft is to care.

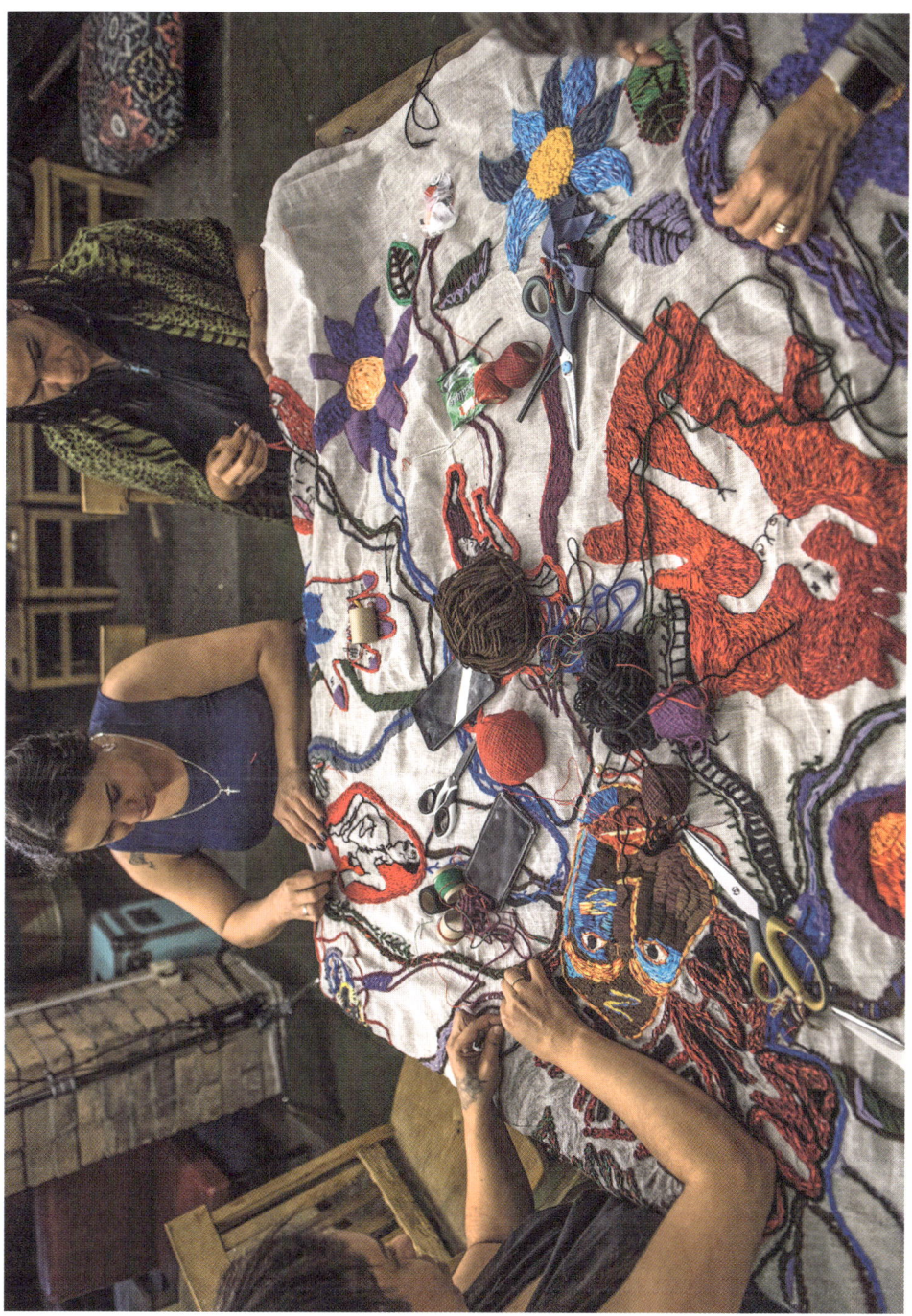

Teresa Margolles, *Tela São Paulo*, 2019, mixed media installation including a cloth that was embroidered in a collective workshop, courtesy of the artist and mor charpentier

The passage through which
we become (wo)men?

The passage through which
we become (wo)men?

Zanele Muholi, *Bester I, Mayotte*, 2015, courtesy of the artist and Yancey Richardson, New York

'My body, my right' was written on a traffic sign in bright letters, words I repeat softly while waiting at the traffic lights with my bike. 'My body, my right', a variation on 'my body, my choice', with which the right to abortion was fought. This time, it made me think of the tattoo on the left shoulder of Zanele Muholi, a womb culminating in a vulva, with the ovaries on each side: their passionate statement for the right to exist, to simply be allowed to live. As a black lesbian woman in South Africa, Muholi does not experience this self-evidence to the full, not even after the abolition of apartheid and the 1996 Constitution, which promises equality. They live in fear. There is regularly hostility from the outside world towards lesbians, and this is far-reaching if you think of the rapes that men carry out in order to 'cure' these women of their sexual orientation. 'I don't understand all that about curative rapes', says Muholi, 'it's raping where you come from.'

The suffering and the fear. Muholi sought a way to set that down on paper and printed a series of red ice crystals using their menstrual blood. *Isilumo Siyaluma*, which means *Period Pains* in Zulu. Vulnerability, pain, and fire—all in one. With the red stars and crystals, they made something beautiful out of all the ugliness in this project that only ends when their menstruation stops.

```
The passage in which we bleed
The passage where we are/ were born
The passage through which we become (wo)men?
The erotic passage meant to be aroused, is raped
The passage we love is hated and called names
The sacred passage is ever persecuted
```

This self-portrait of Zanele Muholi is a tribute to their mother, Bester Mayotte. They look wonderful on it, very black, because they make the black in the photo extra dark in order to emphasise their blackness. The lips are painted a striking white and they also have white lines around their eyes. They are looking straight at you. Clothes pegs are sticking out in all directions from their hair which is drawn up in a bun. Two clothes pegs are hanging from their ears like chic earrings. The light is reflecting from their forehead, focusing extra attention on the slightly drawn-up eyebrows and giving them that worried expression.

The self-portrait is part of the series *Somnyama Ngonyama, (Hail, the Dark Lioness)*, in which Muholi is honouring their ancestors. Muholi grew up under apartheid and when their father died, their mother had to seek work to support the family. As was the case for many others, her only option was to become a domestic worker in a white family, working long days for a meagre wage, with always-serving hands, in a subordinate position. That cruel situation where a mother runs someone else's household, cooks meals, takes care of other people's children, but in doing so has to leave her own children to fend for themselves to a large extent. After slogging away for 42 years, she was burned out and she had woefully little time left to enjoy her family and grandchildren.

My body, my right. My life, my right. So many rights that are continually being trampled on:
- (03) You have the right to life, liberty, and security of person.
- (23) You have the right to free choice of employment, with fair remuneration.
- (24) You have the right to rest, leisure and paid holiday.
  – (Universal Declaration of Human Rights) *[75]

In white families, they often spoke of this indispensable help as 'She was like family' or 'She is a treasure' or 'A pearl', and that sounds really bitter, in view of the circumstances. You would think that the white boys and girls who had been pampered during their childhood by black women would be very warmly disposed towards them. Nothing is further from the truth; it appears that the serving presence of black women only resulted in a widening of the gulf between black and white. *[76]

Sometimes the domestic help appears by chance in a photo album, almost always namelessly. An English first name was enough for the family. Yes, yes, almost family. The black household help lived as a shadow of the woman she truly was, living in her own community and among her own children. That is where her real name is heard.

Writing about *Self-portrait as Bester* confronted me with the plight of the domestic worker: Until then, I'd not been fully aware of the gravity and injustice. I knew the painting *Martha– die bediende (Martha–who served)* (1984) by Marlene Dumas:

The passage through which we become (wo)men?

'I had a single photo (snapshot) of her. She was sitting tensed up, neat and rigid, and was looking into the camera with a rather startled expression on her face. In the larger than life-sized painting, she towers above us. The feeling of discomfort remains in a portrait that alludes to a distrustful space in which surnames vanish and first names are fictitious.' *77

I certainly saw the discomfort in the portrait, but I was not able to feel it enough. Of course, I didn't buy Outspan oranges in order to support the boycott against South Africa (don't squeeze a South African dry), but the consequences of the policy of apartheid remained unimaginable, far away in the Netherlands.

Through their photos, Muholi aims to give their own community pride and self-confidence, building the history of black representation in this way. And that works for me too, in a different way. Thanks to their homage to Mother Bester, I have also been retrained now. Art isn't just a nice picture; Muholi's piercing eyes forced me to delve into history.

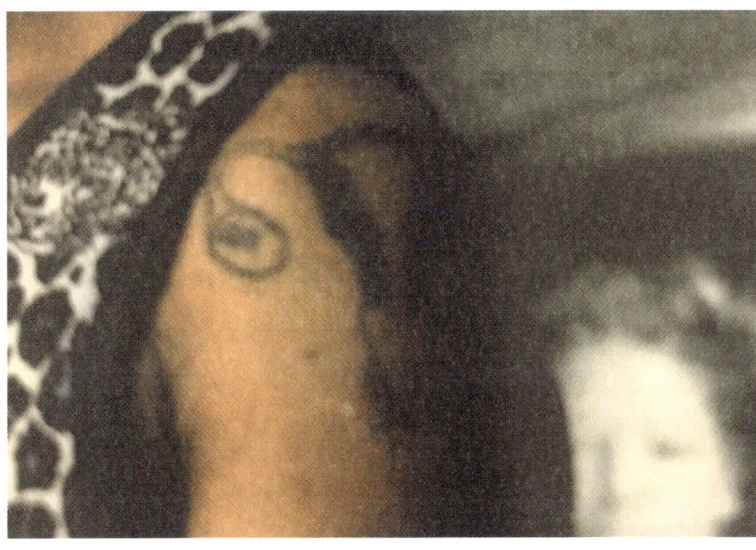

Death and water

Death and water

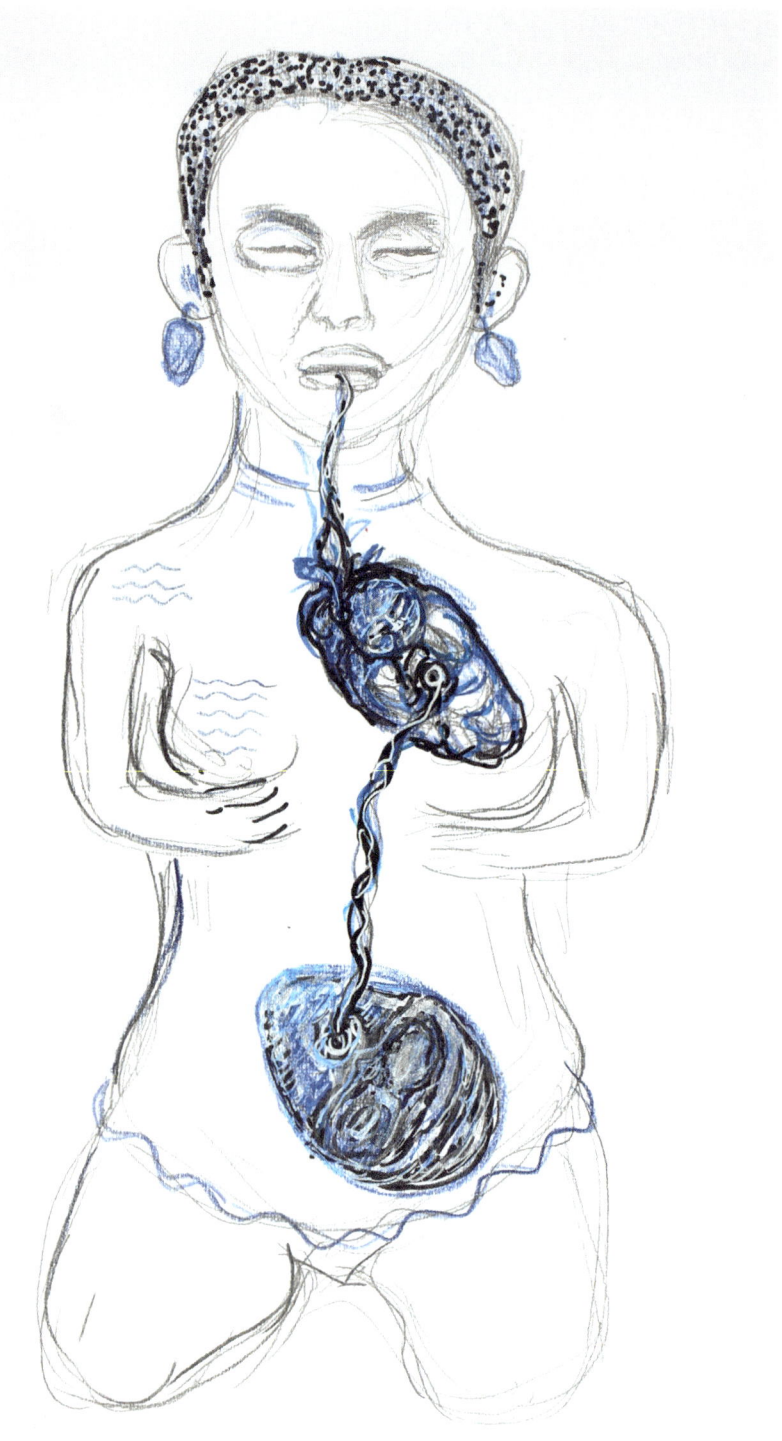

Efrat Zehavi, *Blue Baby Blue Hole*, 2022, from the *Bodybook* series

Death and water

A procession of strange plasticine sculptures passes by during my first visit to the studio of Efrat Zehavi.

A white mask expressing total amazement hides the face of a woman; a similar mask covers her belly, but this time there is water gushing from its mouth. A mermaid. A stern-eyed angel with a fish hook in her chunky clay hand. Long thin rolls of plasticine spiral into arms with clumps of seaweed here and there. A sketch on paper of a woman holding her body firmly in check: her torso is a blue hourglass with a baby floating in the top half and below, in the womb, a tiny human figure stands upright, arms by its sides, wearing diving goggles. Efrat has also carried out this sketch in unfired clay, with the woman pulling the edges of her belly apart so that you can look straight inside, at the man and the baby, which is fastened with a clip. Or the woman whose umbilical cord dangles from her mouth like a liquorice shoelace, only to disappear by means of a foetus into the mouth of a man, who bobs up and down in the region of the womb. A confusing tangle of umbilical cords, diving tubes, oxygen tubes, who is feeding whom, who is saving whom?
The colour blue of the water is dominant.

Efrat's way of thinking is as magical as that colourful procession of sculptures, through which she explores the possible connection between various events in her life. A year before Efrat was born her two-months-old sister died of 'blue baby syndrome'. Her lover died in a diving accident at the notorious Blue Hole in Israel in 1998. And Efrat herself narrowly escaped death through 'water intoxication': a strange little-known disorder which occurs if you drink large quantities of water and are unable to rid the body of it. Through excessive amounts of water and inadequate sodium levels the fluid in the blood vessels increases, which can cause the brain cells to swell.
It happened to her at exactly the same age as her mother was when she lost her first baby. Death and water.

Working from the sketches in plasticine and unfired clay, Efrat has now made ceramic sculptures, five in a row.

> <u>Hanne</u>: Those are quite something, I find those two sculptures on the left scary, quite frightening.

Efrat: People often say they're afraid of my sculptures, I've been hearing that for the past fifteen years. Being three-dimensional makes them so direct, so real.

> Hanne: Yes, that's true. But that in itself doesn't explain the fear. To me, it seems macabre that the clay woman is apparently alive, but is pulling her belly open. It makes me think of hideous rituals. There's something dark in the sculptures.

Efrat: Yes, though for me it's the other way round: I made a preliminary sketch for those women with their open bellies, and then carried it out on a larger scale. That's a rational process, controlled. I'm more afraid of those other three sculptures because they're more a product of my subconscious. They tell me something that I don't yet know.

> Hanne: As an artist of course you never work without an idea, the idea flows via your hands and you have to trust that your hands will pass it on.

Efrat: The most difficult thing is to trust that it will still work out all right without a perfect sketch. Sometimes I create something by chance: I took an egg made of polystyrene and drew a face on it. When I fastened one half of it to the belly the face was suddenly hanging upside down, which made it more like a birth. The image made more sense. But you can't give birth to a full-grown man, that's impossible, and that's why it's so sinister.

> Hanne: The head is more outside the body than in it, it's not growing inside like a baby, but more like a growth that the woman carries around with her. That she may need to get rid of.

Efrat: Now that you put it like that I can see it differently as well: as a sculpture with a healing effect, and that's a direction I'd like to go with these sculptures. With these female figures I was inspired by grave sculptures, and the question of why people used to put so many beautiful objects in graves, objects which would then disappear from sight. In the West we no longer have that ritual so we're more inclined to find it strange. But I understand it very well. The sculptures that I like the most I don't want to exhibit or sell: they belong with me as long as I live, because they remind me of something, of who I am, what I felt. Or of things that I had to overcome, one of those wonderful moments that you really did something for yourself. Maybe they can go in my grave!

> Hanne: And can you suggest an answer to the question why gifts are put in a grave?

Efrat: There's one thing that we can never grasp and that is death. I think that from the very beginning people started anxiously looking for ways to cope with that. Humans try to give that unknown entity a form, to ward it off. Death is so fascinating. If you experience death from close by it's painful, a parting. Those grave goods are there, I think, to ward off death, or as compensation.

These grave sculptures are intended to keep the dead person in the grave. Then you can distance yourself from it and go on with life, that's the only thing we can do. When my boyfriend died I thought, Oh, wait a minute: I can make art from this. It's material. That races through your head for a second, because you don't yet realise how deeply you're affected. So I call my sculptures mourning sculptures, not grave sculptures.

> Hanne: And how do the mourning sculptures that you're now making fit into the past? In what way are they connected to those events?

Efrat: The sculptures don't stand alone, they're a series and they're interconnected as regards subject matter. This is really a journal that I'm making, but in the form of a *body-book*. Instead of analysing my mind, I'm keeping track of the physical body. Are those events connected or not?

That's one of my questions. My mother was 23 when she lost my sister. I knew the story but never really thought about it. But I always felt that grief inside me, an inexplicable grief. I think that my mother passed on her pain to me. Inside my mother's body I was surrounded by the pain that she didn't want to feel but that existed all the same. My parents didn't visit the grave either: this was a baby of two months that wasn't mourned. Perhaps it was because of the Yom Kippur War that broke out the day after her death. Instead of grief my mother suffered from panic attacks, and once again she passed on that panic to me.

In Rotterdam I ended up living next to a graveyard and I saw children's graves there, even of one-day-old babies, with soft toys, little hearts and pebbles. They were being mourned. But if you don't know how to mourn, you store up the grief in your body.

> Hanne: Yes, I recognise that, my childhood was dreadful, with a lot of stored-up grief, and then you don't dare to mourn. A hidden fear whispers to you that once you start you'll set a never-ending stream in motion, that you'll simply be washed away. Too strong, too much, you'd never survive that. So how and where do you begin to feel then?

Efrat: My *body-book* was also intended to ward off evil spirits. A *dybbuk* (from the Hebrew word for attachment) is a disembodied soul that can find no rest and then takes possession of you as an evil spirit. This spirit has to find rest through someone else, sometimes it even has to be driven out.

> Hanne: So your sculptures are also intended as an exorcism, in order to ward off and drive out all that grief, all those tears of water?

Efrat: For a long time it seemed as if a spirit had nestled in me. The grief was not allowed, or not able, to come out, and then you really go mad.

Sometimes all I could do was scream really loudly. I couldn't cry, I was an ocean of grief. During the water intoxication, I couldn't urinate, the water couldn't get out. Perhaps the tears are coming out only now. Perhaps the process of making something causes the water to flow at last. Through that I can ward off evil.

<u>Hanne</u>: How would you describe mourning?

<u>Efrat</u>: Mourning can really hold you prisoner, but in fact it's not-mourning that keeps you locked up in your body. Not-mourning is a physical experience. You freeze. In my case, my breath literally caught in my throat. When my friend stopped living, movement in my life stopped. I couldn't breathe for years–well, I did breathe, I'm alive, aren't I, but it blocked somewhere in my upper body, it was never complete. Life is movement and death is when movement ceases. Everyone thinks that sorrow is about crying. I felt all kinds of things: turmoil, panic, anxiety, but what I couldn't do was cry, my eyes were dry and itchy. Just talking about it now, I feel it all over again. Mourning feels like an enormous liberation. It was only in 2019 when I started doing meditation that I realised that I felt different. The cramped feeling was gone. Since that time my body has begun to accept the loss. Mourning is not just about death, but also about denying yourself any pleasure. For years making portraits was the only thing that gave me pleasure, through the contact, the connection and the conversation. Now that I can experience my own emotions again, life gives me more pleasure. Perhaps I thought I wasn't important enough. Who'd be interested in me, in my sorrow, my petty sorrows in the light of what's happening in the world?

But, says Efrat, now really laughing, mourning and sorrow is exactly what is happening in the world. As it is in me.

<u>Hanne</u>: These women are sea creatures with coral-like hair, shells and a fish. In these three sculptures

> which have such a flow to them I can recognise letting go as a movement through which sorrow flows out. As if the sorrow that first filled your whole body, as in the hourglass drawing, is now coming out of the body and can exist around you, instead of being inside you and controlling everything.

Efrat: That process was really special for me. For twenty years I carried the story and the sorrow inside of me, but didn't speak to anyone about it. If you break a leg everyone can see what you have to contend with, but if you're always smiling or cheerfully complying with social mores, no-one knows about the sorrow that you carry with you. Perhaps this is the first time that I allow myself to talk about this story, and to portray it.

   And now I'm striving for ever simpler forms, instead of realistic representation. Expressing something too clearly limits the freedom of the observer. I use masks so that the viewer is not immediately saddled with a particular emotion, so that the emotion remains open.

> Hanne: And you prefer to leave your own feelings out of it?

Efrat: Through the mask I give the sculpture a particular expression, of fear or puzzlement, for example, but you don't know what's going on in the body, and that's where the past is stored up. That is the story that I tell.

> Hanne: How do you look back at the past now, at the death of your boyfriend and that near-death experience, and how do they fuel the present moment?

Efrat: The time difference has dissolved. The moment that I realised that, I had a feeling of completeness, a benign sense of peace. Death and birth are part of a cycle and that's what it is. And I realise now as well that I am who I am because of all of those events, otherwise I might never have come to the Netherlands, and now I'd be the mother of two children in some mountain village. The experience is still very much with me and determines how I see other people, especially the realisation that every human being carries something with them that is invisible. I do a lot of portraits, and it is precisely that tension between the interior and the exterior that interests me. I get to know the people through their stories, a face is often a façade, after all. In my portraits I bring that together, as I do in my mythical mother-portraits that I make purely on the basis of a story and my own fantasy.

> Hanne: I experience the sculpture of the woman with the fish as a deep sigh. Water garlands the face, it flows down so beautifully but it leaves the face free, the water flows around it.

Efrat: The fish is moving as well, upwards or downwards, that's not clear. I had intended to paint the sculptures blue but instead, they're now white, very clean and pure. The difference in colour comes from two different sorts of clay. The clay, the earth, provides a counterweight to the water. It gives something to hold on to.

   These experiences have woken me up, and still occupy me. I've processed it mentally, but there's more to it. Consciousness gives you the illusion of control. The yearning for control leads to wishful thinking: if I do this, that will happen. A form of magical thinking. Something compulsive. Sometimes I postpone an appointment because the date has some significance for me. But control is an act of despair. The only grip that I have on all these experiences is that I transform them into a work of art. You have control of the story, you can guide that and I have made a fairytale out of it.

Death and water

Efrat Zehavi, *Blue Baby Blue Hole*, 2022, from the *Bodybook* series

Efrat Zehavi, *Blue Baby Blue Hole,* 2022, from the *Bodybook* series

Better not move

Better not move

Petra Noordkamp, cover of the book *Better not move*, 2022

'For Menno' is written on the very first page of Petra Noordkamp's photobook. Her partner died of a cardiac arrest three years ago now. The trip to Japan that she had already planned took on a completely different dimension as a result of his sudden death. There is an image of a stone on the front cover of the book, a rock that can weather any storm. In actual reality, it was a pebble on a pavement in Kyoto. 'I was struggling but also felt unyielding. I knew I could go on', says Petra. She originally wanted to go to Japan to research and photograph silent spaces but now something was added. Mourning. Menno's death had unleashed old fears within her and she wanted to use her journey to overcome these. Her attic apartment often seemed to be spinning around her and she no longer dared to be alone. She suffered from panic attacks. 'I found the mornings particularly awful: there's a brief moment when you don't think anything and then the intense missing sets in. I was so lonely. Everyone else was going on with their lives. I was becoming more and more lonely.' Then she posted messages on Facebook and Instagram, but she would have done better to type in huge letters: 'Can someone please call me?' So she got on the plane to Japan with, on top of her already sensitive nervous system, a throbbing fear of earthquakes. Tokyo lies in a region that is geologically unstable and strong tremors are being measured all the time. That feeling of insecurity was already lurking somewhere inside her and had never really gone away following a serious accident, but Menno's death had stirred up all her fearfulness. She was always on the alert. And yet she got on the plane with all of those fears. Bravely.

In Tokyo, Petra was completely obsessed by the possibility of an earthquake. She showered as quickly as possible, because just suppose a quake started… she'd have to run outside naked. She found her apartment rather claustrophobic because of the small windows with rice paper blinds. The danger never left her thoughts for a moment in fact, except when she went out to take photos. That provided some relief for a while. She was alone and afraid in Japan but not lonely because when you travel you don't have friends around so you can't let that loneliness take hold. There is simply no one close by to help you get through the evening. Such peace.

A stone represents the unchanging and eternal. 'I hold on to emotions for too long. Sometimes they run away with me', says Petra. 'It makes my head spin.' In a dream, she threw a stone through a windowpane. Away with it, away with that craving for control, the idea that you can determine the course of events. In real life, it took somewhat longer to free herself from the thoughts going round and round in her head. In Japan she became fascinated by rituals and the idea of things having a soul. 'No other country has so many objects that bring good fortune: the crane, a turtle, a waving cat, Daruma the monk, or a Hina doll.' Perhaps this is a way to deal with the continuous threat of a natural disaster, like a constant stream of incantations.

 Petra finally made a film and a book in order to continue living, it gave her a purpose in life during a period of mourning. Inspired by the lucky charms, she included a number of Menno's possessions in this book, such as a pair of shoes, a piece of film, a mug, and a Japanese teapot that Menno had inherited from an uncle from Japan. The other images are abstract 'empty' photos of traditional Japanese architecture, stones, tree roots, water and moss. The trip to Japan proved to be a breaking point for her fears, most of which she has now lost. Menno was an editor and they had met while working on one of Petra's films. 'Film is movement', a friend had once told her and, with that instruction in mind, she sometimes made rather forced movements. Nothing stayed still for a moment. 'Better not move', said Menno during that first meeting. Her film consists of a succession of still images; it is only the water that moves, and a porcelain cup tinkles precariously on another cup. Everything else is still.

p. 359-361: Photos from the book *Better not move*, 2022

Living on air

Marlene Dumas, *Nuclear Family*, 2013

Marisca Voskamp is an incomparable being. In her presence I sense that I am dealing with an artist in heart and soul, although without a sizeable oeuvre to support this feeling. She is elusive, cosmic, and at the same time thoroughly earthy. Whenever I arrive by bike she is busy splitting blocks of wood with a big sharp axe, or burrowing in the mud to make a foothold in the earth for young plants.

The first time that I visited Marisca Voskamp at her house in Wormer her husband André was still alive, although everyone realised that it would not be for much longer. We ate with her children in the garden. It was pleasant and the atmosphere was lively. Nevertheless, the knowledge that someone's life will soon be over has a certain effect on you. Not uneasiness, but something fragile that lingers for weeks. I cycled home at dusk, cutting straight through the business park. Now Marisca e-mailed me in answer to my appeal on Instagram. We had lost contact with each other.

> 'Hanne, I would like to take part in your book, at the moment I'm stroking and soothing clay to admit the emotions that I've set aside for the last three years. As I've never worked with clay the result is fragments, memories. I put the fragments in water. The air from the fragments bubbles up in the water, air bubbles that I can't put into breath bags.'

I don't quite understand it but I always have instant faith in her projects. Her best known work is *Ademtocht (Breathing)*, a big cloud of plastic bags containing the breath of people in psychiatric care: staff, patients and their families. In this way she portrayed the motor of life. The breath of fragments cannot be captured. And yet, a mysterious image forms in my mind. Grief breathes in and out too.

> 'I don't get it, all around me I see reflections of what I make, or the past that has passed away, passed away in the past, and I move among them against a new horizon, I breathe, I wake, and read the newspapers that André always read aloud, because that's what he did. Wake up, look at the wall, the title of his work from 2003, is that you, death? Those yellow stickers, why don't I take them off?'

The artworks are just as elusive as Marisca herself, rather than hang on a museum wall they prefer to hide away in a desk drawer. Or on a table at the top of the house, where you can hardly stand, after climbing two steep flights of stairs. Where printed A4 sheets of paper are strewn about, with little domestic scenes, the evening sun, two grimy beer glasses stacked together. A bit of mould on a grapefruit. A drying rack hung with washing. Beautiful. Every print fixed to a gallery wall with two pins, that could be my favourite exhibition. But meanwhile they are lying hidden here, in the attic. Marisca is one of those rare artists who just keep on going, but in the seclusion of her own house, in her own world, and in theory that is enough for her. The work has no need to enter the outside world. Though sometimes it is allowed to (with the accent on 'allowed').

'Embracing what is missing. He's still here and that's good, I'm happy this way, I'm Indonesian, we live life and death. We celebrate life and celebrate death. I was brought up with both Indonesian and Dutch culture. My Indonesian nature tells me that you shouldn't feed sadness, because people don't die to make you sad. It's more an attitude of keeping the dead alive. Cherishing, honouring, besides, his soul is still here and sometimes more or less perceptible. So it's all very positive. Different from the Dutch version of death, then there's nothing, gone. I don't believe in that. For the rest, that's just how it is, life together is 1 plus 1, together in being alone. I get a lot of energy from this. I love life. That's why the air bubbles from the fragments are so good in this context. I haven't yet made a work to commemorate him. Or to mourn him.'

Now I'm sitting at her table again. Beaming, she tells me that she has just sold her car, that gives her power, more daring. Away with all that ballast. 'It's better to live on air.' Her son Parker came and stayed with her for a while, she taught him to cook, he found peace and warmed her with his company. On the neighbouring farm there was a new dog running around. 'Tell you what, come and give her a stroke every day'. Now the dog Louise lives with Marisca. The year after André's death she did nothing but chase after the dog, who kept running off. It kept her busy. Marisca is the most intuitive artist I know, who feels her way through the world, constantly taking one step backwards, then another step forwards but in another direction, perhaps further backwards, from the world to her own garden and house. To make her art there.

'I don't want to make any more works of art', she says, sitting at the kitchen table. 'You start on something, then it becomes reality, work also becomes therapy, a way of dealing with dead reality. But as for putting something small and precious on a plinth? You could also keep it for yourself.'

The art stays at home. As a lodger? A tenant? We shall see.

'You have to feel right in your body. With a commission it's hard to feel that freedom. In a plan for the NS I wanted to project the world onto slabs of baked clay. When the projection touches the ground it becomes like a hologram. I had to get into a commission frame of mind, cancelled the project. It made me nervous, because it thwarted my own life.'

Most artists live to make art. Just as I live to write, or to make an exhibition. Something that enters the world. That I can share. But for Marisca it works differently. Art has to adjust to her life, has to fit into it. Too much administration, too many applications, technical problems, then a 'no' rises to the surface. It's not allowed to thwart her life.

Sitting at the table she tells me how she managed to go on after André's death. Impulsiveness and freedom. Producing testosterone, gathering strength. 'Now that Daddy isn't here anymore, we're going to start by doing everything we couldn't do with him.' A month after the funeral they all went to Egypt without planning ahead. Gave a garden party for eighty guests.

Marisca and André had known for some time that he was dying, he was suffering from an incurable disease. They kept quiet about it, just kept going. But you are both living then with approaching death. Time spent in a wine press gives a bitter taste. During this period and with this knowledge Marlene Dumas painted the family, a painting with the aura of eternity.

Marisca lives on. A postcard landed on the doormat, of the Monet landscape that hangs in the Zaans museum round the corner. Marisca wanted to do something with it.

Heaven and earth lying side by side. Where is the horizon in the cosmos? Marisca made a scan of the postcard, and made a fold in the copy.

> 'Looking for a new horizon, if you look at the fold, you see that I've moved the horizon. Creating a landscape that comes into being through my own choices. Without him, in which he is absent. We live in the unknown, what holds us fast is the known. In this fold is room for our existence.'

The card with the fold now hangs opposite the Monet painting. It breathes out and completes the circle of time.

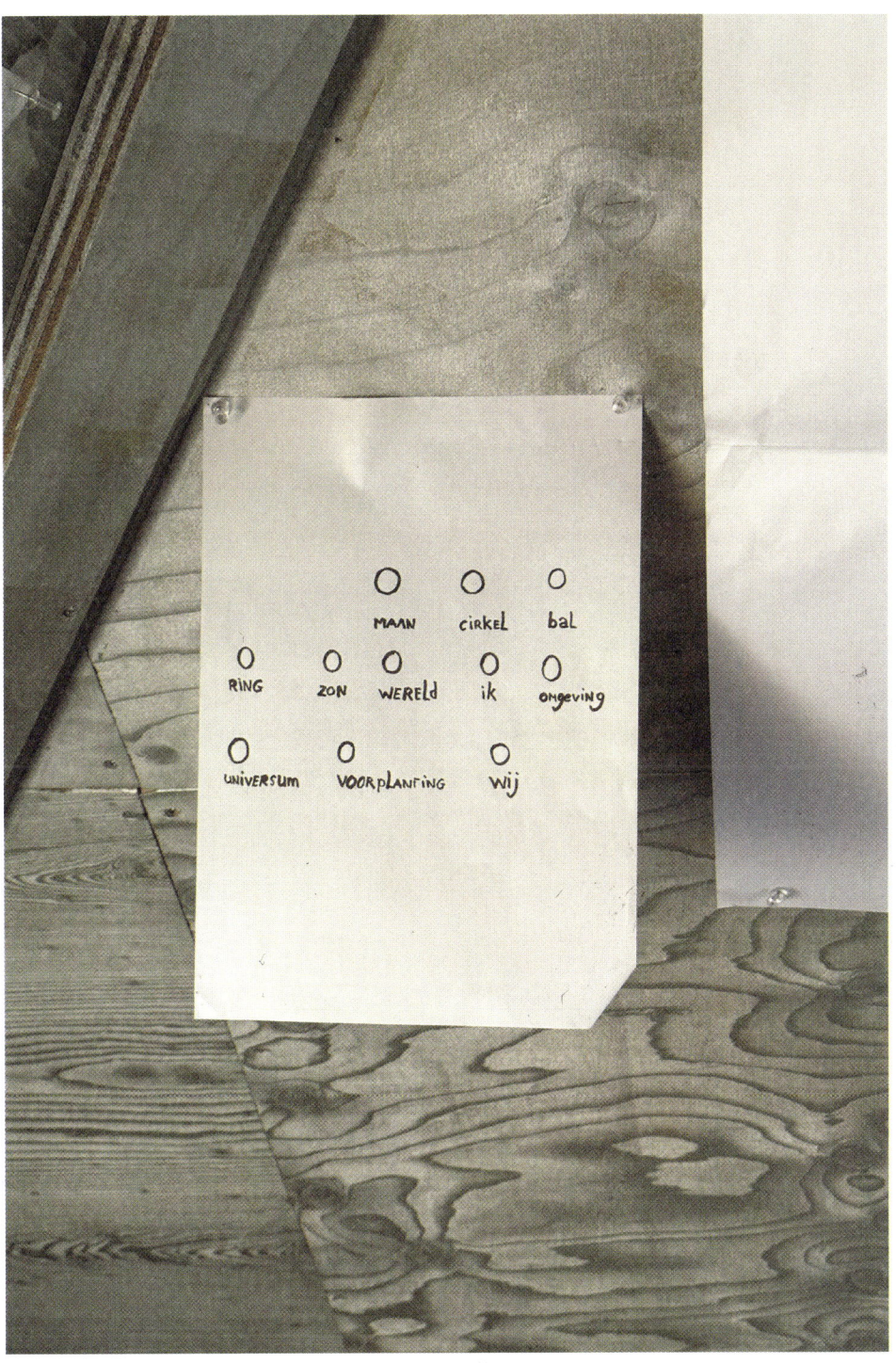

Marisca Voskamp, *Compass in universe (movement between work and life)*, 2004, (number 17)

Marisca Voskamp, *View of the ocean floor*, 2020, (number 658)

Marisca Voskamp, *The day with light and darkness,* 2022, (number 1197)

Mending

Mending

You cannot really leave your childhood behind you, it hangs around you like the flayed pelt of a sweet little animal, it tickles you and keeps you warm.

In this book, I went in search of my grief, but it was mostly the non-grief that I encountered. Yet, I did find something: after all those months of writing, I look back and notice that a beautiful and sometimes strange process has been set in motion.

The black and white, good and evil, that overshadowed our family was gradually dissipating. There were more and more memories of small loving gestures by my father, Toon. The round wicker basket of dried flowers that he brought me after the death of my new-born daughter. The fact that he asked someone to talk with me when my mother's death was drawing near, because he had the feeling that I couldn't comprehend it. And that was true. It was thanks to my father that I was able to go to university (my mother was more likely to think of Schoevers, the secretarial college).

In our family, he was the great evil that messed the family up, but now I can see the sorrow in his life. As the psychiatrist Bessel van de Kolk states, people who have experienced great trauma are less able to let love flow. I saw that empty, emotionally barren life more and more. The loneliness, his disappointments.

Mama, perhaps you were the only one who really understood Toon, who was prepared to make the effort to stay with him, even though he denied that after your death. ('Ans didn't understand me')—but understanding can actually be very threatening. It was you who came closest to his secrets, his burdens, his nightmares, his addiction to drinking. He yearned to have a family that would finally give him love, but we didn't do that. In one of my sessions with therapist Vera, there was a painting of a landscape on the wall, and I suddenly pictured Toon sitting on my shoulders while I rose up out of the river and allowed him to vanish into the air: fare well, fare better in a next life.*[78]

Dear mama, I understand that your emptiness was of a very different nature to Toon's, an emptiness arising from an inexhaustible gentleness, a great cloud of love that turned to mist in that void and became almost invisible. As a child, I felt your loneliness, but was unable to fill it, in spite of cleaning the kitchen until everything shone and buying new tea towels with my pocket money. Doing everything to please. A big heart and a cuddle would have been better. Perhaps we were too close to each other in our loneliness.

Mama, what I do remember clearly are the beautiful dresses you wore with such style, the ones we bought together for you, I looked with you, glowed with you, and saw clearly what suited you eminently. What a joy. It was part of our times together. I have made the clothes again, smaller, the clothes as I remembered them. As a way of doing something for you, after all the dresses and shirts you sewed for us children and that we received so ungratefully. With each stitch, I drew closer to you. With each dress, we converged more.

    All those garments are now hanging from pins on a piece of yellow checked fabric, around the piece for Martha. I can cherish your love and kindle a little flame.

(1) After a poem by Neeltje Maria Min: 'For my love I will be named'. Translation David Colmar. http://www.verseville.org/neeltje-maria-min.html

(2) In 1988 Nel Draijer's groundbreaking research was published, which showed that almost one in seven women had experienced sexual abuse in her youth.

(3) This text is based on the introduction to the book *The Ballad of Sexual Dependency*. The film *All the Beauty and the Bloodshed* was recently released in which this period is much more extensively discussed; I have left the text as it is because the core of the text remains intact.

(4) Robbert Dijkgraaf, *Het zwarte gat is het atoom van de 21ste eeuw*, NRC Handelsblad, 11 April 2019.

(5) VPRO, *Andere tijden*, 25 May 2004 (1979).

(6) Carlijn Visser, *Hoge bomen in Hanoi*, 2017.

(7) *Dodental Vietnamoorlog hoger dan verondersteld*, NRC Handelsblad, 4 April 1995.

(8) Quoting from a letter from Ted Hughes to his daughter Frieda, 12 February 1995. *The Letters of Ted Hughes*, edited by Christopher Reid, Faber 2007.

(9) Nicolaas Quaghebeur, HUMO, 20 March 2017. The interview itself was a conversation with his friend Plinio Apuleyo Mendoza in the book *The Fragance of Guava*.

(10) For this text I have used two catalogues of the work of Ana Mendieta:
– *Ana Mendieta, Traces*, Hayward Publishing 2013.
– *Ana Mendieta*, Xunta de Galicia 1996.

(11) As formulated by Xandra Schutte in in De groene Amsterdammer, nr. 33, 'Een sensuele maar achterlijke plek'.

(12) Jane Weinstock, *Interview with Martha Rosler*, October Vol. 17, *The New Talkies* (Summer, 1981), pp. 77-98.

(13) https://www.nytimes.com/2020/01/05/arts/john-baldessari-dead.html

(14) According to Chinese medicine.

(15) *The Perfect Medium, Photography and the Occult*, Yale University 2005.

(16) https://www.lebohangkganye.co.za/context

(17) https://www.vogue.com/article/rombaut-vegan-lettuce-slide

(18) Rodaan Al Galidi, 'Koelkastlicht', gedichten, Maas, 2016.

(19) Marije van Beek, *Predikant Mpho Tutu van Furth: 'De Bijbel maakt helemaal geen enorm punt van homoseksuele relaties'*, Trouw, 24 December 2022

(20) Peter de Waard, *Miekes dood was niet tragisch, haar leven was niet zinloos*, de Volkskrant, 13 January 2011.

(21) https://www.artforum.com/print/198308/alice-neel-35457

(22) Patricia Hills, *Alice Neel*, Abrams Publishers, New York, 1983, p.81. All following quotes and the poem 'The great Renunciation' are from this book unless otherwise indicated.

(23) https://www.groene.nl/artikel/de-moeder

(24) https://www.artforum.com/print/198308/alice-neel-35457

(25) I used the following books to write this text:
– Patricia Hills, *Alice Neel,* Harry N. Abrams Publishers, New York, 1983.
– Kelly Baum and Randall Griffith, *Alice Neel: People Come First,* the Metropolitan Museum of Art, New York, 2021.
– *Alice Neel, Portret van het moderne leven,* Haags Gemeentemuseum, 2016.

(26) The helmet was on display in the exhibition 'Fetisj, schrijvers en de dingen' in the Literary Museum in The Hague, now the Museum of Literature.

(27) Bas Heijne, *Iedereen is in zijn hoofd altijd ergens,* NRC Handelsblad, 19 February 2010.

(28) Marcel Proust, *Time regained,* Independently published, 10 Jan. 2021. http://margotdijkgraaf.nl/blog/100-jaar-a-la-recherche-du-temps-perdu-over-het-lezen-van-proust/

(29) Maarten Buurman, *De essentie van Spinoza,* ISVW Uitgevers 2019.

(30) Lao Tzu: *Tao Te Ching, A Book about the Way and the Power of the Way, Ursula K. Le Guin,* Shambhala Publications Inc, 2019.

(31) Rainer Maria Rilke, *Auguste Rodin,* Translated by Daniel Slager, Archipelago, 2004.

(32) A performance by William Marx of John Cage's *4'33*. Filmed at McCallum Theatre, Palm Desert.

(33) Translations of the poems of Mahmoud Darwish by Munir Akash and Carolyn Forch (poem on p. 201) Nezar Andary (poem on p. 202).

(34) Nizar Qabbani, 'Jogging'. https://allpoetry.com/poem/14328800-Jogging-by-Nizar-Qabbani

(35) Yasser Arafat on 13 November 1974, speech to United Nations General Assembly. https://al-bab.com/documents-section/speech-yasser-arafat-1974

(36) Cécile Koekkoek, *Elke keer dat ik mijn ouders zag, voelde ik mijn bloed koken,* interview with Philip Huff, De Volkskrant, 14 Februari 2022.

(37) Marja Pruis, *Ik heb het huis niet verwoest. Ik heb het schoongemaakt.* Interview with Manon Uphoff, De Groene Amsterdammer, 15 December 2021.

(38) Bessel van der Kolk, *The Body keeps the score,* Penguin, 2015.

(39) *Strands of Steel:* http://poetsglobal.blogspot.com/2009/05/caged-bird-deprived-of-flight.html
Translations by Khizra Aslam.

(40) Word of thanks.
Forever grateful for the contributions of Suyoung Yang, Flora van Dullemen, Isabel Pereira, Berk Duygun, Iver Uhre Dahl, Frederica van Mastrigt, Bo Wielders, Tamim Mohammadi, Nagim Mohammadi, Siadhail Augusteijn, Lui Macrae, Philip Groubnov, Erik Kameletdinov, Naomi Moonlion, Jeremi Biziuk, Niam Madlani, Fatima Jabor, Shirin Mirachor, Reda Senhaji, Lema Ahmadi, Ella Wang-Olsson, Leonardo Scarin, Diane Mahín, Julia Sterre Schmitz, Yannick Verhoeven, Mayis Rukel, Joost Koster, Hannah Reede, Io Alexa Sivertsen, my mother and my grandfather. Thank you, without you it wouldn't have been the same.

(41) http://poetsglobal.blogspot.com/2009/05/caged-bird-deprived-of-flight.html
Translations by Khizra Aslam.

(42) Stephan Sanders, *Godschaamte*, Van Oorschot 2021.

(43) Gerard Reve, *Nader tot u* (Nearer to Thee), 1966, De Bezige Bij, 2001.

(44) https://www.crescas.nl/columns/zomerschrijvers/aigoz/Zeven-dagen-Grunberg/

(45) Wim Kayzer, *Of Beauty and Consolation*, English; Dutch 2006. Patricia de Martelaere, De groene Amsterdammer, 19 August 2000.

(46) Bianca Stigter, *Kijk mama, een uitgekleed dier,* NRC Handelsblad, 15 February 1991.

(47) Wim Kayzer, *Van de schoonheid en de troost,* book and TV series, 2006.
Patricia de Martelaere, De groene Amsterdammer, 19 August 2000.

(48) Peter Wohlleben, *The Hidden Life of Trees:* William Collins, 2017.

(49) https://www.nature.com/articles/nature.2016.19839
https://www.ema.europa.eu/en/news/diclofenac-use-animals-poses-risk-european-vultures

(50) Poem: 'To My Daughter' by Joseph Brodsky.

(51) Joseph Brodsky, Anna Achmatova, *Maatstaf.* Jaargang 31, 1983, New York, August 1982.
https://www.dbnl.org/tekst/_maa003198301_01/_maa003198301_01_0002.php

(52) Luc Sante, *Evidence: NYPD Crime Scene Photographs: 1914–1918,* January 1, 2006.

(53) The Crucifixion, The Crucifixion, Duccio (c.1255–before 1319) (school of), Manchester Art Gallery.

(54) Longinus van Caesarea, The Bible, (John 19:34).

(55) Robert Musil, *Man Without Qualities, Picador Classic,* 2017.
https://erikgveld.wordpress.com/2020/06/09/robert-musil-de-man-zonder-eigenschappen-boek-1-1930-1932/

(56) A.L. Sötemann, *J.C.Bloem, Media Vita,* October 1989.
https://www.dbnl.org/tekst/anbe001lexi01_01/lvlw00039.php

(57) Gerrit Komrij, *De gestorvene,* NRC Handelsblad, 10 August 1995.

(58) Lo Woudstra, *Eli Content in de Neie sjoel.*
https://lowoudstra.wordpress.com/2020/01/07/eli-content-in-de-neie-sjoel/

(59) C. van der Kooi, *Sterker dan de dood?,* 2002.
https://www.dbnl.org/tekst/_lit006200201_01/_lit006200201_01_0009.php

(60) https://www.biblegateway.com/passage/?search=Song+of+Solomon+8%3A6-7&version=ESV

(61) https://www.cultuurschakel.nl/media/7681/werksessie-3-en-5-language-is-the-only-homeland-nl.pdf

(62) https://47canal.us/media/pages/exhibitions/cici-wu-lantern-strike-strong-loneliness/1991828547-1626977703/lanternstrike_pr_en.pdf

(63) https://www.moussemagazine.it/magazine/cici-wu-billy-tang-2020/

(64) https://www.poetryinternational.com/nl/poets-poems/poems/poem/103-29777_XURONG/#lang-en
Translation by Zhou Xiaojing.

(65) http://www.bristol.ac.uk/religion/buddhist-centre/projects/bdr/chaplains/online-guide.html

(66) China is of course a country with great cultural diversity. I found this information on the pages of various funeral organisations, e.g. https://www.funeralguide.co.uk/blog/death-around-world-chinese-funeral-customs-and-traditions]

(67) https://www.artsy.net/article/artsy-editorial-moving-new-exhibition-pays-tribute-christina-yuna-lees-start-art

(68) Katie Roiphe, *The Violet Hour,* The Dial Press, 2016.

(69) Peter Wohlleben, *The Hidden Life of Trees:* William Collins, 2017.

(70) Julian Baggini, The Guardian, 8 January, 2009.
In: https://www.360magazine.nl/andere-manieren-%E2%80%A8om-naar-tijd-te-kijken/

(71) Nick Cave, *The Red Hand files,* issue #6, October 2018.

(72) Ines Minten, *Kunst uit het morturarium,* De Standaard, 1 oktober 2019.

(73) https://www.meer.com/en/16643-we-have-a-common-thread

(74) Thanks to Diana Blok for watching and translating the film.

(75) The Universal Declaration of Human Rights (UDHR) was adopted by the United Nations General Assembly on 10 December 1948 (A/RES/217) to outline human rights (basic rights/fundamental rights). Eight states abstained: the Soviet Union plus five other states from the Eastern Bloc, Saudi Arabia and South Africa.
1. Everyone is born free and with equal rights.
2. Human rights apply, whoever you are, wherever you are.
3. You have the right to life, liberty, and the security of person.

(76) In books and films archives: '… it is dominated by a white perspective. The migration of black women to cities and the work they did in the private spaces of white households led to a special kind of entanglement, and, in particular, to the racist assumption by even the youngest white child that black hands do the dirty work.' https://www.newframe.com/new-books-domestic-workers-south-africa/

(77) https://www.litnet.co.za/marlene-dumas-spui25-martha-die-bediende/

(78) The police actions in Indonesia were unlawful and misleading propaganda was conducted in the Netherlands. With the knowledge of then and now, the Netherlands had no business in this country and the colonial regime has brought an incredible amount of injustice to the population of Indonesia.

Colophon

APE #216
The roundness of loss
Hanne Hagenaars

© 2023 Art Paper Editions
ISBN 9789464665192
www.artpapereditions.org
www.hannehagenaars.nl
First edition, 500 copies
July 2023

Author: Hanne Hagenaars
Editor: Rens van der Knoop
Proofreading: Floor van Luijk and Doina Kraal
Translation: Kathryn Westerveld
Translation *Living on Air, Violence is a Language, Death and water:* Jo Nesbitt

Thanks to: Diana Blok, Inge Breedveldt Boer, Moon Crow (shaman), Doina Kraal, Aida Kashani, Manu Keirse, Rens van der Knoop, Paul Kooiker and Esther de Vries.

Design & edit: Hanne Hagenaars and Lien Van Leemput for 6'56" (www.6m56s.com)
Printed in Tallinn.

This publication was made possible with support of the Mondriaan Fund, Prins Bernhard Cultuurfonds and Jaap Harten Fonds.

All rights reserved. No part of this publication may be reproduced or transmitted in any form or by any means, electronic or mechanical, including photo-copy, recording or any other information storage or retrieval system, without prior permission in writing from the publisher and the editors.